# THE TEACHER'S HANDBOOK

## ON THE SCHOOL LIBRARY MEDIA CENTER

BY
BETTY MARTIN
AND
LINDA SARGENT

First published 1980 as a Library Professional Publication (LPP), an imprint of The Shoe String Press, Inc. Hamden, Connecticut 06514

Library of Congress Cataloging in Publication Data

Martin, Betty, 1910–
   The Teacher's Handbook on the School Library Media Center.

   Bibliography: p.
   Includes index.
   1.   Instructional materials centers.   2.   Teaching—Aids and devices.   I.   Sargent, Linda, 1942–      II.   Title.
LB3044.M37                          027.8                          80–24542
ISBN 0-208-01854-9
ISBN 0-208-01847-6 (pbk)

# Contents

Table of Figures                                             6

Foreword by Elizabeth Duncan Koontz                          7

Preface                                                      9

Part I. Basic Information
Chapter 1.  "I should like to have a clearer under-         15
            standing of the scope of a media
            center."
Chapter 2.  "It would help me to know more                 27
            about the activities of the media
            specialist and about how we can work
            as a team."
Chapter 3.  "I should like to know the ways in             45
            which the media center can be used
            most effectively."

Part II. The Teaching-Learning Process
Chapter 4.  "I should like to know what help I can         71
            expect in the design and implementa-
            tion of curriculum components."
Chapter 5.  "I should like suggestions which would         99
            help me develop creative learning
            experiences."
Chapter 6.  "The process of selecting media to be         134
            used in instruction is important, and I
            need to know acceptable procedures."

Part III. Meeting Students' Special Needs
Chapter 7.  "I could use help in developing ways          159

to foster desirable student attitudes
and values."

Chapter 8. "I need assistance in finding ways to        177
challenge the gifted student and to
motivate the slow learner."

Chapter 9. "One of the most difficult things I          212
have to do is to select appropriate
materials and instructional strategies
for mentally and physically handicapped students."

Chapter 10. "Support and suggestions for solving        246
special reading problems are my
greatest needs."

Part IV. Professional Growth
Chapter 11. "I would benefit from encouragement         275
to grow professionally and from more
information about in-service education
opportunities."

Chapter 12. "My media skills need updating so           285
that I can function effectively in a
multi-media learning environment."

Chapter 13. "I am interested in the design, crea-       296
tion, and production of non-print
materials related to instruction."

Chapter 14. "My greatest weakness is the promo-         312
tion of good school-community
relationships."

Summary of Guidelines for use of Media Center           324

Appendixes
    I. Selected References on Learning Packages.        329
    II. Selected References on Learning Centers.        331
    III. Independent Study
        III-A. Independent Study Guidelines For         333
        Students.

4

III-B. Commitment of Teacher-Consultant. 335
III-C. Teacher Recommendation Form. 336
III-D. Independent Study Application. 338
III-E. Selected References on Independent 339
Study.
IV. Tutorial Program
IV-A. Letter to Parents. 340
IV-B. Memo to Teachers. 342
IV-C. Selected References on Student 343
Tutors.
V. Selected References on Simulations. 345
VI. Selected References on Inquiry and 346
Discovery.
VII. Guidelines for Group Leadership. 347
VIII. Selected References on Small Group Work. 350
IX. Selected References on Oral History. 352
X. School Library Bill of Rights for School 353
Library Media Programs.
XI. Selection Aids for Printed Materials.
XI-A. Book Selection Aids. 355
XI-B. Current Selection Aids. 359
XI-C. Free and Inexpensive Materials 361
Selection Aids.
XII. Selection Aids for Non-Print Materials. 362
XIII. Sources of Information and Materials for 366
the Handicapped.
XIV. Suggested Ways to Share Books. 370
XV. Suggested Library Activities for Reading, 376
Viewing, Listening, and Personal
Guidance.
XVI. Selected References on Production of 381
Non-Print Materials.
XVII. Some Basic Reference Materials for 383
Teachers to Know.

Index 391

# Table of Figures

Figure No.
1. Summary of Facets of Media Center                          23
2. The Roles of Media Specialists and Teachers in            41
    Implementation of Curriculum
3. Types and Results of Inequality of Teaching              101
4. A Formula for Creativity                                 126
5. Steps in Valuing Process                                 161
6. Reading Guidance for the Gifted                       184–85
7. Checklist for Independent Study Assignments             194
8. Techniques and Behaviors for Working with              207
    Slow Learners
9. General Services of the Media Specialist for          220–21
    Handicapped Students
10. Media Center Services that Promote                   281–83
    Professional Growth
11. Media and Activity Suggestions for Diversified         286
    Teaching
12. Skills for Teacher Use of Non-print Materials          290
13. Media Center Skills for Teachers                     292–93
14. Production Skills                                    303–04

FOREWORD

The Teacher's Handbook on the School Library Media Center provides an easy-to-read, practical source of help for educators, whether experienced or new to the field. It can also serve a needed function for prospective teachers and administrators. The education professional has a general knowledge of the developments that have occurred in various aspects of the education world — curriculum, methods, approach, materials, administration, and supervision. But this book gives a closer look at one of the most dramatic: the advent of intrinsic, instructional use of materials and technology, media and media centers as a component of classroom operation.

The perception of media as encompassing all forms and channels of communication used in the transmittal of information opened new directions and concepts. The uses of old and more recently developed materials and processes described in the handbook offer guidance for the creative person, direction and reinforcement for the beginning teacher. It offers know-how and techniques to one who may be experiencing difficulty in the proliferating tasks of teaching today's youth.

The authors, Betty Martin and Linda Sargent, have captured the everyday concerns of teachers and spoken to them with cogent responses. Preservice teacher training institutions will find the handbook a valuable reference and study guide for prospective teachers; its uses for in-service staff development are almost unlimited. Through it, administrators will develop deeper insight into the relatedness

7

of a good school library media center to classroom teaching and learning.

I recommend it to any practitioner as a book well worth owning.

ELIZABETH DUNCAN KOONTZ
*Assistant State Superintendent for*
*Teacher Education*

North Carolina State Department
of Public Instruction

During our combined thirty-nine years of professional experience in public elementary and secondary schools we have heard many teachers express various needs. We both believe strongly that a good library media program, administered by a competent library media specialist, has valuable contributions to make toward meeting many of those needs and bringing depth and vitality to the total school program. The purpose of this book is to define and interpret these contributions to teachers. Each chapter is devoted to one area of teacher concern, and its content is designed for reference according to an individual teacher's specific interest. There are many "see also" cross-references to other chapters. Overlapping among areas necessitates repeating in one chapter some information in another.

The terminology used is generally that of the guidelines of the American Association of School Librarians, prepared and published by the American Library Association and the Association for Educational Communications and Technology, *Media Programs, District and School.* It should be noted that the word "library," eliminated from this 1975 publication in an effort to emphasize the non-print and active instructional role rather than the old-time passive and supplemental responsibilities of the library media center, has now been widely restored to use by the profession. Wherever in this book the designations "media center" or "media specialist" are employed, it is understood to be a shortened form of "library media." Also, on the subject of words and phrases that "stand in" for others to avoid length or awkwardness, wherever "he" is used, it should be understood to mean he or she.

Definitions include:

*Media* — all forms and channels used in the transmittal of information process. *Both print and non-print materials* and their accompanying technologies are included.

*Media Specialist* — a person with appropriate certification and broad professional preparation, both in education and media, with competencies to carry out a media program.

*School Media Center* — an area or system of areas in the school where a full range of information sources, associated equipment, and services from a media staff are accessible to students, school personnel, and the school community.

*Media Aide* — a member of the media staff who performs clerical and secretarial tasks and assists as needed in the acquisition, maintenance, inventory, production, distribution, and utilization of materials and equipment.

*Media Technician* — a member of the media staff with technical skills in such specialized areas as graphics production and display, information and materials processing, photographic reproduction, operation and maintenance of audio-visual equipment, operation, and maintenance of television equipment, and installation of systems components.

The specific purposes of our book are:

1. to provide information concerning the role of the media specialist in relation to the overall school program;
2. to offer suggestions about ways in which to use the media center and the services of its staff as resources for more productive learning;
3. to describe ways in which to stimulate student interest in learning;

4. to project and specify some cooperative teacher-media specialist activities;
5. to assist in fostering creativity in the teaching-learning process;
6. to suggest ways to provide more effective learning experiences geared to each student's individual needs and goals.

Each chapter was submitted to several teachers at both elementary and secondary levels. Each was asked to comment, and their comments are given at the end of the appropriate chapters, with our response to the affirmations, disagreements, or uncertainties expressed. This was extremely helpful, as it gave us reactions to what we had said and the opportunity, in some cases, to clarify it. All but three of our South Carolina respondents were from the Greenville, South Carolina, public school system, two from Furman University, also in Greenville, and another from the Greenville County schools. Two North Carolinians from elsewhere helped us enormously too.

We express our great appreciation to the following, who read all or part of the manuscript and offered their comments and suggestions:

Dr. Hazel Harris, Furman University
Dr. Jim Mahaffey, Furman University
Ms. Jane Satterfield, Greenville County Schools
Dr. Denny Wolfe, North Carolina State Department of Public Instruction

And our thanks also to those who wrote comments about specific chapters:

Joanne Alexander, Wade Hampton High School
Evelyn Anderson, Riverside High School

Lillian Brock, Southside High School
Gloria Brooks, East North Street Elementary School
Larry Greer, Beck Middle School
Hope McCleskey, Augusta Circle Elementary School
Laura Pfister, Brook Glenn Elementary School
Betty Reagan, J. L. Mann High School
Pat Taylor, Hughes Middle School
Polly Wallace, Special Education Consultant
Celio O. Wolfe, Broughton High School, Raleigh, N. C.
Louise Wykes, Wade Hampton High School

And, finally, we express our appreciation to the staff of
the Furman University Library for their assistance in
locating materials.

# PART I

## BASIC INFORMATION

# 1

## "I Should Like To Have A Clearer Understanding Of The Scope Of A Media Center."

The library media center contributes to the educational growth of students through the learning experiences offered in its central facility and through the broad range of services that enhance and expand these experiences by carrying them beyond the physical boundaries of the center itself into other areas of the school and community. All these experiences and services comprise the media program.

Library media program learning opportunities may best be defined by describing at least eight of the program's aspects. These aspects do not "stand alone," but overlap and are interrelated.

The first of these eight aspects is that of the media center as a **Multimedia Resource Center.** Those of you who teach in a school with an excellent media resource center know the great variety of media that are available. Those who are not as fortunate might like an inventory of some of these:

15

Books
Newspapers
Pamphlets
Periodicals
Charts and Maps
Globes
Study kits
Art prints
Audio disk and tape recordings
Study guides
Video tapes
Filmstrips
Laboratory manuals
Microcards
Microfilms
Games and puzzles
Microslides
Motion pictures (8mm or 16mm)
Slides
Programmed learning packages
Transparencies
Models and realia
Toys (elementary)
Small animals (elementary)
Community resources access

In addition, there are materials in new formats which will be coming on the market in future years. Equipment needed to use the non-print materials as well as that for producing one's own unique instructional materials should be in good supply and maintained in working condition. Such rich resources offer stimulating possibilities for the enterprising, versatile teacher and for students. However, this abundance might as well be under lock and key if the media staff has not organized the resources so that they will be easily accessible to teachers and students, and helped them learn to use these effectively.

This accessibility requires the orderly arrangement of the materials according to a standard classification system, usually the Dewey Decimal Classification. It requires that the files providing the key to finding all these materials must be so placed as to make them easy for the students to consult. The files should not be sequestered in an office, nor separated according to print or non-print format. Accessibility is achieved in some schools by arranging non-print materials on the open shelves with the books, but this is not possible or desirable in all schools.

Closely related to the first aspect is that of the media center as a **Communications Center.** The wisdom, the mistakes, conjectures, and reflections of past and present ages as well as the facts, are communicated to students by printed, visual, or aural symbols. They can select the information best suited to their purpose and learning style, decode it, organize, analyze, synthesize, and apply it. This application usually takes the form of presenting the results of their work to teacher and class. In the process they develop the skills of communication with others, including the media staff, which guides and facilitates the process of learning communication skills. This staff is in the business of helping students to look and see (visual literacy), to listen and hear by means of both non-print productions and the written or spoken word.

This leads directly into one of the most valuable characterizations, or aspects, of the media center, that of a **Learning Laboratory.** Students can go to the media center to locate and use information to verify, broaden, and apply and experiment with the facts and concepts presented in their textbooks. They learn skills not only of location but also of discrimination in selection and more effective ways to utilize materials. In a good library media situation students come individually to look at a filmstrip, to listen to a recording, to make transparencies or slides, to find several books on a subject and compare the facts, to consult an article in a periodical, to learn how to use specific reference books, to work on an independent study report, to learn how to operate a particular piece of equipment, to receive help from a volunteer tutor, to plan a bulletin board display for a classroom, to borrow a camera for a special project— and more. Reasons for going to the media center may spring from personal interest or from teacher motivation. It is important that no one and nothing—not the media staff, nor the teachers, nor administrative structures—erect barriers limiting such individual student access.

Small groups of students may also make much use of the media center as a learning laboratory. This depends a great deal upon the degree to which teachers' instructional strategies include the use of small group work. The prognosis for improved student learning with this mode of teaching is often a good one, and more and more teachers are turning to this strategy when they know that the media center is capable of supporting it. Some of the media staff's most productive work is done with small groups, where there is an identified, common learning purpose or a common interest. These small groups use the media center to locate materials, to receive instruction on a needed skill, to research a project, to produce non-print materials, to plan their work together, to review a film or video tape, to consult a study guide, to analyze critically an account in several newspapers, to make a tape recording of their report, and many other activities. Small group work in the media center develops student interest, involvement, and responsibility for learning.

Visits by a whole class to the media center were once the standard formula for insuring minimal exposure to the library, but they had little impact on the truly integrated instructional use of books and other media. Now that we know more about individual abilities and the variety of learning styles among students, and, above all, because of the transformation of the use of the media center from supplemental/enrichment to fully instructional status, this way of using the media center doesn't seem to be profitable. However, there are occasions when it is practical and effective if properly planned for. For instance, a teacher might wish to take a whole class to the media center because a different topic had been assigned to each of four groups and they all planned to gather materials. Or a teacher at the beginning of a unit requiring a lot of periodical work might take the entire class to the media center for introductory instruction on the *Reader's Guide to Periodical Literature*, to be followed up later by a small group instruction. Care should be taken in whole-class use of the media center that the needs of individual students are not overlooked.

Discussion of the media center as a learning laboratory emphasizes that one of its most valuable aspects is the opportunity to teach students, and to help them to practice, *how to learn*. The ability to *think* has long since been identified by the Educational Policies Commission of the National Education Association as the central purpose of American education.(6) As the student reflects on ideas, examines them critically, and works with them creatively, adapting them to his own uses, he is on his way toward being an independent learner and to developing patterns of thinking, conceptualizing, and decision-making which can be followed all his life in coping with, and solving, problems of home, community, work, and national life.

Teachers may also think of the media center as a learning laboratory for their professional or personal learning. Through available professional books, magazines, pamphlets, tapes, and other materials, they can keep up to date in their areas of specialization. In-service workshops can sharpen their own skills and make them more aware of skills needed by students. Teachers and media specialists can use materials to learn together how to design improved instructional units and teaching aids. Familiarity with the collection in the media center can greatly help teachers in understanding its desirable uses and applications for special student needs.

Still another aspect of the media center is **Recreational**.

19

Lest anyone think that it is "out of character" to provide for such a function in a school, it should be remembered that the ideal in the world of school (as in the world outside it) is to bring work, learning, and leisure closer together, not to emphasize their separateness. Often insufficient attention is given to providing time for students to unwind, to relax, to let their minds wander and wonder a bit, to "re-create" themselves. Just possibly the library media center could introduce the concept that exercising the mind can be as pleasurable as exercising the body. It is true that some media staff members do not take kindly to those students in the media center who are apparently doing nothing, even when they are not interfering with the work of other students. But this activity may fill a real need, and a teacher can interpret this to the media specialist on a student's behalf if necessary. Students who browse among books or magazines, look at a filmstrip, listen to a recording just for fun, play checkers or chess, work a puzzle, or merely daydream will probably come back to their work refreshed and recharged. In addition, they are developing desirable habits for the use of leisure time. These extra-curricular experiences often include learning aspects, and, most important, they mean that a student feels pleased and comfortable with the media center's surroundings.

The media center may, in another of its aspects, be described as a **Teaching Center**. The media staff instructs students in the skills of locating and using materials and operating equipment. They may also teach, according to their competencies, lessons in various courses, as requested by teachers. For example, a media specialist who had visited Williamsburg might teach a lesson about Colonial Williamsburg to an American history class. An important part of instruction is teaching students to be discriminating in their selection of materials and to work with the data they have gathered. Research skills, coordinated with the work of subject teachers, are often taught by the media staff. Students are also taught to evaluate motion pictures, TV, and recordings, and to recognize and appreciate those of high quality.

In many schools literacy and developmental reading skills are taught in the media complex. One-on-one tutorial work takes place, also seminars and small-group discussions for talented and gifted students.

It may be evident, from comments already made, that the media center functions as a **Production Center** for teachers and students. The facilities and equipment are available for teachers to produce materials for their classes, and for students to design and create materials to illustrate a project, present an independent study report, describe a process, or clarify an event. These activities are a valuable addition to the media program, although some schools have not yet acquired the equipment and staff to put them into effect. They are so significant in broadening the horizons of the gifted and in stimulating learning by average and slow students that every effort should be made to provide them. Production facilities are especially helpful in bringing the life of the school—its clubs, its special interest groups, its events, its PTA and community—swirling through the media center and, conversely, in sending the media center out into the mainstream of school life.

A closely related facet of the media center is that of **Resource for Student Personal and Social Development.** The opportunities here for students to become self-directed learners and more confident persons are numerous. There is also the possibility of learning to share with others, consideration for the rights of others, responsibility and dependability. Working in the media center, students learn the give-and-take of relationships with their peers and with those younger and older. There are many occasions for them to become sensitized to the needs of others and to practice making adjustments in their own behavior. Above all, the climate of the media center, the nearness of so much to know and think about, can inspire.

The media center is also a **Consultation Center**. Both teachers and students can "try out" their ideas on the media specialist and expect empathetic and interested help on a variety of subjects. Some examples of teacher consultation with the media specialist are:

—The design of a learning package.
—A suitable speaker on a certain subject.
—Materials to achieve a particular objective.
—Ways to stimulate slow learners.
—Appropriate design for a learning center.
—Suggested materials to introduce a unit.
—Ways to evaluate a unit.
—Media skills needed during a unit.

Samples of student consultations are:

—An effective way to report on research.
—Suggested organization of data.
—An interesting way to share a book with the class.
—Advice on the technique of interviewing people.
—Sources for current material on a subject.
—Guidance in making a sound-slide program.
—Ways to determine the authority of an author.
—Suggestions for broadening personal reading.
—Help with information about a hobby.

Some teachers do not take advantage of the consultant expertise of media staff members. On the other hand, in some schools the media staff members are not qualified by training or experience to serve in this capacity. If teachers were to make them aware that such consultative help would be welcome, media staff members might be motivated to acquire the needed training.

The following chart (Figure 1) presents a summary of the various aspects or characterizations of the media center.

FIGURE 1
SUMMARY OF FACETS OF THE MEDIA CENTER

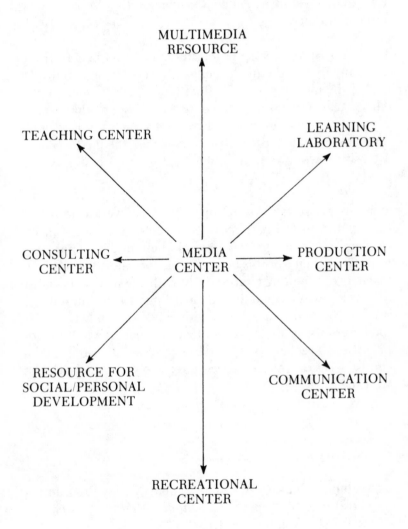

MULTIMEDIA
RESOURCE

TEACHING CENTER

LEARNING
LABORATORY

CONSULTING
CENTER

MEDIA
CENTER

PRODUCTION
CENTER

RESOURCE FOR
SOCIAL/PERSONAL
DEVELOPMENT

COMMUNICATION
CENTER

RECREATIONAL
CENTER

The focus of this chapter has been on the learning experiences in the media center. The next chapter, which is concerned with the role of the media specialist, will treat these experiences in more depth and will indicate how they are expanded and extended throughout the whole school and community.

TEACHER'S RESERVATION: Often students do not benefit from the many uses of the media center. In theory these multiple uses of the media center are fine, but in reality many high-school teachers do not have time to use media center resources to such an extent. Frequently such use is seen as supplementary to basic instruction. To use the media center extensively would require planning time that is simply not available.

WRITERS' RESPONSE: This point of view is a very traditional one in that in the past the media center was not seen by teachers as an integrated part of their instructional program. The theme of this book is to explore the advantages to teachers of planning continuously with the media specialist to develop ways of making the learning process interesting, productive, and geared to individual needs. While time—or the lack of it—is always a problem, it becomes a question of priorities. Teachers who make a practice of using media center services and resources extensively consider it time well spent.

BIBLIOGRAPHY

1. Adams, Charles W. "The School Media Program: a Position Statement." *School Media Quarterly*, 2:127–43, Winter, 1974.
2. Beatty, LaMond F. "Do Media Specialists See Them-

selves as Others See Them?" *Audiovisual Instruction,* 21:44–45, November, 1976.

3. Clark, G. "Echoes of the 60's Advocacy in the School Media Center of the 80's." *American Libraries,* 10:369–72, June, 1979.
4. Cyr, Helen W. "Why Not the Instant Media Center?" *School Libraries,* 20:21–23, Spring, 1971.
5. Davies, Ruth Ann. *The School Library Media Center: A Force for Educational Excellence.* New York, R. R. Bowker, 1974.
6. Educational Policies Commission. *The Central Purpose of American Education.* Washington, D. C., National Education Association, 1961.
7. Goodwin, Georgie. "An Educational Tool for All." *American Libraries,* 1:164–65, February, 1970.
8. Gambell, Trevor T. *Developing Children's Language Through the Elementary School Media Center.* Edmonton, Alberta, University of Alberta, 1976.
9. Gillespie, John T. *A Model School District Media Program.* Chicago, American Library Association, 1977.
10. Gillespie, John and Diane L. Spirt. *Creating a School Media Program.* New York, R. R. Bowker, 1973.
11. Goodlad, John J. *Facing the Future; Issues in Education and Schooling.* New York, McGraw-Hill, 1976.
12. Jay, Hilda. "Increasing the Use of Secondary School Libraries." *School Libraries,* 20:23–26, Summer, 1971.
13. Henne, Frances. "Learning to Learn in School Libraries." *School Libraries,* 15:15–23, May, 1966.
14. Hug, William E. *Instructional Design and the Media Program.* Chicago, American Library Association, 1975.
15. Hunt, Lyman C. "The Lively Learning Center and the Alert Librarian." *Wilson Library Bulletin,* 45:293–97, November, 1970.
16. Kingsbury, Mary E. "Future of School Media Centers." *School Library Quarterly,* 4:19–26, Fall, 1975.

17. Klonz, Mary P. "The Role of the Media Center in the Education of Disadvantaged Children." *Southeastern Librarian*, 20:158–65, Fall, 1970.
18. Lacey, R. A. "Taming King Kong: Lessons of the Recent Past." (Setting up a School Media Program.) in *Center for Understanding Media. Doing the Media*. Chicago, American Library Association, 1979.
19. Leviten, Karen. "The School Library as an Instructional Information System." *School Media Quarterly*, 13:194–203, Spring, 1975.
20. *Media Programs, District and School*. Prepared by the American Association of School Librarians, American Library Association, and the Association for Educational Communications and Technology. Chicago, American Library Association, and Washington, Association for Educational Communications and Technology, 1975.
21. Pearson, Neville P. and Lucile Butler. *Instructional Materials Centers; Selected Readings*. Minneapolis, Burgess Publishing Company, 1969.
22. Prostano, Emanuel T. and Joyce S. Prostano. *The School Library Media Center*. Littleton, Colorado, Libraries Unlimited, 1971.
23. Smith, George N. "Modern School Media Centers," *School Media Quarterly*, 3:10, Fall, 1974.
24. Sullivan, Peggy. *Impact: The School Library and the Instructional Program*. Chicago, American Library Association, 1967.
25. Ward, Pearl L. and Robert Baron. *The School Media Center, A Book of Readings*. Metuchen, New Jersey, Scarecrow Press, 1973.
26. Whitenack, Carolyn J. "The School Media Program: Emerging Multi-media Services." *Library Trends*, 19:410–17, April, 1971.

# 2

## "It Would Help Me to Know More About the Activities of the Media Specialist and About How We Can Work as a Team."

There are some teachers who actually envy or even resent media specialists because they think being a media specialist is such an easy job. In these cases teachers have either been victims of a false image and not in close enough contact to learn the true facts, or their experience has been with a media specialist who has been inadequately trained or who is neglecting the responsibilities of the position. Can anyone be said to have an "easy job" who is responsible for the acquisition, organization, storage, distribution, retrieval, maintenance, administration, and evaluation of a large quantity of materials and equipment, not to mention the accompanying, and even more time-consuming, program of utilization? Add to this continuing research and development for the improvement of the media program, and one can understand that it is difficult for a single person to perform all of these tasks well. For proper operation of the media center, adequate support personnel, technical and clerical aides, must be added to the media staff. However, the media professional, or the head of the media program where there is more than one specialist in the school, is accountable for the total operation and program. A multi-faceted program, operating at optimum effectiveness, requires a qualified media specialist for every 250 pupils.

The media specialist functions in partnership with the school faculty to devise and put into effect an instructional program that implements school objectives. The media program is a vital component of this schoolwide program. According to Davies, "The function of the library media program is to support, to implement, to enrich, to vitalize, and to humanize the educational program as it strives to attain excellence in content, process and product."[4]

The media specialist's activities are a response to the needs of the school program as it is implemented by the strategies jointly developed by teachers and the media specialist. Responsibility for these activities is assumed partly by teachers, partly by the media specialist, and by both working together cooperatively. It may be a new idea for the teacher to perceive the media specialist as a collaborator in the planning and development of both curriculum and teaching strategies, and many teachers may not realize that in most states media specialists are now certified as teachers as well as in the media field. They may be considered as competent as other teachers involved in curricular decisions and plans. For too long the capability of media specialists in these areas has not been recognized or utilized. Largely because of the lag between perception and reality, work with media is still seen by some as being technical or clerical in nature, and library media specialists have been limited to serving as the collectors, organizers, and distributors of materials and equipment.

The following outline of the updated, expanded role of the media specialist focuses on activities in relation to the implementation of curricular objectives. Today's library media specialist may be expected to

28

ORGANIZE SPACES SUITABLE FOR VARIOUS ACTIVITIES.

*For teachers and students*, the media specialist
Provides a physically attractive and pleasant environment in which many interesting exhibits and displays arouse curiosity and appeal to interests.
Administers efficient work spaces for individual, small-group, and whole-class reading, viewing, and listening.
Makes available the facilities and equipment for the production of materials.
Provides space for the evaluation of new media.
Makes all spaces easily accessible, and comfortable.

*For teachers* the media specialist
Maintains an area where teachers may consult and/or review professional and instructional materials, including books, pamphlets, tapes, films, sample instructional units, new curricular trends, and notices of workshops, meetings, etc.

SUPPORT AN EXCELLENT TEACHING/LEARNING PROCESS

*For teachers and students* the media specialist
Carries out research to assess the responsibilities of the media program in relation to the school program and cooperatively sets objectives.
Gathers, organizes, distributes, and promotes an extensive general collection of print and non-print materials and equipment.
Has a thorough knowledge of these resources and provides guidance in their use.
Makes available special collections, such as paperback books, vocational guidance materials, materials for minorities, books with high interest and low vocabulary level.

Locates specific materials for identified ability levels and purposes.

Maintains flexible circulation procedures to accommodate diversified learning needs.

Is alert to new media as they are issued and adds them to the collection.

Trains students and teachers to use mediated instructional units.

Compiles bibliographies as needed.

Maintains an ongoing evaluation of the media program.

*For teachers* the media specialist

Plans instructional modules with individual teachers or teaching teams, assists in identifying objectives, activities, evaluation methods, and available materials.

Works with teachers to develop learning packages or other special material for the slow students.

Designs with teachers special projects to help identify and challenge gifted students.

Makes up collections of materials for use in class areas.

Advises teachers concerning effective ways to use different types of media.

Locates speakers who can contribute to the study topics and identifies relevant places in the community with educative value for class visits.

Plans jointly with the teachers various ways in which the whole class, small groups, or individuals may use the media center.

Offers to visit class areas to participate in discussions, give book talks, teach skills or other lessons, evaluate student work, etc.

Evaluates units already taught, material available, and future need for additional supportive materials.

Keeps up-to-date on topics being studied in each class.

Identifies skills that students will need and the strategic times they should be taught in relation to instructional units in the classroom.

30

Advises teachers about new materials as they are received.

Plans with the principal for appointment of a school media advisory committee to suggest ways to improve the media program and to resolve problems. Both students and parents may be asked to serve on this committee.

*For Students* the media specialist

Helps individual or groups with reference work and research.

Assists students in the efficient processing of the information they have gathered as they evaluate, analyze, synthesize, organize, and apply it.

Helps students develop problem-solving skills and establish desirable learning patterns.

Suggests creative and imaginative ways for students to report the results of their research or share the books they have read.

Plans for slow-learning students to use appropriate materials and to engage in those activities that will assure success.

Suggests for talented and gifted students the materials and projects that will employ their full capabilities.

Encourages students to make use of nonprint materials as well as print resources. Develops procedures for home use of these materials and equipment necessary to use them.

Helps students to become independent learners.

Displays student work in the media center.

Sets up a student media committee to discuss problems and to make suggestions for a more effective media program.

DEVELOP POLICY FOR A WISE SELECTION OF NEW MEDIA

*For teachers and students* the media specialist

Organizes workshops on evaluation techniques.

Orders media for assessment purposes.

Supplies and circulates lists of new media.

Sets up groups to evaluate new media and make recommendations, or participates in and promotes such a district-wide plan.

Compiles these recommendations and publicizes them.

Calls attention to reviews in professional publications.

Arranges for a commercial house to offer a training session on utilization of new curriculum components.

## PROPOSE ACTIVITIES TO WIDEN HORIZONS

*For teachers and students* the media specialist

Plans bulletin board displays on the background of current events.

Jointly with teachers and/or students plans displays and activities on such subjects as the frontiers of science, various aspects of the economy, the government, international relations, etc.

Jointly with teachers and/or students fosters projects on other countries, their cultures, history, and their places in the community of nations.

Publicizes educational programs and events in the community.

Compiles lists of materials on subjects of personal interest to students or teachers, or related to such interests.

Sets up a TV and motion picture corner featuring related materials.

*For teachers* the media specialist

Assists in keeping them abreast of educational innovations and trends.

Plans with them various workshops as needed.

Displays exceptional student projects that illustrate creative teaching.

Edits a media news sheet with notes of productive uses of media in teaching.

Establishes a professional area in the media center for professional materials and notices.

Places displays of professional materials in the teachers' lounge and sets up a self-charging system.

Offers to secure professional materials from other sources.

Promotes vertical articulation in professional concerns by arranging for communication with teachers in schools in levels immediately above or below. For example, middle school teachers could participate in workshops with elementary or high-school teachers.

Encourages teachers to write articles for professional publications.

Keeps teachers informed about local, state, regional, or national professional meetings, conferences, etc.

## PROMOTE PERSONAL/SOCIAL GROWTH

*For teachers* the media specialist

Keeps relations with teachers free from bias, prejudice, or school politics.

Accepts and values each teacher.

Gives recognition to productive activities that have resulted from good working relationships among teachers.

By words and actions promotes good rapport among teachers and between teachers and administrators.

Jointly with teachers organizes a workshop on human relations.

*For students* the media specialist

Informs teachers and counselors of observed developing student problems.

Keeps in close touch with counselors to make contributions to the guidance program.

Serves on faculty committees seeking to help students

who have adjustment difficulties.

Maintains a close, warm, accepting relationship with students.

Allows students to serve as media student assistants if it seems possible that the responsibilities will have a positive effect upon their personal or social behavior.

Encourages teachers to use the strategy of small group work so that students have opportunities for social interaction.

## Aid in the Development of Competency in Basic Skills

*For teachers and students* the media specialist

Locates and orders pertinent materials.

Has a thorough knowledge of the collection of materials and the skills for which they may be used.

Suggests and, cooperatively with teachers, puts into effect many strategies that will stimulate students' motivation to read.

Sets up displays demonstrating the value of being a good reader, of being expert with words.

Has available an extensive collection of paperback books that appeal to students; circulates some of these in collections to class areas.

Implements special projects on authors, their work and lives.

Keeps in close touch with teachers, especially reading specialists, to ascertain students' interests and reading levels; initiates joint reading projects.

Publicizes materials on these interests.

Encourages students to increase writing skills by writing reviews of books read, to be posted in media center or published in a media news sheet.

Jointly with teachers undertakes a project for students to write letters requesting free and inexpensive materials.

Participates with teachers in the process of publishing a school magazine featuring student creative writing.

34

Secures, publicizes, and makes available tapes, transparencies, and other materials for mathematics instruction.

Encourages the use of reference sources in the media center for students to find the many practical applications of mathematics in everyday life.

## ENCOURAGE DEVELOPMENT OF AESTHETIC APPRECIATION AND KNOWLEDGE

*For teachers and students* the media specialist

Motivates enjoyment of literature of the highest quality with individual students and groups.

Puts into effect a continuing program on outstanding authors; also artists, musicians, film-makers, dancers, and actors.

Posts notices of local or regional cultural events and significant TV programs or motion pictures.

Cooperates with teachers in designing lessons on critical evaluation of TV programs and motion pictures.

Supports the programs of the English, art, and music teachers.

Sets up an "art corner" in the media center with frequently changed displays.

Offers study courses for teachers to familiarize them with outstanding books being written today for young people.

## HELP ESTABLISH AND MAINTAIN GOOD COMMUNITY/SCHOOL RELATIONS

*For teachers and students* the media specialist

Develops and maintains a community resource file of people and places that have educative value.

Helps to identify and schedule volunteer tutors from the community.

Welcomes the assistance of volunteers in appropriate tasks

in the media center (not all of them menial or routine). Develops programs for PTA meetings to interpret the media program.

Offers to serve as a speaker on general school topics at community meetings.

Involves community members in groups discussing educational programs or other subjects of interest.

Invites parents to discussions about the books their children are reading, and about other media experiences they are having.

Asks parents to participate in media selection and evaluation groups.

Invites parents to serve in an advisory capacity in setting media program goals.

## Foster Desirable Habits and Attitudes

*For teachers and students* the media specialist

Encourages habits of using media resources by maintaining a welcoming receptive attitude toward all teachers and students and their requests.

Builds a favorable attitude toward the media center by encouraging interest and eagerness to help in the projects and programs of other departments and teachers.

Is consistent in providing the assistance requested, in offering helpful suggestions, and in following through on plans made with teachers.

*For students* the media specialist

Makes the media center an interesting, exciting place for learning.

Gives recognition to those students demonstrating desirable habits and attitudes.

Is pleasant, firm, and fair toward those students with negative attitudes and disruptive habits.

Administers the media center with as few rules as possible

governing the use of the center, and states these rules in positive form.

*For teachers* the media specialist

Gives orientation to all teachers new to the school.

Gives instruction to teachers on the use of new media as they are acquired.

Gives instruction to teachers on other skills as the need arises in the instructional program.

Makes sure that teachers have the opportunity to become skillful in the production of non-print materials.

Develops a handbook for teachers listing objectives, activities, materials, and evaluation for each skill.

Plans skills instruction with teachers so that lessons are woven into the curriculum and are taught when students need to use the skills.

Identifies weaknesses as students are observed using media resources and notifies teachers which skills should be taught.

Urges teachers to provide many opportunities for students to make use of skills taught.

Devises diagnostic instruments to assess students' progress in learning skills.

*For students* the media specialist

Teaches skills individually or in small groups.

Varies instruction and materials according to ability levels of students.

Emphasizes reteaching and review as necessary.

Develops learning centers and learning packages on various skills.

Teaches students the skills of producing transparencies, sound-slide sequences, video tapes, and other non-print materials.

Is quick to assist students when they are spending an inordinate amount of time locating information.

Gives much attention to assisting in study skills and habits and encouraging their practice, especially organizing time, materials, and data.

## PROVIDE FOR DIVERGENT STUDENT ABILITIES

*For teachers* the media specialist

Makes available materials for special needs on specified reading and ability levels.

Works with teachers to develop special learning centers and learning packages or other specialized instructional modules.

Advises teachers concerning media skills appropriate for gifted students.

Cooperates with administrators and teachers in securing student or volunteer parent tutors for the slow learners.

Gives teachers information on applicable innovative teaching techniques as these appear in professional publications.

*For students* the media specialist

Encourages independent study for students who qualify.

Secures advanced materials from state libraries and from universities and special libraries for gifted students.

Provides accessible media facilities for the physically handicapped.

Provides ways to use equipment they can handle.

Secures books in braille for those visually impaired.

Has on hand filmstrips with captions for those with hearing deficiencies.

Initiates a workshop on signing for teachers and students.

Works in small groups with students, using books and related sound filmstrips.

Finds students and volunteer adults to assist the handicapped and slow learners and works with them on a
one-to-one basis.

Teaches all handicapped students simple skills of producing non-print materials, with other students
assisting if necessary.

Reads or arranges for reading to small groups, and stimulates discussions.

Works individually with students on finding and using
information and selecting books for recreational
reading.

In addition to the activities listed above the media specialist also has curricular responsibilities in relation to the
school principal. These usually involve conferences. Martin
and Carson have listed the significant areas of consultation.(9) They are as follows:

The assessed needs of the media program
Basic policies of the media program
Immediate and long-range goals and objectives
A review of operational routines
Plans for a flexible use of the media center
In-service education activities
Curriculum planning with staff members
The media budget
Ways to increase teacher and student use of the media
center
Service to atypical students
Trends in media service and innovative uses of media
Special projects suggested
A review of the media specialist's annual and/or monthly
reports
Deficiencies in media staff
Media quarters and equipment and collections
Student behavior problems
Evaluation structure

Publicity concerning media services
Selection of new media
Assignment of media personnel to extra duties
Circulation of non-print material for home use
Continuing education of the media staff
The climate and opportunity for innovative activities
Stimulation of the integration of media with school
    programs

It is self-evident that the media specialist cannot afford to neglect these conferences with the principal. The decisions that are reached concern the total school program, and definitely have implications for teachers.

In reading and absorbing this review of the media specialist's role a teacher will see many opportunities, we hope, for effective partnership with the media specialist in turning student apathy into eagerness, teaching drudgery into enjoyment, and learning deficiencies into progress. To achieve these goals the media specialist and the teacher must respect each other's competencies and be prepared to meet each other halfway. Champlin found in a survey in 1969 among ninety-one teachers that there seems to be "only a limited amount of cooperation" between teacher and media specialist, and advocated that each try to understand the role of the other "in order to aid the student in obtaining a truly broadening education."(3)

As we said at the beginning of this chapter, a single media specialist with no support staff can hardly be expected to provide all of these services all the time, but a competent, energetic person should be able to handle many of them most of the time, given encouragement and high expectation on the part of teachers. There are unwilling, incompetent, unimaginative, rigid, uptight, and even downright disagreeable people among school library media specialists, probably in about the same proportion as among other groups of people. Admittedly, with often just one media

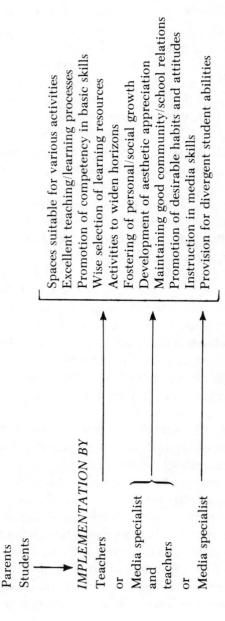

Figure 2

The Roles of the Media Specialist and Teachers in Implementation of Curriculum

INPUT FROM
Principal
Parents
Students

IMPLEMENTATION BY
Teachers
or
Media specialist
and
teachers
or
Media specialist

Spaces suitable for various activities
Excellent teaching/learning processes
Promotion of competency in basic skills
Wise selection of learning resources
Activities to widen horizons
Fostering of personal/social growth
Development of aesthetic appreciation
Maintaining good community/school relations
Promotion of desirable habits and attitudes
Instruction in media skills
Provision for divergent student abilities

specialist to choose from per school, a poor one will show up as very poor indeed and can make the kind of program we project well-nigh impossible. But even in real hardship cases teachers who know what they want in the way of services from the library media center and program, what in plain fact they have a *right to expect*, can press for and achieve changes for the better, whether these take the form of support staff, more attention and understanding from the administration, more budget, or even a personnel shift.

If you see the value of the expanded role of the library media specialist to the learning process in your school, you should confer with your principal on plans to make these services available. Teachers are being brought into the decision-making process more and more, and you have the opportunity to make your needs known and to investigate ways to provide for them.

TEACHER'S RESERVATION: The chapter expresses an ideal. It is not possible for one person to do all these things, and in most cases the media staff is too limited. . . . Media specialists know techniques, but they are not familiar with all content areas. It is true that teachers need to work more closely with media specialists, but to expect a media specialist to be an expert in all subject areas is unrealistic.

WRITERS' RESPONSE: These comments point up the need for expanded staff in media centers. It is to be hoped that teachers will make principals aware of the need for increased personnel. With adequate staff a wide range of services can be provided.

Teachers should remember that media specialists are certified as teachers in most states before they become media specialists, so they do have a degree of expertise and experience in many content areas. In their role as media specialists they read widely in educational literature and conduct extensive reviews of books in subject areas. These readings and

42

reviews give them considerable knowledge of subject area content.

BIBLIOGRAPHY

1. Beeler, M. G. Fancher et al. *Measuring the Quality of Library Service*. Metuchen, New Jersey, Scarecrow Press, 1974.
2. Boyland, Michael W. "The Media Specialist Involvement with Media." *Drexel Library Quarterly*, 9:47-57, July, 1973.
3. Champlin, Constance J. "Use of the Elementary Library by Classroom Teachers." Thesis. Nashville, Tennessee, George Peabody College for Teachers, 1969.
4. Davies, Ruth Ann. *The School Library, a Force for Educational Excellence*. New York, R. R. Bowker, 1969.
5. Forum, "What is a School Media Specialist?" *Tennessee Librarian*, 30:32-36, Fall, 1978.
6. Gillespie, John T. and Diane L. Spirt. *Creating a School Media Program*. New York, R. R. Bowker, 1975.
7. Hall, A. "Social Role of the School Librarian." *School Librarian*, 26:322-28, December, 1978.
8. Hug, William E. *Instructional Design and the Media Program*. Chicago, American Library Association, 1975.
9. Martin, Betty and Ben Carson. *The Principal's Handbook on the School Library Media Center*. Syracuse, New York, Gaylord Professional Publications, 1978.
10. Martin, Gordan E. "The Industrial Arts Teacher and the Media Specialist." *Audiovisual Instruction*, 21:36-38, April, 1976.
11. *Media Programs, District and School*. Prepared by the

American Association of School Librarians, American Library Association, and the Association for Educational Communications and Technology. Chicago, American Library Association, and Washington, Association for Educational Communications and Technology, 1975.

12. Penn, Vivian-Sue. "19 Ways to Love a Librarian." *Instructor*, 85:40–41, May, 1976.
13. Pillon, Nancy B. "Media Specialists Work with Teachers." *Drexel Library Quarterly*, 9:59–69, July, 1973.
14. Schmid, William T. "The Teacher and the Media Specialist." *Media and Methods*, 13:22–24, October, 1976.
15. Swenson, Evelyn T. "Library Science Training in Teacher Education." *Journal of Education for Librarianship*, VIII, Winter, 1968.
16. Taylor, Kenneth J. "Instruction First and Media Next." *Wisconsin Library Bulletin*, 68:81–88, March-April, 1972.
17. Taylor, Kenneth J. "Librarians, Audiovisual Consultants, and Instructional Planning." *Illinois Libraries*, 53:174–79, March, 1971.
18. Wehmeyer, Lillian Biermann. *The School Librarian as Educator*. Littleton, Colorado, Libraries Unlimited, 1976.

# 3

## "I Should Like To Know The Ways In Which The Media Center Can Be Used Most Effectively."

Whether or not a teacher considers that the use of the media center and its services is vital to the instructional program for *all* children depends upon past teaching experience, the competency of the media specialist or librarian with whom the teacher came in contact, and the quality of the media center or library in the school. In a survey of 91 teachers in the public schools of one city Champlin found that "most teachers view the main value of the school library as a reinforcement of classroom learning and not as an important agent in the actual learning process." Teachers reported their reasons for not using the library as follows:(8)

| | |
|---|---|
| Lack of time | 14.28% |
| Lack of access | 9.89% |
| Lack of materials | 9.89% |
| Inadequacy of physical facilities | 6.59% |
| Unpleasant personality of librarian | 3.29% |

Another point of view is that of the students. In a study among 1,240 students Jay found the following reasons given for not using the library:(14)

45

Too much lecture by teachers
Course content irrelevant or repetitive
Too little choice in assignments or topics
Too little student participation in classroom planning
Too cold a student-teacher relationship and classroom
    atmosphere
Too much dependence on textbook alone
No facilities for group work in the school libraries
Almost no student access to non-book materials
Restrictive pass system limiting access to the library

If both teachers and students feel frustrated and unhappy about the media center, the use will be minimal and many thousands of dollars will have been spent in vain. Yet we know that information is expanding at such a rapid pace that only one media center in a school will soon not be enough to supply the variety and quantity of current material required by an up-to-date curriculum. Interlibrary loans and access to other resources are already being required in some school programs, and this practice will increase. Before long, computer transmission through terminals located in the media center will be common so that regional or national data bases can be tapped.

When one thinks of the many ways in which media centers *can* be used, it is surprising that they aren't all overflowing with students all day. Here are some of the reasons that students might go to the media center:

To learn the skills of locating and using material and
    equipment.
To secure information to be used in achieving instructional objectives.
To secure materials for recreational purposes or for personal interests, e.g., books, recordings, filmstrips,
    magazines, etc.
To use the community resource file.

To work with a tutor.

To use a conference room for group planning or other activity.

To use a carrel for individual use of media.

To have a conference with the media specialist.

To design and produce transparencies, slides, filmstrips, or recordings.

To preview a film or filmstrip, or to audit a recording.

To secure materials and/or equipment for use in the class area or for home use.

To use a learning center.

To pursue an independent learning project.

To use an educational or simulation game.

To borrow materials such as a reproduction of a painting or other art object.

To fulfill responsibilities as a member of the media student assistant group.

To secure material to meet a special need, such as a reading problem, a sight disability, or advanced study.

To assist the media staff in selecting new materials.

To assist in planning an instructional unit or special project.

Students who engage in the above activities will most likely require the services of the media staff. In addition, many services of the media specialist and, to a lesser degree, of other media staff members are performed outside the media center and benefit not only students but also teachers and administrators. These services and activities include participation in curriculum meetings, in media selection conferences, in conferences with the principal, in planning with teachers, and in visits to class areas to talk about new books, to teach media skills, and to discuss critical handling of data.

Media resources have direct implications for all teaching strategies except perhaps the lecture method and programmed teaching, and even with these there are follow-up functions and possibilities. The contract plan, discovery method, individualization, inquiry method, problem solving, project method, team teaching, independent study, learning centers, learning packages, research assignments, etc.—all become more effective and productive when diversified resources are utilized which appeal to different interest and ability levels and which tailor learning opportunities to the individual student. In order for the media center and all its resources to be used effectively it is essential that

All media be organized for easy accessibility for students and staff members.

There be unrestricted use of all media in the media center except in situations where there is a lack of space or where some students consistently disregard the rights of others.

Teachers and media staff be committed to the belief that the integrated use of all relevant print and non-print materials is vital to an excellent instructional program.

All students be given instruction so that they may be self-directed and skillful in locating and using all types of media and that this instruction be directly related to the student's needs as they arise from his program of study.

The student's program provide many opportunities for functional use of these skills through quest-type activities or discovery projects.

There be continuing communication between teachers and media staff on the design of instructional programs and ways to utilize all media effectively as part of this design.

The use of media by individual students, small groups, or large groups be governed by the needs of the instructional program.

Teachers and the media staff guide student use of media

so as to encourage and foster critical thinking, creative
analysis and skill in organizing data and producing
media.

Teachers and the media staff build into the curriculum
many opportunities for students to make choices
among materials to be used and ways in which to use
them.

As students use media they be continuously guided in the
development of effective individual and group work
habits by teachers and media staff.

Teachers and media personnel involve students in selecting media, planning for its use, and evaluating its use.

Input from people in the community be given consideration in planning and promoting an instructional program which incorporates a wider and more productive
use of all media.

The media staff assist teachers in developing multimedia
kits or learning activity packages and in setting up interest centers in class areas and in the media center.

There are three aspects of the use of resources in the
media center which will have a significant effect upon the
quality of the experience: the teacher's own attitude toward
the media center and its staff; the teacher's preparation of
the student to use the media; and the teacher's assessment of
the student's work in the light of his freedom to make his
own selections and choices.

Attitudes are catching. If the teacher projects interest and
enthusiasm for going to the media center and working with
the staff there, students will be more apt to exhibit eagerness and a desire to participate in media center activities instead of considering it a "drag." In some schools the teachers
do not go with their classes to the media center when the
whole class goes, and thereby send the message that such a
visit is unimportant. If teachers show that they don't think
that the media center is worth a visit, their students will

almost surely adopt the same attitude. Teachers subtly advertise their advocacy of the media center by frequently making such remarks as: "Who would like to see if there is any more recent information in the media center?"; "Let's check the media center for the latest statistic about this"; "The media specialist will be able to help us find some poems on this subject." Such habitual references and questions on a wide variety of subjects will pique student curiosity and point up the value of a place where so many answers are available and where different paths to learning are respected and encouraged.

The success of the media center experience also depends upon how thoroughly students are prepared before they leave the classroom to use the media center. Students should be aware of the skills they are going to need there. If they are weak in some of them, the teacher can arrange for the media specialist to give the needed instruction. Students need to understand the purpose of the work they will be doing as well as terms and projected activities. In some cases they will need suggestions as to sources for information and subject headings to consult. The media specialist might be invited to the classroom to brief students on this. Teacher planning in advance with the media specialist will have helped to ensure that suitable and sufficient material is available.

Do teachers sometimes send students to the media center haphazardly with no particular purpose? Unfortunately they do. Maybe the media specialist has not been diligent about establishing good communications with that teacher and arranging planning sessions. Or maybe the teacher wanted a break in a trying day filled with behavior problems. It is unrealistic to expect great benefit from such a media center session. This is not to say that individual students should not be encouraged to make unstructured "just looking and relaxing" visits to the media center at appropriate times.

Do teachers sometimes declare they have in their classrooms the commercially prepared materials that accompany their instructional programs and therefore they don't need to use the media center? Such comments are sometimes heard, and the usual result is that students are limited to very meager fare. A teacher cannot possibly have in the classroom all the materials in different formats and of diverse reading levels and interests related to any one unit of study. A teacher who says this kind of thing is guilty of stifling independence and limiting the capacity for choice and self-direction by students.

Another significant concern in preparing students for activity in the media center is the current list of rules and regulations governing use of the media center. Teachers may need to discuss and explain some of the rules and also should be involved at some point in evaluating them. Are there too many to be reasonably kept in mind? Are they too rigid? Are they stated too negatively? The answers to these questions may indicate that indeed the rules limit access to the media center and contribute to a poor student attitude.

A final consideration in the process of using the media center is the follow-up when the students return to the classroom. Did they carry out plans? Did they locate the material they needed? Did they accomplish what they set out to do? How could the next visit to the media center be made more effective? The media specialist should be asked to contribute to this evaluation.

To illustrate the many ways that media resources can be used to vitalize learning, examples will be given in the areas of social studies, science, and language arts (omitting reading, which will be discussed later.) These examples represent a "dipping into" various instructional units at certain times. From these illustrations the contributions of media resources to the other areas of the curriculum, for example, mathematics, music, home economics, can be inferred. Since media are employed to implement instructional objectives, the samples of media experiences will be discussed in relation to these objectives.

In these examples the term "media specialist" will be used frequently. Some schools have a media staff consisting of one or more media specialists, one or more media aides, and a media technician. However, many schools have only the one media specialist and no supportive media personnel. In the case of the former schools the media aides or media technician would assist with some of the activities described. It is understood that in each of the examples cited the teacher and media specialist together formulated the objectives for that instructional unit.

An abbreviated summary of the social studies objectives listed by Clark are used here.(10) The social studies curriculum seeks to develop the concepts and competencies listed below.

OBJECTIVE: *An understanding of the social world and how it has been conditioned by the physical world.*

In a study of geography a class learned about the climate and topography of different countries from wall maps and atlases borrowed from the media center, which the media specialist taught them how to use. Information was found on the products, industries, exports, and these were discussed in relation to the geography. A useful film was *Three Families in Different Environments* (BFA Educational Media). The media specialist suggested to the teacher that three groups of students role-play the home life of families in different countries. The media specialist also showed students how they could illustrate the information by drawing on blank film to make a filmstrip. Other materials used included two sets of filmstrips, *World Geography* (McGraw-Hill) and *Man's Earth Home* (Encyclopedia Britannica Educational Corporation), which showed the influence of geographical features on man. Also useful was a series of study prints, *Climates of the World* (Coronet). Information was found in reference books, such as Grolier's *Lands and Peoples*. The media center's vertical file yielded brochures on the areas studied, as well as mounted pictures. The media specialist taught students how to use the *Readers' Guide to Periodical Literature* in order to find articles in the *National Geographic* and other magazines. A small group needed a review on the use of encyclopedias, and was sent to the media center for instruction.

OBJECTIVE: *An understanding of change in our culture and the knowledge that change is continuous.*

A group of students in a class used tape recorders to interview grandparents and older members of the community to learn about the "old days." The media specialist worked with others to find books that describe customs of even earlier times, such as Langdon's *Everyday Things in American Life, 1607-1776* and Tunis's *Frontier Living*. Filmstrips such as *Profile of Americans* (New York Times Company) that give an overview of changing trends in the United States were helpful. Another group of students found magazine articles with the projections of futurists who pictured the world of tomorrow. One student carried out a study showing how inventions have changed our lives. The media specialist alerted the teacher to an educational television program on life in the early 1900's. Small groups of students listened to recordings of early American folksongs and compared them with popular songs today, using the media center conference room for this activity. The class set up an exhibit entitled "Then and Now" with examples of books, cooking utensils, clothes, etc.

OBJECTIVE: *An understanding of interdependence among nations.*

An economics class studied how the flow of raw materials and manufactured products caused nations to depend upon each other. Information was gathered from many reference books in the media center, including *The Worldmark Encyclopedia of the Nations*, Paradis's *The Economics Reference Book*, and the United States Department of State *Fact Book of Countries of the World*. Up-to-date statistics were needed, and the media specialist gave instruction on the use of *The World Almanac and Book of Facts* and other yearbooks and the *Statistical Abstract of the United States*. Instruction was also given on how to read graphs and charts. The opaque projector was used in a media center conference room to project charts from books and to enlarge some of them for use as posters. Assisted by the media specialist, students made transparencies to report their research. Some students prepared a sound-slide presentation showing imports and exports of various countries.

OBJECTIVE: *An appreciation and understanding of the role of all races, religions, and cultures.*

This class had chosen races for a study. The teacher divided the class into three groups, and each selected one of the three major racial groups to study: Negroid, Caucasoid, and Mongoloid. Each class group made many visits to the media center to find information about the characteristics, cultural aspects, and subdivisions of each race. They consulted filmstrips, one of which was *Why Skin Has Many Colors* (Sunburst Communications), listened to recordings of representative music, and used *National Geographic* on microfilm. With the help of the media specialist, each group made a set of transparencies to present the many facts they had learned and the conclusions they had reached.

OBJECTIVE: *An understanding of the problems, history, tradition, beliefs, values of peoples of other countries.*

Students in one class decided to select a country from each of the continents for an in-depth study. The countries were Australia, Greenland, Canada, Brazil, Germany, Egypt, and Russia. Students came to the media center individually, in small groups, or as a whole class as they worked on the information in a variety of books, encyclopedias, pamphlets, magazine articles, filmstrips, recordings, sets of transparencies, atlases, and other special reference books such as Grolier's *Lands and Peoples*. Examples of the filmstrips used were *Brazil* and *The Soviet Union* (both EBEC) and *Documentary on Canada* (Society for Visual Education). Both the media specialist and the teacher worked with the students in the media center, giving them guidance in the selection and use of materials. Some of the materials were chosen to be taken to the classroom. There were lessons on critical reading and on evaluating, analyzing, and organizing data. Before the beginning of the study the media specialist gave students a review of media skills and worked separately with groups that were deficient in one or more skills. The media specialist was able to locate people in the community who had visited the countries and who came to the class to talk about their personal observations of customs, traditions, and history of each country. Some brought slides and artifacts to illustrate their talks. The class had a grand finale of the study by presenting a festival of folk songs and dances of the countries. This was videotaped.

OBJECTIVE: *An understanding and appreciation of our American heritage and our democratic form of government.*

A study of world governments brought into relief the many advantages of a democracy and the necessity for an informed citizenry. This class divided into groups to study monarchies, oligarchies, republics, and democracies, as well as socialism, communism, and fascism. Special reference books used included Ketchum's *What is Democracy* and Ebenstein's *Today's Isms*. For the slow readers the media specialist introduced Abramowitz's American History Study unit on *Documents of Freedom* (Follett). Students made excellent transparencies illustrating the dif-

55

ferent forms of government and comparisons between them. The sound filmstrips that were useful were *Our National Government: How it Developed* (Society for Visual Education), *Communism in Yugoslavia* (Zenger), and *Fascist Dictatorships* (Educational Audio Visual). Films also provided much information. Some of those used were *What Liberty and Justice Mean* (Churchill Films), *Marxism: The Theory that Split a World* (Learning Corporation of America), and *Hitler, Part I: The Rise to Power* (McGraw-Hill). The media specialist secured a state legislator to speak to the class, and trips were made to observe the city council and the state legislature in action. Some groups made sound-slide sets to describe the information they had gathered. The class organized and held a simulated national election, with conventions to nominate candidates, primaries, campaigns, and voting. Much information for this activity was found in the media center, and the *Readers' Guide to Periodical Literature* was used extensively to locate recent articles on elections. The necessary skills were taught by the media specialist.

OBJECTIVE: *The development of competence and self-direction in skills basic to social studies.*

As demonstrated in the examples above, the instructional program supplied the impetus for the teaching of media skills. When it became apparent that skills were needed to use materials and equipment, they were taught. Practice and many opportunities to use new skills developed assurance and competence in students. Most skills were taught to small groups with common needs. Learning centers on certain skills were set up in the media center, and learning packages for various ability levels were developed. Diagnostic tests were given periodically to identify deficiencies.

OBJECTIVE: *An understanding of the structure and function of our economic system.*

One class made a study of capitalism and its history. Students consulted books in the media center, including such titles as Forman's *Capitalism*, Galbraith's *Capitalism*, and McGraw-Hill's *Dictionary of Modern Economics*. Magazine articles, films, filmstrips, and pamphlets all proved useful. A simulation game entitled *Market* (Benefic Press) about consumers and retailers aroused interest, especially among the slower students. The media specialist taught students individually or in groups how to evaluate sources of information and how to work efficiently with data. The teacher and media specialist working together set up in the classroom a learning center on the features of capitalism. With the guidance of the teacher and media specialist two students developed independent study projects, one on banking, the other on taxation. One used a tape recorder to interview a banker, the other interviewed a member of the city council. They made transparencies and sound-slides to summarize their projects. The class illustrated what they had learned by setting up a business, designing, manufacturing, and selling a small box to hold such things as paper clips and other items. One group, representing workers, constructed the boxes; some class members posed as owners of the company; others bought stock in the company. A price was put on the box, and many were sold to other students. There were meetings of the board of directors, the workers' wages were set, and dividends declared. There were many visits to the media center to find all the information they needed.

In considering media center involvement in the science area, the objectives used are summarized from those quoted by Carin and Sund. (6)

OBJECTIVE: *Knowledge of certain scientific facts and concepts.*

A class studying seeds found, with the help of the media specialist, books in the media center suited to their reading levels. Advanced students found facts in Comstock's *Handbook of Nature Study*. Others used Hammond's *The Riddle of Seeds* and additional books for facts and experiments. Much interest was shown in a film employing time-lapse photography to show how a seed develops into a plant. An 8mm loop film showed this growth in simpler form, and the media specialist suggested that the teacher send some students individually to use this in a carrel. The sound filmstrips which provided information were *Seed Plants* (Coronet) and *Plants—How They Live and Grow* (EBEC), and also the film *Seed Dispersal* (EBEC). The teacher used the overhead projector to show the different shapes of the seeds collected by the students. The class made and illustrated booklets on seeds and selected the best of these for the media specialist to fit with board backs and to prepare pockets and cards for circulation from the media center. The students' exhibit of different seeds planted in glass jars was displayed in the media center.

OBJECTIVE: *The manipulation of basic science equipment, and the interpretation and preparation of maps, graphs, charts, tables.*

Students studying the preservation of foods performed many experiments on the different processes used. In considering how milk is kept pure, they put on slides drops of milk from samples kept at different temperatures and made counts of the microorganisms as they examined the slides under the microscope. The media specialist assisted with instruction on making and reading charts and graphs of their findings and set up a learning center on interpreting charts and graphs. Students found information on microscopes in the media center. They also looked for material on the history of preservation of foods and made an interesting sound-slide presentation of this. With proper instruction and guidance they found magazine articles on the current and future methods of preservation. Among the books they used were the U.S. Department of Agriculture 1979 Yearbook, *What's to Eat*, and Tannebaum's *Feeding the City*. The class visited a local cannery and a food-freezing plant. They made an 8mm film of these processes and gave it to the media center for use by other classes.

OBJECTIVE: *The ability to demonstrate problem solving skills.*

One class studied the various kinds of pollution. When considering noise pollution, they decided to try to solve the problem of the high level of noise in the cafeteria during the lunch hour. Among the books they used was Steven's *Sound and Hearing*. They also used many magazine articles and pamphlets on noise pollution. They learned more about sound from the recording *Science of Sound* (Folkways Records) and from the filmstrip *Learning about Sounds* (EBEC). Small groups came to the media center to listen to the recording on the wireless listening system. Students used the filmstrip individually in the media center carrels. Students studied the ear and made slides from diagrams in books to demonstrate how we hear. They performed experiments with mice to decide whether loudness, pitch, or tone quality caused changes in behavior. They studied whether changes in the environment, such as numbers of people present or the playing of soft music, affect the degree of noise. They also carried out surveys among the students. Throughout their study students used the scientific method, stating the problem, formulating hypotheses, gathering data, analyzing the findings, and drawing conclusions. At the end of their study they made recommendations to the principal for improving the cafeteria situation.

OBJECTIVE: *An understanding of the uses, benefits, and limitations of science to society.*

A great interest in cloning led one science class into the field of genetics. As they searched the media center for all the recent magazine articles on cloning, the media specialist found that some students needed a review lesson on how to use the *Readers' Guide to Periodical Literature*. The teacher divided the class into groups, each of which chose a topic: genes, chromosomes, heredity, mutations. As the groups consulted books, filmstrips, films, transparencies, etc., the media specialist instructed them in needed skills and helped them with analyzing and organizing data. Materials that proved useful were McGraw-Hill's *Encyclopedia of Science and Technology* and accompanying *Yearbooks*, and a kit, *Straight Hair, Curly Hair* (Crowell), which contained a book, a filmstrip, and a recording. A filmstrip, *Why You Are Not an Elephant* (Guidance Associates), was enjoyed. Students used the kit and the filmstrips in the media center carrels. The media specialist invited a science professor from the local university to speak to the class on genetics. The groups made slide and transparency presentations to summarize their research for the class. The media specialist helped the students plan a debate at the end of the study, "*Resolved*, Experiments with cloning are a menace to our society." This was video-taped for other classes.

OBJECTIVE: *The development of an interest in reading, collecting, studying, or becoming involved in some scientific activity as a leisure time pursuit.*

Seeking to promote a lifetime interest in some aspect of science, a science teacher scheduled a browsing period for his class in the media center with the assignment of scanning science materials and selecting some topic of interest. Prior to the period in the media center, the media specialist visited the classroom, briefed the class on sources of science materials, and described the content of the special science reference books. The media specialist suggested to the teacher that the class become familiar with the science magazines in the media center and suggested an outline for students to use in examining the content of the magazines. After each student had selected some scientific interest, the media specialist offered to compile a brief list of materials on each subject, using information on reading levels supplied by the teacher so that students could pursue their interests.

In the area of language arts the objectives used are those listed by Smith.(18)

OBJECTIVE: *Each child needs to experience language in dynamic and relevant ways all day, every day.*

The media specialist encouraged students to tape record reactions, experiences, and creative works ranging from stories and poetry to reviews and directions. After the reading of a story, the students were given an opportunity to express their reactions to it and discuss it. Some practiced writing and taping commentaries to slide and filmstrip programs. One group of students wrote and taped the directions for operating different pieces of equipment. Students wrote on cards brief reviews of books they had read, and these were filed in the media center for other students to consult. Students wrote and acted in a play they videotaped and presented to other classes. The media specialist secured the names of pen pals in other countries for students to correspond with. The media specialist worked with some groups on role-playing and dramatizations. One class liked to put on puppet plays in the puppet theater in the media center, and the media specialist helped with this. Students were encouraged to use the media center conference rooms to practice reports, debates, dramatizations, or choral reading. The media specialist held poetry appreciation sessions in which students found recorded music to use as background for the poems they chose to read. Students were shown how to make characters for their favorite story to use on the flannel board while they told the story. The media specialist conferred with teachers to select upper grade students to read to small groups of primary children.

OBJECTIVE: *Each child must acquire necessary communication skills so that he may express himself effectively in all media and find lasting satisfaction.* (Reading skills are treated in a separate chapter.)

To improve oral expression the media specialist and teachers collaborated on these activities: asked students to tape original stories; encouraged students to make a slide sequence and tape the commentary; directed students in role-playing, shadow plays, puppet shows, etc.; suggested that students participate in panel discussions; planned for upper grade children to tell stories to younger children; arranged debates and informal discussions; read the bare facts of a story to students and asked them to supply the descriptive adjectives and adverbs; led a discussion comparing two art prints as to style, use of color, subject matter; encouraged students to express their feelings and reactions to a story read to them; helped students make their own cutouts to use on the overhead projector or flannel board to illustrate the stories they told.

To improve written expression, the media specialist and teachers worked on these activities: planned a learning center in which students follow a taped story on a dittoed copy and put in the necessary punctuation marks; sponsored a writing club to encourage creative and personal writing; had an above-average student work in the conference room with a small group of slow students on writing advertisements of books they had read to "sell" them to the class; used the sound filmstrip, *Getting Ready to Write Creatively* (Troll) with groups; invited students to write letters requesting free material, expressing appreciation to authors or thanks to speakers, or requesting permission to visit a place;

planned correspondence with student media assistants in other schools; asked students to write a commentary for the slides they had made; arranged a poetry or story file in the media center where students could file original work for others to read; sponsored a media news sheet written by students; invited students to write stories with illustrations to be made into booklets with pockets and cards for circulation; suggested that upper grade students write a history of the school; had students write myths, fables, fairy tales, and displayed these with related books; asked students to write new endings to stories; asked students to write "I was there" experiences such as "coming over on the *Mayflower*," "going West," "living on a plantation," etc.; asked students to write additional stories about the book characters they like; asked students to write their reactions if confronted with the same situation as a book character; suggested that upper elementary grade students work on a research paper complete with outline and bibliography.

To sharpen listening skills the media specialist and teacher worked with students on the following activities: taped sounds at home and asked students to guess what they were; with primary children, used the recording *Accent on Listening* (Xerox Education); gave upper grade students a list of questions to answer after watching a certain TV show; asked students to close eyes and make a list of sounds heard in two minutes; used a toy telephone and asked one student to carry on a conversation while the others tried to guess to whom he was talking; had students listen to a segment of a recorded speech and then write a summary of it.

To promote communication in the medium of non-print materials, the media specialist helped students design and produce transparencies, slide sequences, recordings, filmstrip presentations, videotape programs, and 8mm films. In using these types of communication students expressed feelings and criticism about poems and books, or recorded accumulated data from research, reactions to topics of study, descriptions of field trips, interviews with various people, dramatizations, reports on independent study or special projects, etc.

OBJECTIVE: *Each student needs to come to apppreciate the beauty of language itself, the effective use of words, and the creative way they may help him express his own original thoughts.*

Many of the activities listed above may also implement this objective. In addition, many media specialists and teachers have used these experiences with words: played beautiful records and had students write their reactions; had students write three paragraphs expressing the same thought in three different ways; had children read Haiku poems and write examples of their own; quoted a phrase from a story and asked students to write it in a more colorful way; suggested that students keep a list of the most beautiful words in the English language (their opinion); asked upper grade students to look at a certain TV drama and write a critical comment about the dialogue; asked these students to write a review patterned upon those appearing in book review journals; read excerpts from the classics and asked students to select the expressions they thought were the most effective.

These are just a few examples of the ways in which the media center and media services can become an integral, vital part of the students' learning experiences. In order to accomplish this each teacher must be alert to the many opportunities that present themselves each school day and consider such questions as:

Do I collaborate with the media specialist on planning instructional units, implementing these plans, and evaluating student progress?

Am I concerned that students learn how to learn and to

master lifetime media skills?

Do I plan flexible use of the media center by the whole class, individuals, and small groups so that students go to the media center when there is a need?

Do I demonstrate an active interest in developing the media collection in my own field?

Am I knowledgeable about media center resources in my subject area?

Do I plan continuous, purposeful use of the media center?

Do I participate in the selection of new media?

Do I emphasize by attitude and example the value of using information sources and make a practice of providing many opportunities for students to use the school media center?

Do I value the competencies of the media staff and use them to enhance my instruction?

Do I plan projects with the media specialist to develop student love of reading and the habit of reading?

What can I do to assist the media specialist in efforts to make the media center an attractive inviting place which is easily accessible to everyone in the school community?

How can I cooperate with the media specialist to maintain desirable student behavior in the media center?

How can I use more fully the talents of the media specialist as a resource person when planning teaching strategies for varying ability levels and learning styles?

How current are my own media skills?

When was the last time I sought the media specialist's aid in the design and production of instructional materials or encouraged student production of non-print materials?

With the firm foundation of a clear understanding of the potential role of the media specialist and the functioning of the media program the teacher, any teacher, can proceed with confidence in partnership with the media specialist to build a superior teaching-learning program.

TEACHER'S RESERVATION: As I have read this chapter I have found some conflict with the idea of having an open media program, as we have now, instead of a scheduled class time, as we had in past years. It seems that you advocate teachers accompanying their classes to the media center, as we used to do.

I find that most children need instruction in how to use equipment, such as film viewers and tape recorders. Should it be the responsibility of classroom teachers or of the media specialist to provide this instruction?

Some suggestions for involvement of the media specialist seem unrealistic. Involvement in science experiments or in making charts and graphs isn't possible, given the limits on time and space that most media specialists must face.

WRITERS' RESPONSE: Perhaps we did not make ourselves clear regarding the teacher's role. We recommend that when an entire class goes to the media center, the teacher should accompany the class. But we certainly favor individuals and small groups going independently to the media center when they need to make use of resources.

Teaching the skills of using equipment is the mutual responsibility of teachers and media specialists. It is best to teach a skill when it is needed, so that the task may fall to the teacher on occasion and to the media specialist at other times. Any formal presentation designed to teach media skills should be planned cooperatively by the teacher and media specialist.

The comment regarding unrealistic suggestions for involvement of the media specialist simply emphasizes the need for increased media center staff. In several places throughout the handbook we encourage the identification and enlistment of volunteer assistants. We do not encourage use of volunteers *in place of* professionals, but, given the situation as it is in schools now, the media center is one place where volunteers can make a valuable contribution.

BIBLIOGRAPHY

1. Balzek, Ron. *Influencing Students Toward Media Center Use.* Chicago, American Library Association, 1975.
2. Bell, Caroline R. "Library for All, All for Library." *Journal of Reading,* 17:119–21, November, 1973.
3. Bell, Jo Ann. "The Technical-Vocational Student and the Library." *Southeastern Librarian,* 20:241, Winter, 1970.
4. Bixler, Dorothea. "Planning with Teachers. "*Illinois Libraries,* 53:179–80, March, 1971.
5. Bussis, Anne M., Edward A. Chittenden, and Marianne Amarel. *Beyond Surface Curriculum; an Interview Study of Teachers' Understandings.* Boulder, Colorado, Westview Press, 1976.
6. Carin, Arthur A. and Robert B. Sund. *Teaching Science Through Discovery,* 3rd ed. Columbus, Ohio, Charles E. Merrill Publishing Company, 1975.
7. Casciano-Savignano, C. Jennie. "Interpersonal Relationships in Secondary Schools." *National Association of Secondary Principals Bulletin,* 60:26–30, April, 1976.
8. Champlin, Constance J. "Use of the Elementary Library by Classroom Teachers." (Thesis) Nashville, George Peabody College for Teachers, 1969.
9. Christine, Emma R. "Saturation Situations." *School Media Quarterly,* 3:16–20, Fall, 1974.
10. Clark, Leonard H. *Teaching Social Studies in Secondary Schools.* New York, Macmillan, 1973.
11. "Five-day Program of Activities Encourages Student

Use of the Library." *Mississippi Library News*, 42:103–04, June, 1978.

12. Fleischman, Helen J. "A Study of the Classroom Teacher's Role in Library Skills Lessons." Thesis. Brookville, New York, Graduate Library School of Long Island University, 1971.

13. Frary, Mildred P. "School Library Service to the Disadvantaged Student." *Library Trends*, 20:405–15, October, 1971.

14. Jay, Hilda. "Increasing the Use of Secondary School Libraries." *School Libraries*, 20:23–26, Summer, 1971.

15. Kennemore, Florence and Mary Ann Wickwire. "Planning for Educational Initiative." *School Libraries*, 20:16–20, Spring, 1972.

16. Martin, Betty and Ben Carson. *The Principal's Handbook on the School Library Media Center.* Syracuse, New York, Gaylord Professional Publications, 1978.

17. Rogers, J. V. "Media Center Resources and Appalachian Secondary Teachers." *Southeastern Librarian*, 28:149–57, Fall, 1978.

18. Smith, James A. *Creative Reading and Literature in the Elementary School.* Boston, Allyn & Bacon, 1973.

19. Taylor, Anne P. and George Vlastos. *School Zone: Learning Environments for Children.* New York, Van Nostrand, 1975.

20. *The Teacher and the Library.* (Tape recording) Westport, Connecticut, Charles Burke, nd.

21. Van Orden, Phyllis. "Science Literacy Skills and the Media Specialist." *Illinois Libraries*, 3:37–38, Winter, 1970.

# PART II

## THE TEACHING-LEARNING PROCESS

# 4

## "I SHOULD LIKE TO KNOW WHAT HELP I CAN EXPECT IN THE DESIGN AND IMPLEMENTATION OF CURRICULUM COMPONENTS."

Traditionally, teachers have looked upon librarians as card-sorters and shelf-arrangers, whose major challenge was to get the books back! In recent years, however, a major change has occurred. As outlined in previous chapters, the library has evolved into a media center designed to be the hub of learning activity within the school, and the librarian has become a media specialist whose knowledge and expertise far exceeds organizing and keeping records.

Unfortunately, many teachers still view the library media center as an old-fashioned "storehouse." They might ask the media specialist about the availability of a book, periodical, or filmstrip, but they would neither expect nor solicit any broader assistance in planning. They may be unaware that the media specialist offers numerous skills and has many areas of expertise that can contribute to better planning and happier results in the classroom.

The evolution of the library media center and of a more significant instructional role for its staff has been, in fact, a direct result of the knowledge explosion, which has demanded a new approach to the teaching/learning process. Teachers can no longer be expected to meet, by themselves, armed only with a textbook or a series of textbooks, the informational needs of students. The accelerated pace of change demands flexibility in curriculum as well as in methodology. The educational process must therefore teach students "*how* to learn a subject, how to go about gathering the materials that will enable them to teach themselves." As the amount of information, as well as the sources of information, multiply, the need for individualized instruction and independent learning grows. At the very heart of an effective program of individualized instruction is a vital media program. The application of advanced technology has increased the feasibility of true, individualized instruction. "Media have become the instruments of learning and the transmitters of information." Thus education has molded a new role for the media specialist, who now becomes a *partner* with teachers in providing a learning environment that "challenges intellect, sparks curiosity, stimulates creativity, and generates enthusiasm for the joy of discovery."(43)

The effect of these changes on curriculum has been dramatic, and sometimes chaotic. The current economic "crunch" and resulting retrenchment in the schools has added to the problems. Yet the process of helping students learn *how* to learn is increasingly the crucial purpose of education. Robert Pickering, President of the American Montessori Society, points out that in real life people seldom find anyone who has "the answer." Rather, each person must analyze a situation for himself, usually in the face of conflicting or ambiguous claims, and must select among alternatives with limited or incomplete information. In these terms education can best serve students by equipping them to explore for meanings, not memorize answers. In this type of educational process the teacher functions with the media specialist as a team whose job is to equip the student with competency and confidence in the "tools" that will enable him to solve problems. The mastery of tools is an ongoing process, just as mastery of content is an ongoing process.

This means that curriculum development, too, must be an ongoing process, and also that the traditional roles of

72

teachers, media specialists, and other school personnel change in relation to each other. The rethinking of personnel roles includes understanding of curriculum development as a continuous process. In a sense, one is an outgrowth of the other.

A discussion of curriculum development could fill several volumes. "Curriculum" can refer to a total K-12 design embracing all subject areas; it can mean the core composition of a specific subject area course; or it can mean anything in-between the two. The same principles apply whatever the scope or the range of the curriculum being planned. In this chapter, however, the emphasis is on planning lessons or units of study in a specific subject area at a particular grade level, because this is generally the concern of an individual teacher in curriculum planning. The focus is on cooperative planning between teacher and media specialist, and the scope of the chapter is limited to this. It does not attempt a full discussion of curriculum development in its larger sense. There are many excellent works that address this subject quite adequately, some of which are cited in the bibliography.

Media specialists should as a matter of course be included in curriculum planning at all levels, district- or statewide, as well as individual classroom planning. Knowledgeable in subject matter and in methodology, they are familiar with many resources and skilled in previewing materials. They have expertise for matching method to content, and these to student interests and abilities. Teachers who are not accustomed to seeking assistance from the media specialist in their schools are overlooking a potential source of ideas and assistance in making instruction more interesting to themselves as well as to students.

In curriculum planning there are basically six elements to be considered:

1. One must decide what the primary goals and objectives are—the outcomes being sought for students.

2. One must select the content to be covered.
3. Classroom activities or educational experiences that will enable students to achieve the objectives must be determined.
4. Relevant materials in terms of the content and activities need to be selected.
5. Classroom experiences must be organized in a meaningful way that will enhance their effectiveness.
6. Evaluation must be devised that will indicate whether or not specific objectives toward the ultimate goal have been achieved.

There is often confusion about the terms "goals" and "objectives." Usage can vary from one author to another. In this chapter definitions for these words are taken from Ehman, Mehlinger, and Patrick, as given in their book, *Toward Effective Instruction in Secondary Social Studies*.(8) An educational goal is a long-range outcome. It is usually stated in general, even abstract, terms, and it represents development or growth over a long period of time. An objective is a "measurable statement describing what the student can do or will produce following instruction." It is stated in precise, unambiguous, achievable terms, and it represents an immediate outcome of an educational experience. Educational goals "act as a compass to keep teachers on course," while objectives remind teachers and students what is to be accomplished on a daily or weekly basis.(8)

The sources of educational goals are varied. The goals set for any group of students by a given teacher will inevitably reflect to some extent that teacher's own values and experience, but they should reflect also the highest standards and needs of the society, the values of the community and the values and aspirations of the students themselves. The Board of Education for the school district may have provided some educational goals as stated in a policy manual, or the state may have published curriculum guides that indicate goals for teachers to pursue. An individual school may have developed goals for its own instructional program. Professional reading in one's own field can help identify goals projected by experts that seem valid for the teacher's situation. In any case, it is essential to set goals that are understood and generally accepted by students so that the educational experiences planned for them have greater meaning as steps toward achievement of these goals. By the same token it is important for the teacher to make the media specialist in the school aware of these goals so that they may be effective partners as a teaching team.

Objectives for a single lesson or a unit should be aimed at helping students achieve the long-range goals. They may be identified in a number of ways. If the state or district has stated a list of objectives in relation to goals in a subject area, it is simply a matter of choosing from this predetermined list those objectives that best meet the needs of the students. In most cases, however, state or district guidelines are written in terms of concepts or skills and do not spell out specific objectives, so it is up to the teacher to translate these into objectives. Instructional objectives define the knowledge to be gained, the skills to be acquired or exercised, the feelings or attitudes affected, and sometimes the time limit involved. Thus they state in measurable terms the behavioral change that is to take place in the student. For example, in working with elementary students to develop the concept of "Family" the objectives of the lesson might read as follows:

Students will be able to
1. describe possible family units;
2. classify a series of pictures as "nuclear family" or "extended family";
3. "introduce" via verbal sketches their own families to the class.

At a higher level, objectives in a study of the concept of

"Family" would focus on the family as a cultural institution. Objectives might be as follows:

Students will be able to

1. distinguish the nuclear family from the extended family;
2. list the functions of the family in society;
3. predict (with supporting information) the future of the family as an institution in society.

In other words, the objectives will state in behavioral terms what students are to know about a concept or what skill they are to exercise in terms of that concept.

In the event that there are no guidelines from either the state or the district, then the responsibility for setting goals and objectives falls heavily upon the teacher. "A variety of criteria can be used to select the basic ideas (which will be the goals of instruction): they must have scientific validity; they must be learnable at the age level at which they are offered; they must have utility in our current culture."(35) These basic ideas—the goals—must be translated into objectives that define the understandings, the knowledge, the skills, and the attitudes to be developed in the students.

If one of the goals is improvement of student self-concept, a supporting objective might define ways in which the student would demonstrate a realistic understanding of his assets and his weaknesses. A long-range goal such as an understanding of the interrelationship of science and technology would impose objectives which require a student to define both terms, list examples of technology as applied science, and perhaps make a value judgment on the consequences of modern scientific and technological developments. It becomes easier to narrow down the possible objectives as the teacher becomes familiar with what students already know and what skills they have already acquired.

In writing objectives it is important to think in concrete terms. The more precise one can be in stating a desired outcome, the more likely students are to achieve it. Certain verbs are more fitting in objectives than others. The following list was compiled by Ehman, Mehlinger, and Patrick:(8)

| | | |
|---|---|---|
| identify | synthesize | extrapolate |
| distinguish | evaluate | state |
| write | name | construct |
| recite | order | transfer |
| solve | rank | differentiate |
| list | describe | reject |
| contrast | design | choose |
| compare | apply | select |
| analyze | interpret | |

As experience in writing objectives is gained, this list may be expanded. Examples of appropriate objectives would include the following:

Students will be able to identify five factors that may produce change in a community.

Students will be able to distinguish statements of fact regarding the energy crisis from statements of opinion.

Students will be able to write in their own words a definition of the term metamorphosis.

Students will be able to locate on a world map areas or countries where drought is common.

Students will be able to describe the applications of Newton's laws in the machinery used in the space program.

As the lesson plans are developed there may be any number of objectives, depending on the results expected. The media specialist in the school can assist the teacher in formulating and clarifying objectives and can suggest appropriate ways and times to include research and media skills in stated objectives.

Selection of content to be covered is often a problem to teachers. Many teachers feel an obligation to "cover the book." Some teachers teach as if they want their students to learn everything *they* have learned. Obviously, they can't do that in one year, much less teach all there is to know beyond their own knowledge! Some selection must be made of what information students should acquire. Goals and objectives will help determine content selection, and availability of resources and materials also influences content selection. The teacher, with the media specialist's help, can keep in mind what materials are available on relevant subjects in the school or district. If the media specialist is apprised well in advance of the subjects to be covered, new materials that would be useful can be identified or new ones obtained. Together, teacher and media specialist can plan appropriate acquisitions for the media center.

Having identified the goals and objectives of the lessons and the specific content to be covered in them, the teacher's next concern is to devise activities and experiences for students that will enable them to achieve the specific objectives set for them. The media specialist can be a valuable source of assistance. If there is no one set of materials appropriate to the lesson plan, the media specialist can help the teacher to adapt or modify available resources. The resources themselves may at times influence the choice of activities, or the media specialist can assist in matching materials from the media center to specific plans. The media specialist can be of great help to teachers in judging whether the activities planned will in fact result in students reaching the objectives. Ideas for activities are discussed in more detail in Chapters 3 and 5.

Organizing planned activities in a meaningful way is one of the most important and most difficult duties of the teacher. Many teachers plan exciting activities and stimulating lessons, but give little thought to how one lesson or group of lessons relates to another. Continuity and reinforcement are lacking. District- or statewide curriculum guides may provide an overall plan which insures continuity in the curriculum, and those fortunate enough to have such guidelines are in general wise to work within them. Having no overall curriculum design in the district for a subject area can be a real handicap to a teacher's efforts to coordinate current student instruction with previous learning experiences as well as future ones. Vertical integration of learning experiences (that is, between grade levels) is never easy. The media specialist can play a vital role in facilitating this vertical integration within a school, and for this reason should be included in departmental as well as school-wide curriculum planning.

In the horizontal integration of learning experiences, that is, the correlation of science studies to math, math to social studies, social studies to language art, etc., at the same grade level, the media specialist can also be of tremendous assistance. The reinforcement of learning from one subject area to another underscores the relevancy of that learning and helps students to see relationships between ideas. Thus they begin to learn how to generalize from their experiences. The media specialist is familiar with multimedia approaches to teaching that facilitate and enhance interdisciplinary learning, and can help each teacher to coordinate lessons from different subject areas. Interdisciplinary teaching is very rewarding both to teachers and students.

Assume that a teacher has planned a unit study and has received enthusiastic response from students as they engaged in the series of activities. How can one know whether or not the desired outcome has been achieved? Is enthusiasm enough? To be sure, a teacher is to be congratulated when students have been enthusiastic about their work, but evaluating the success of the unit goes much further. If ob-

79

jectives for the unit are written in terms of measurable or observable behavior, a major segment of the evaluation is already provided. The teacher knows rather quickly whether or not the students can perform the tasks outlined in the objectives. Furthermore, it is also possible for the student to monitor his own progress. Students need to know the objectives they are working toward so that they can have the satisfaction of knowing when and what they have achieved. Such satisfaction acts as a stimulus to further achievement.

Frequently a unit of study ends with a major test. If no objectives have been written for the unit, "neither the teacher nor the students will be clear about what is to be learned until the teacher writes the test at the end of the unit."(8) Obviously this misses the whole point of testing. Evaluation is a part of the learning process. It is not a contest between teacher and students to see who can outwit whom. Testing should define for students what information they have gained, what skills they can apply, and what objectives they have yet to reach.

Teachers often feel threatened by standardized tests or other instruments they have not developed themselves. But the teacher who can identify what his objectives have been and can measure student achievement against these objectives need not fear standardized testing or any other. The purpose of a specific test must be considered before the test results can have any meaning. Standardized tests are generally norm-referenced, which means they compare the performance of a student or group of students to other students in the class, district, state, or nation. Test data from a standardized test can be used by teachers in identifying needed goals. If students in one school or one district show weakness in certain skills, emphasis in the curriculum can be shifted to correct this deficiency.

Criterion-referenced tests are coming more and more into use. This type of test reveals mastery by a particular student of specific skills, information, or concepts. No comparison is involved. Teacher-made tests that measure achievement of objectives fall into this category. Test data from this type of test enables a teacher to individualize instruction to meet each student's needs.

Even at its best, testing can measure satisfactorily only the cognitive and psychomotor domains of learning. It is difficult to measure affective learning. Evaluation in the affective domain must rely primarily on indirect measures or on observation of student behavior. Subtle changes in a student's attitude will more likely be revealed in a teacher-student conference than on a paper/pencil test. Conferences between a teacher and parents may reveal progress made by the student that a test could never show. In other words, evaluation rests on many criteria besides test results. The media specialist, made aware of the behavioral changes desired in a student or students, can be of valuable aid in observing students and offering assistance with evaluation. The key to this potential assistance is the concept which the teacher has of the media specialist. If the media specialist is viewed as a *partner* in the teaching/learning process, the entire process at every step can be made more effective.

The following dialogue between a teacher and a media specialist planning a unit of study illustrates the manner in which the media specialist contributes to the development of the unit. This contribution is not limited to the selection of materials. Topics that may be discussed between teacher and media specialist include lesson objectives, student activities, materials that support lesson objectives, possible student production of non-print materials, media skills students may exercise, suggestions for culminating activities, and recommendations for evaluation procedures.

MEDIA SPECIALIST/TEACHER PLANNING SESSION
A UNIT OF STUDY ON THE ARAB-ISRAELI CONFLICT

Teacher:  I have already outlined the major objectives of this unit. I'd like you to look these over and make comments or suggestions before we go any further. There are nine objectives that I have listed so far:

1. Students will advance their research skills.
2. Students will locate the area of study on individual desk maps and will describe the physical features of the area.
3. Students will write a brief paper describing the historical background of the area.
4. Students will list the principal issues of conflict.
5. Students will list cultural characteristics of the Middle East.
6. Students will give the names of major leaders by countries.
7. Students will prepare a time-line of events in this century.
8. Students will predict what may happen in the future in the Middle East.
9. Students will propose a peace plan.

Do these seem realistic to you? Are they inclusive?

*Media*      They look fine. I think objectives 8 and 9 might
*Specialist:* be restricted to your very talented students. How about expanding 7 to include preparation of a map showing territorial changes correlated to events on the time-line. Objective 1 needs to state more specifically what exactly students will do. What did you have in mind?

*Teacher:*   I was vague there because the amount of skill acquired varies from one student to another. Basically what I want is for them to expand their knowledge of sources. Some students can use standard reference materials pretty well, but need to learn how to use other sources. Then some students can't even use encyclopedias very effectively.

*Media Specialist:* We can set up learning centers on use of standard references such as *The Readers' Guide*, atlases, *Facts on File*, and so forth. Only the students requiring help with these would need to use the centers. Perhaps we should include as an objective the development of critical-thinking and problem-solving skills. (Teacher makes note of these suggestions.)

*Teacher:* I need some suggestions for activities for some of these objectives, particularly 1 and 4. The learning centers you've suggested help with 1, but we'll need to decide how to work with other students. For objective 3 I also need help in compiling a bibliography.

*Media Specialist:* Depending on how you want to organize that part of the unit, I can prepare a bibliography of books on each Middle Eastern country or a bibliography by topics. I can also make a list of the standard subject headings under each country in the card catalog, including:
Social life and customs
History
Description and travel
Politics and government
Art (country)
This should be helpful to the students.

*Teacher:* I agree. Your going over the subject headings with the class would be a good demonstration to them of how to "think" their way through a card catalog. Do you suppose you could develop some type of work sheet for them to complete as an exercise in using the card catalog?

*Media Specialist:* Yes, I've done that before. Give me a couple of days on that, and I'll see what I can come up with.

How do you plan to begin this unit?

*Teacher:* I thought I would open with a film on the Middle East as an introduction to the region. Such a film as *Promised Land, Troubled Land,* perhaps, although I haven't previewed it. Are you familiar with it?

*Media Specialist:* Yes. I think that film would help students with objectives 3 and 7. We will work out a work sheet for the viewing of the film. I believe that the sound filmstrip *What is the Middle East?*, which we have here in our collection, would serve well as an introduction to the unit. Why don't you look at it sometime tomorrow, then we can make a final decision. It is one of a series. The others are on individual countries in the Middle East and might be used by students in their research.

*Teacher:* I want to follow the introduction with a brief description of the problem of the study unit. Then you could discuss research techniques as a means of exploring the problem and suggesting a solution. That would give you a chance to mention the various learning centers set up on use of reference materials for students who need help.

*Media* What are the broad topics you want students to

*Specialist:* pursue? Will they make individual reports or do you plan to assign group work?

*Teacher:* They need to learn about the history and the government of the various countries, the dominant religions, the cultural practices, the social life of the people, the economic and educational systems, the resources, the climate, the geographic features as they affect the culture, and other relevant facts. I thought you could set up a reserve shelf that would include low-level reading materials as well as standard studies on this topic.

*Media Specialist:* I believe it is always better to let students find their own materials—that's the skill you want them to develop. Why not assign students to groups, give each group a topic, and let the group survey the materials and select titles for the reserve shelf. I can add any they miss. We have some good materials on some of these topics, such as the 8mm film *Three Religions in Jerusalem.* We also have an excellent filmstrip sent from Scholastic on the Middle East. These are particularly good for students with below-average reading ability. I can set some of these up for individual use.

*Teacher:* I was thinking about giving group assignments on these broad topics and then having group reports given to the entire class. I guess their first activity could be to find and select materials for the reserve shelves. If I assign a topic like religions, for instance, then within the group they could choose individual topics to research, such as Judaism, Islam, Christianity.

85

| | |
|---|---|
| *Media Specialist:* | We have excellent facilities, equipment, and materials for students to use in making their own sound-slide productions. Or they may wish to make transparencies, a videotape, even an 8mm film. |
| *Teacher:* | I have prepared a general work sheet for them on the governments and the economic systems of the area. If each group reports on one large topic, the other students can take notes and complete the work sheets as a summary activity. I will need to make similar work sheets on each topic. |
| *Media Specialist:* | *The Christian Science Monitor* has some good articles on the economy of the region. We could clip some of these and set up a supplementary learning package either for the group that has that topic or for the entire class. I'll be glad to work with you on developing learning packages for different ability levels on the history of the area. |
| *Teacher:* | Good idea. I think learning packages could be helpful to students in completing the various work sheets after the group presentations. Probably a good many students will want or need additional information. |
| *Media Specialist:* | I noticed in a recent copy of the *National Geographic* an excellent article on the Middle East. For a cultural study students could compare this article to similar articles from the nineteen-thirties and forties. Our file goes back that far. I can show the class how to use the *National Geographic* cumulative indexes. In comparing the articles they would be able to note the con- |

stants of the culture as well as the changes. And, naturally, the early articles make no mention of Israel. The students would be able to see what changes the founding of Israel has caused. They could make a set of transparencies to illustrate the comparisons.

Teacher:   I have four or five students who need some independent study assignments. I want to allow them to choose their own topics for research. That comparative study would be one option. I hope one or more of them will be interested in studying the involvement of the United States and Russia in the Middle East. That would give them an opportunity to make some value judgments about our role there. Can you think of any other possibilities?

Media Specialist:   Our students know so little about the literature of the Middle Eastern countries. We have some writings by Jewish authors, and our world literature anthologies will contain some selections by Arab authors. One student might make a critique of these.

Teacher:   I want the other students to have to make some value judgments, too. I thought I could pose some questions for them regarding distribution and usage of resources. Can you suggest any other suitable topics?

Media Specialist:   Perhaps population control. Another good topic for value judgments is the importance of Jerusalem as a holy city to each of the major religious groups. I'll need to work on bibliographies for these. Let me start identifying materials on all these topics, and then we can talk again in a day or two. By then I'll know which topics we have adequate resources to cover.

*Teacher:* Okay, great! I'll work out the details for group as well as individual assignments to be sure each student does have an opportunity to meet each of the first seven objectives. I agree with you that 8 and 9 should not be general objectives for the whole class. Once we've outlined the unit in more detail we will need to look at evaluation.

In subsequent meetings the teacher and the media specialist mapped out a detailed plan for the complete unit which listed each objective, the activities (group and individual) for each objective, and the method of evaluation for each objective. They also listed the major materials and resources needed for each activity. The teacher reviewed the organization of the activities to make sure adequate time was allotted for each. The media specialist suggested some additional activities, worked on identifying materials, and began putting together various learning centers and learning packages. Together they discussed evaluation of each objective and worked out a method of self-evaluation for students using the learning centers. The result was a carefully planned unit that provided a variety of activities for a variety of ability levels, yet held together to achieve a single set of objectives for the class. The objectives of the study were realistic, the activities were appropriate for the objectives, and the necessary materials for each activity were readily available. At the end of the unit both the teacher and the students had a means of evaluating their progress.

This type of planning session between the teacher and the media specialist should be a frequent occurrence. The ways in which this team can interact in planning teaching activities are almost unlimited. Planning individual lessons or single units of study is, however, only one aspect of curriculum development in which teachers and media specialists should collaborate. Broader, long-range planning also requires input from both. In many school districts teachers and supervisors are now developing or updating a scope and sequence of skills and concepts in all subject areas. The media specialist can assist in keeping this planning varied yet integrated from one level to the next. Elimination of repetitious and overlapping use of supplementary materials can be avoided with input from the media specialist. In addition, the media specialist can incorporate an appropriate sequence of research skills into the planned activities. Likewise, the suitability of activities can be reviewed and new ways suggested to give students a chance to be directly involved in their own learning. The media specialist can assist in reinforcing concepts and ideas identified at each level or plateau in the total sequence. Being involved in and aware of the goals of the total program, the media specialist can better coordinate new purchases, media center displays, and community resource files to supplement teaching programs.

Some examples of collaboration between teachers and media specialists may serve to generate other ideas of ways teachers can work with the media specialist in their own schools. Let's call these examples case studies.

*Case Study A.* A guidance counselor is working with several students who have failed to graduate after four years. He asks the media specialist to discuss with each of them some readable materials on careers of possible interest to these students. The media specialist prepares a custom-tailored list of stories, pamphlets, articles, and filmstrips after a friendly conference with each student about possible career interests, and follows up by arranging for community resource people to meet with students interested in similar careers.

*Case Study B.* A first year, eighth-grade music teacher asks how the media specialist can help her with a large class composed of a few unruly boys who refuse to sing and the disgruntled majority of students who resent the distraction. She has never used a media center in her teaching. The media specialist suggests some topics appealing to this age group in which the media center has extensive holdings. The teacher selects folk music. From Carl Sandburg's *American Songbag* they identify ten categories of folk music that might be used for small group study as an alternative to group singing with the rest of the class. The media specialist and the teacher discuss ways in which to direct the work of each group, and the teacher skims a selection of books and recordings to formulate guide questions. It takes several planning sessions, but the enthusiasm of her students during "research" periods in the media center and the quality and imagination of their group presentations to the class convince the teacher not only that the extra effort was worth it, but that the media specialist is a valuable ally.

*Case Study C.* Students in Mr. B's industrial arts class have been assigned as a term project development of a comprehensive report regarding either a process in industry that affects consumers or a product that is used by most consumers. The report is to include sound-slide productions, demonstrations, displays, or other appropriate visuals. Each student is told to arrange an individual conference with the media specialist, who will help the student finalize selection of a topic and begin to organize appropriate reference materials. The media specialist will assist students in evaluating material gathered, in preparing layouts and lettering, developing photographic displays, and in organizing the format of a sound-slide production. This contributes greatly to the success of the students in preparing their projects. It gives the media specialist "teaching" opportunities to reinforce research and media-communication skills as well as thinking skills.(21)

*Case Study D.* An experienced senior high-school teacher experimenting with a new design for his sociology classes brings his course outline to the media specialist. He wants his students to learn through wide collateral reading, to translate into human terms the factual data in their new textbook. He asks the media specialist to identify compelling and provocative books related to various social problems to which these students might respond. He and the media specialist discuss points of view to which he hopes his students will be exposed. Reporting back to the teacher, the media specialist examines each biographical, fiction, and other title with the teacher to make sure that the treatment, theme, and style are in line with his aims. Finally they talk about ways to obtain student reactions to the books as a guide for future selections.(12)

*Case Study E.* A teacher of United States history consulted with the media specialist to develop assignments requiring students to use primary sources. The teacher and media specialist together worked up a list of events in history on which the media center had appropriate resources. Students were to choose one event and write a paper describing the social conditions at that time. For example, one paper described "how people lived in Illinois" at the time of the Mexican War. The students were to read newspapers and magazines, fiction, biographies, diaries and journals of the period. Where applicable, original photos were used. Students who chose more recent events were to interview older citizens in the community. For each time period the media specialist prepared a core bibliography that the students were to expand. The media specialist assisted in scheduling work periods for students in the media center. These students were spared the frustration of writing on a topic for which resources were too limited, and the media specialist was spared the onslaught of twenty-five students demanding assistance at once. The results, gratifying to all concerned, were interesting, authenticated reports.

These examples of cooperative planning from the start of a lesson, unit, or project point up the role that the media program can play in education. There are many ways the media specialist can work with a teacher in planning. The following list summarizes a few that have been discussed:

—Assemble, preferably with student participation, materials on a specific topic for reserve shelves.
—Recommend high interest/low vocabulary titles on specific topics.
—Correlate specific topics to available fiction.
—Make recommendations to teachers for best use of specific materials.
—Prepare learning packages or learning centers on specific topics or skills.
—Suggest or develop learning activities for specific objectives.
—Assist students in creating and developing non-print materials.
—Develop "bibliographies" on specific topics, for particular needs, of materials in all formats.
—Develop appropriate displays for media center.
—Prepare transparencies for teacher on a specific topic.
—Preview materials.
—Recommend resource people in community.
—Recommend relevant field trips.
—Suggest appropriate objectives for study units.
—Suggest motivating activities for students based on individual interests.
—Examine materials for a multimedia approach.
—Help teacher to assess reading or skill level needed for specific materials, kits, learning packages.
—Assist in observing student behavior.

—Suggest methods or strategies for, and assist in, evaluation.
—Evaluate commercially produced curriculum packages in terms of teacher's goals and objectives.
—Assist in conducting needs assessment prior to curriculum planning.

The teacher has much to bring, too, to this partnership, the very foundation of which is the teacher's perception of the media specialist as a member of the teaching team. Cultivating the habit of seeking assistance is important, keeping the media specialist informed of goals, objectives, and content areas, long before materials are actually needed. The teacher should remember to:

—Include the media specialist in department meetings.
—Consult the media specialist for suggestions on including variety of media in assignments when planning lessons or units.
—Make suggestions for acquisitions to the media specialist.
—Always consult the media specialist before taking classes to media center.
—Prepare students for visit to the media center by explaining purpose of visit, what should be accomplished.
—Get the media specialist's advice about most appropriate ways to use specific materials.
—Ask the media specialist's advice in setting objectives, particularly when research skills are involved.
—Seek help of the media specialist in dealing with special student learning problems.
—Suggest to the media specialist displays that reinforce class work.
—Invite the media specialist into classroom to discuss books on current topics.

—Consult the media specialist regarding community resource people.

—Preview materials for the media center.

—Assist in retrieval of the media center materials.

—Require courteous behavior of students in the media center.

—Show enthusiasm for the media center and encourage fellow teachers to utilize it fully.

Just as success stimulates a student to further achievement, so one satisfactory team-planning experience of teachers with media specialists will lead to others. Little by little, by working together, the team will discover ways to add to each other's effectiveness in guiding learning. The more this partnership expands in scope, the more students will be using the "laboratory of learning." They will acquire more than just knowledge; they will develop lifelong learning skills, which is the real goal of education.

TEACHER'S RESERVATION: This chapter suggests many pathways to use of the media center by the teacher-student team. It is to be hoped that the media specialist has as much expertise in curriculum-planning as the chapter implies, and that the teacher will have the expertise to use the media center in the manner these writers project.

The format of the example for a unit study to be worked out by the teacher and media specialist on a topic such as the Arab-Israeli conflict seems interesting and feasible. The latter part of the chapter seems to be repetitious; these duties were clearly stated previously, and the case studies do not add new information.

WRITERS' RESPONSE: There are, of course, varying degrees of skill, competence, and experience among teachers and media specialists alike, but for those who desire to grow professionally this handbook should help delineate ways in

94

which they can work more effectively to improve their performance.

Repetition at the end of the chapter is by way of summary and emphasis. We wanted to present as many examples of cooperative planning between media specialists and teachers of as many subjects as possible. The case studies were included for those reasons.

## Bibliography

1. Adams, Charles W. "The School Media Program: A Position Statement." *School Media Quarterly*, 2:127–43, Winter, 1974.
2. Balzek, Ron. *Influencing Students Toward Media Center Use*. Chicago, American Library Association, 1975.
3. Belland, John, C. "Educational Media: Why Bother?" *School Media Quarterly*, 3:219–22, Spring, 1975.
4. Bixler, Dorothea. "Planning with Teachers." *Illinois Libraries*, 53:179–80, March, 1971.
5. Champlin, Constance J. "Use of the Elementary Library by Classroom Teachers." (Thesis) Nashville, George Peabody College for Teachers, 1969.
6. Davies, Ruth Ann. *The School Library Media Center: A Force for Educational Excellence*. New York, R.R. Bowker, 1974.
7. "Dear Principal, Dear Librarian: A Dialog on the Heart of the Matter." *Wilson Library Bulletin*, 48:54–57, September, 1973.
8. Ehman, Lee, Howard Mehlinger, and John Patrick. *Toward Effective Instruction In Secondary Social Studies*. Boston, Houghton-Mifflin, 1974.
9. Foshay, Arthur. *Curriculum for the 70's: An Agenda for Invention*. Washington, D.C., National Education

Association, 1970.

10. Goodlad, John H. *Facing the Future: Issues in Education and Schooling.* New York, McGraw-Hill, 1976.

11. Goodwin, Georgie. "An Educational Tool for All." *American Libraries,* 1:164–65, February, 1970.

12. Grazier, Margaret Hayes. "A Role for Media Specialists in the Curriculum Development Process." *School Media Quarterly,* 4:199–204, Spring, 1976.

13. Hanny, Robert J. "A Process for Deciding How to Teach." *Clearing House,* 49:279–81, February, 1976.

14. Hug, William E. *Instructional Design and the Media Program.* Chicago, American Library Association, 1975.

15. Jay, Hilda. "Increasing the Use of Secondary School Libraries." *School Libraries.* 20: 23–26, Summer, 1971.

16. Kalison, Mildred K. "An Evaluation of the School Librarian's Role in Curriculum Development." (Thesis) Southern Connecticut State College. April, 1974.

17. Kibler, Robert J., Donald J. Cegala, David T. Miles, and Larry L. Barker. *Objectives for Instruction and Evaluation.* Boston, Allyn and Bacon, 1974.

18. Kingsbury, Mary E. "Future of School Media Centers." *School Library Quarterly,* 4:19–26, Fall, 1975.

19. Kitchen, Lynne Jackson. "Teacher-Librarian Cooperation." *Contemporary Education,* 41:69–71, November, 1969.

20. Mager, Robert F. *Preparing Instructional Objectives.* Palo Alto, California, Fearon Publishers, 1962.

21. Martin, Gordon E. "The Industrial Arts Teacher and the Media Specialist," *Audiovisual Instruction,* 21: 36–38, April, 1978.

22. Miller, Rosalind. "Curriculum Delusions." *School Library Journal,* 21:38–39, November, 1974.

23. National Education Association, Research Division. *School Library Personnel Task Analysis Survey.* Chicago, American Library Association, 1969.

24. Ossefort, Joan. "Teamwork Tells at Woodrow Wilson

Junior High Library." *Illinois Libraries*, 58:563–65, September, 1976.
25. Paulin, Mary Ann. "A Study of the Materials Used in the Teaching of Reading by Teachers With and Without a Library Media Center with a Full-time Media Specialist." (Thesis) Kalamazoo, Western Michigan University, 1971.
26. Penn, Vivian Sue. "19 Ways to Love a Librarian." *Instructor*, 85:40–41, May, 1976.
27. Pickering, Robert. "It's All a Matter of Method." *Learning Today*, 9:44–53, Winter, 1976.
28. Pillon, Nancy B. "Media Specialists Work with Teachers." *Drexel Library Quarterly*, 9:59–69, July, 1973.
29. Rossoff, Martin. *The Library in High School Teaching*, 2d ed. New York, H. W. Wilson, 1961.
30. Rubin, Louis. *Curriculum Handbook: Administration and Theory*. Boston, Allyn and Bacon, 1977.
31. Rubin, Louis. *Curriculum Handbook: the Disciplines, Current Movements, and Instructional Methodology*. Boston, Allyn and Bacon, 1977.
32. Schmid, William T. "The Teacher and the Media Specialist." *Media and Methods*, 13:22–24, October, 1976.
33. Sullivan, Janet. "Instructional Development in Media Programs." *School Library Journal*, 25:340, April, 1979.
34. Sullivan, Peggy. *Impact: The School Library and the Instructional Program*. Chicago, American Library Association, 1967.
35. Taba, Hilda. *Curriculum Development: Theory and Practice*. New York, Harcourt, Brace and World, 1962.
36. Tassia, Margaret. "It's Not Just a Game." *School Library Journal*, 25:105–07, March, 1979.
37. Taylor, Kenneth J. " Creative Inquiry and Instructional Media." *School Media Quarterly*, 1:18–36, Fall, 1972.
38. Taylor, Kenneth J. "Instruction First and Media Next."

*Wisconsin Library Bulletin*, 68:81–88, March-April, 1972.

39. Taylor, Kenneth J. "Librarians, Audiovisual Consultants, and Instructional Planning." *Illinois Libraries*, 53:174–79, March, 1971.
40. "Team-Teaching Used." *California School Libraries*, 44:27–30, Summer, 1973.
41. Tyler, Robert W. *Basic Principles of Curriculum and Instruction*. Chicago, University of Chicago Press, 1949.
42. Wong, Laverne. "Meeting Place for the 'Total Educator,'" *Wilson Library Bulletin*, 50:390–94, January, 1976.
43. Wood, Johanna S. "The Role of Media Specialists in the Curriculum Process." *School Library Journal*, 23:20–21, September, 1976.

# 5

## "I Should Like Suggestions Which Would Help Me Develop Creative Learning Exeriences."

Creativity is defined in two ways. One definition describes creativity as the origination of a product, process, or activity that has never been known to man. A second definition, as Smith states it, "is the ability to tap past experience and come up with something new. This product need not necessarily be new to the world, but new to the individual."(48) This second definition is the one used in this chapter.

It is possible to be satisfied with one's present teaching methods, to use last year's lesson plans and tests, lectures or explanations of concepts which have been used many times before, and the same classroom routine. But this *can* be the path to "intellectual stagnation." Perhaps this is a time to evaluate methods: What are the strategies used? Are they productive? Do they spark student interest? How do I feel about my teaching? Is it boring, a deadly routine? Have I used one new activity in the past week? It could be very revealing to use an anonymous questionnaire and get an honest evaluation of teaching from students, and/or listen to an audio or video tape made in the classroom while teaching.

Such an evaluation might indicate that one or more improvements could be made. It is all too easy for us to become defensive and to think of reasons why it is impossible to change any of our methods:

Subject matter must be covered.
An achievement test must be prepared for.
There is no time to plan variety in activities.
Students will become disorderly.
If students learn what's in the textbook, they will be doing well.

The schools are committed to offering the best possible learning experiences for *all* children. Consider the picture Frazier gives of children who are victims of unequal or inept teaching: (22)

Teachers need constantly to look for innovative additions to their repertory of strategies and approaches in order to find those which best fit the learning patterns of various types of students.

A teacher may at first feel insecure with a new instructional method. It is natural to fear what we don't understand. It is the purpose of this chapter to try to throw a little light on creative teaching. The emphasis is not on promoting creativity in students, though that might well be one result, but on helping each of our readers to find ways to diversify and vitalize their teaching. No attempt is made here to outline a complete orientation to educational philosophy, theory, goals, administration, and related matters. That is outside the scope of this book.

Let us begin with some fairly conventional elements for creating a climate or framework for creative teaching in a traditional classroom:

An atmosphere that is free from repression and en-

## FIGURE 3
### TYPES AND RESULTS OF INEQUALITY OF TEACHING

| TYPE OF INEQUALITY | RESULTS OF INEQUALITY |
| --- | --- |
| Children who are undertaught | Fail to learn what they could learn<br>Fall behind others and become discouraged<br>Develop dislike for school<br>May escape from schooling at earliest opportunity<br>Find themselves boxed in by lack of education |
| Children who are overtaught | Waste time in overlearning<br>Become bored with school<br>May develop distaste for learning<br>May fail to find themselves<br>Find themselves boxed in by lack of education |
| Children who are mistaught | Limit interest to subjects thought appropriate to sex role or social status<br>May learn to dislike or fear some subjects<br>Fail to develop broad base for further learning<br>Grow up half-educated<br>Find themselves boxed in by lack of education |
| Children who are not taught some things at all | Respond less fully to total environment<br>May develop prejudices against the arts<br>Function at less than best in some aspects of human relationships<br>May remain ignorant of important realms of human experience<br>Find themselves boxed in by lack of education |

101

courages students to express themselves. Peters states that "teachers need to build a learning environment which minimizes threats to learning, and maximizes attractions to learning and personal growth so that students elect to become involved in the learning process rather than being defensive and self-protective."(42)

An atmosphere of empathy and pleasantness, sensitivity to the feelings of students, and acceptance of individual personalities. Students' attitudes and expressions are usually a reflection of the teacher's. Pleasantness begets pleasantness.

Respect for the uniqueness of each individual student, and less emphasis on conformity. The rigidity of "one best teaching method" or "one best set of materials" should be banished.

Alertness to student needs, personal as well as academic.

Determination to use all resources available to meet those needs, and realistic standards.

Emphasis on the activation of the learner. Time provided for individual effort and small group work. Expectation, constantly demonstrated, that students will be responsible for their own learning. Opportunity for students to make choices, be involved in planning, choose the materials they will use, the activities they will pursue.

Patience and avoidance of rushing or pushing, tolerance for uncertainty, and recognition of honest, even if unproductive, effort.

Time for students to think and digest. Determination to

preserve diverse thinking, and to emphasize thinking over memorizing.

Avoidance whenever possible of the closed question with only a right or wrong answer. Open-ended questions can open doors to new questions and require more thought and the translation of thought into words.

Refusal to let overconcern for discipline and orderliness kill attempts to bring variety and flexibility into teaching. Innovation, injection of surprise and variation might take care of some discipline problems that are the result of student boredom or failure to see any relevancy in classroom activity.

A climate in the classroom of curiosity, the best of motivations for learning, making it a habit to tie what is learned today to new fields to conquer tomorrow.

Emphasis on the interaction between the learner and the subject matter rather than on the subject matter alone. A student's progress measured in terms of his own starting point.

We have all heard the above suggestions many times before. But how many of them have we deliberately set out to put into practice? They are listed here simply as reminders of the importance of attitude and of the general behavior practices that can put new life into the classroom and increase the possibility that students will learn and enjoy learning. In addition to these general elements conducive to creativity, there are some teaching strategies which, although they have been utilized long enough to be considered now basic to some teachers, may still be innovative for others. They have two things in common: first, they all involve a wider than traditional use of media and call for participation by the media specialist; second, these teaching techniques will make learning more interesting to students because they are actively involved in it. Specifically, these include: learning packages, learning centers, independent study, peer teaching, role-playing, educational and simulation games, inquiry and discovery methods, small group work, use of community resources, student production of non-print materials, and oral history.

Learning packages are a boon if one is conscientiously trying to provide for the individual differences of students, whether remedial work for the slow student or advanced work for the more able one. These packages can be designed in booklet form and duplicated as needed, or they may be taped for students to use with work sheets. Some teachers devise packages on three levels on the same study topic for three different ability levels. These can be revised from year to year to be made suitable for other students. A class can rather easily be organized to allow time for this individual work. Exactly how this is done depends upon the number of students in such a program.

Dunn and Dunn (19) give a clear description of how to construct a multi-sensory learning package on tape:

1. Identify the topic. List the concepts and skills related to the study topic, which might be a country, the parts of speech, pollution, etc.
2. List the things you want students to learn about the topic.
3. Plan to tape-record simple learning objectives for students such as this example: "By the time you finish this package, you will be able to explain what a noun is and recognize one in a sentence."
4. Write out what you would say if teaching this topic to a class and tape this.
5. Develop visual, tactile, and kinesthetic activities that emphasize these aspects in different ways.

6. Write out the directions for each activity and tape.
7. Make up a short test which may be recorded.

We would also include a list of relevant materials, both print and non-print, for students to consult.

The same procedure is followed for a learning package in booklet form. To the above should be added a pretest to be given to the student who thinks he knows the material covered by the package. Conferences should be held periodically with individual students and group discussions arranged for frequently.

In a tape format the package must be done rather carefully so that students can use it independently. The following are recommendations:

1. Find a quiet place. Put a sign on the door saying "Recording. Do not disturb." Turn off any electrical appliance that might cause a background noise. Avoid the school bell. The acoustics of the recording area will greatly influence reproduction quality.
2. Place the microphone 10 to 12 inches from the mouth. Place a sponge or handkerchief under the microphone to cut down on vibration.
3. Set volume control to provide the best level for recording. (Experiment).
4. Speak slowly, and vary the tone, pace, and inflection to add listener interest.
5. Speak past the microphone, not directly into it.
6. Allow a few feet of lead tape before recording. Cassette tape should be allowed to run past the leader before beginning to record.
7. Be sure directions are explicit and are on the correct level. Pause after a direction so that the student has time to consider it and carry it out.
8. Students are more attentive if they are expected to car-

ry out directions as they listen, marking answer sheets, manipulating objects, answering written questions, or following a diagram.

9. Include some music, poetry, or a short story at the end. This stimulates effective listening and lessens boredom.

Obviously, the resources of the media center will be most helpful in developing these packages. Many of the materials referred to in the packages will be available there, and many of the open-ended activities can be carried out there with the assistance of the media center staff. For the package to be truly individualized, students must be allowed choices of some of the materials and activities listed. In this way you can provide for their various learning styles and preferences.

A word of caution is necessary. Learning packages will not be useful for those students who need much interaction with peers or daily direction from teachers.

Some teachers like to use learning contracts, which are somewhat similar to learning packages. With a contract, a student agrees to complete certain designated activities in order to earn a "C," or other activities for a "B," or still other (or additional) activities for an "A." In some variations, students agree or contract to complete certain work without a specified grade.

(See Appendix I for a selected list of references on learning packages and contracts.)

Another way to individualize instruction is to develop learning centers in which students may learn by pacing themselves. The media specialist can be an especially valuable partner in this kind of enterprise, designing the centers in terms of the objectives defined, the activities selected, the materials identified, and the evaluation procedures formulated. Collaboration with the media specialist in setting up the centers can be effective whether they are to be set up in the classroom or in the media center.

Suggested planning steps are as follows:

1. Determine the number and kind of centers: It's usually best to start with one or two at first. Though teachers always use some direct teaching, those with much experience with learning centers may use them as the dominant teaching strategy.
2. Determine objectives for each center and clarify them for yourself and student.
3. Decide which centers children will be required to use weekly and those from which a child may choose daily.
4. Keep directions for children as simple as possible.
5. Give each center an eye-catching title with attractive pictures and objects.
6. Gather needed materials. Use various print and non-print materials. Provide for different reading and ability levels. Use of two or three different materials may be required, but choices permitted from the rest. Laminate materials so that children may write on them with water-based, felt-tipped markers.
7. Provide a variety of activities: reading, listening to tapes, looking at filmstrips, using teacher-prepared materials, using games and puzzles, locating information in the media center, examining relevant realia, etc. Allow choices. Avoid the use of too many work sheets.
8. Devise a student self-evaluation plan. Find a simple way to keep records. Record progress in the skill areas.
9. Plan with students an effective way to use the centers. Usually more than one can work at a center at the same time. It is important for students to participate in formulating the rules for use of the centers, which should be posted. The following are suggested rules:

   Stay at a center for the full time specified.
   Talk quietly with anyone who is working with you.

Read the directions slowly and carefully.

Get help from the teacher if you do not understand the directions.

Follow directions in the order in which they are given.

When you have finished put materials in order.

There are some good descriptions of centers in books and magazine articles. (See the selected references in Appendix II.)

Independent study is another means of dealing with the wide range of differences among students, and is more loosely structured than learning packages or learning centers. Of course, any student working by himself might be said to be engaged in independent study. The strategy described here is a long-term study in depth of a topic selected by the student, a flexible but specific program designed to meet the basic and unique needs and interests of that student. Independent study in these terms involves a guidance procedure by the teacher and/or the media specialist in which goals are set cooperatively with the student and a general procedure for reaching these goals is outlined. The teacher is directly concerned with process and only indirectly with content. Communication between teacher and media specialist is essential. The student selects his own sources of information and must know or learn media skills. The student's work is evaluated by the quality of his final summary of the project for which he chooses the format, for example, a sound-slide presentation, an 8mm film, charts, transparencies, etc. The evaluation also determines the extent to which the student has increased in his ability to manage, sustain and obtain personal satisfaction from study on his own.

Before launching an independent study program it must be remembered that not all students are able to work independently. Selection of students for such work should be based on their maturity and responsibility rather than on high achievement. Instead of being assigned a topic for this type of study, the student should choose one in which he is interested. Consultation times should be available. Although the teacher should be informed about and interested in his progress, there should be no attempt to check all his work. His final report will reveal his achievement.

Directives on independent study that were sent to students, teachers, and parents at Greenville (South Carolina) Middle School are included in Appendix III-A-D.

Peer teaching, or student tutoring, is another strategy for meeting individual needs and can often be even more useful for the tutor than for the tutee. The goals of such a program are as follows:

To help boost the tutee's confidence in himself, both in his school work and with his friends.

To widen the horizons of the tutee through the tutor's friendship and new ideas.

To help the tutors learn for themselves the value of being on time, planning, organizing, evaluating, and working with others.

To help the tutors develop continuing patience, responsibility, and willingness to work.

To give the tutee the extra help he needs to make progress.

Those teachers who would involve student tutors should be guided by certain rules. Tutors should not be asked to work with children who are discipline problems. Directions to student tutors should be explicit and suggestions offered to them about ways to organize the work. A few minutes each day should be set aside to talk with them about the work they are doing. Tutors need to be encouraged to be creative and to challenge themselves as well as the students they are helping. The areas in which they will work must be carefully chosen, usually with such skills as reading, listening, spelling, basic math operations, and making use of the media center.

Students are selected to be tutors by their teachers, and selection should not be limited to the most able students. It has been found that tutoring others is a motivating factor for slower students. Students may tutor others in their classes or in classes below theirs. The latter works better. Middle-school students often tutor in elementary schools and high-school students in middle schools. A three-grade spread has been found to make for the most effective pairing.

Media specialists help tutors select suitable materials and advise on effective usage.

Materials related to planning a student tutoring program at Greenville Middle School are found in Appendix IV-A–C along with selected references.

Other forms of creative teaching activities that are used with groups rather than with individuals are role-playing, dramatic play, and educational and simulation games. These techniques are "attention-getters" which create and sustain student interest.

Small group role-playing involves the determination of roles for a certain scenario and the assigning of these roles to students in the group. The roles may be swapped later, especially those that represent adversary positions, to give each an understanding of different points of view. Zeloney gives the following steps in the development of role-playing:

1. Teacher-student selection of a problem and/or goal.
2. Search for information about the problem.
3. Organization of compatible groups for interaction.
4. Comparison of student findings in small groups.
5. Identification of roles and role-playing in small groups.
6. Presentation before and with the whole class.
7. Interpretation which includes analysis, identification

of alternate solutions, replaying alternate solutions, and selecting the most suitable.(64)

Role-playing can be as simple as a child coming to school and telling the teacher something that happened at home or on the way to school and being asked, "Would you like to show us what happened? Carol and John can help you." Or role-playing can be more sophisticated, such as a high-school class role-playing the heads of nations meeting in a crisis situation. In this case, though the conversation will be extemporaneous, the students need to research the problem thoroughly beforehand. In this type of role-playing the need for utilization of media resources and the assistance of the media specialist are evident.

Role-playing is more meaningful when it is integrated into other classroom experiences and activities. For instance, the following situations might occur:

Language Arts

Three or four students who have read the same book could role-play the climax or a different ending.

Several students role-play incidents in an author's life.

A small group originates in a few minutes a short skit illustrating an incident which results from poor listening skills. The dialogue would be impromptu.

Using conflict in a piece of literature being studied, a group role-plays the way *they* would have reacted in the situation.

Social Studies

A group role-plays colonists expressing their opinions about the Stamp Act.

A group role-plays the statesmen at the Yalta Conference.

A class role-plays a mock Greek forum.

Students role-play two couples living many miles apart on the western frontier who meet for the first time.

Science
> Imagining that all the trees have disappeared, students role-play the results.
>
> Imagine a whole town inside a plastic bubble because of the pollution. Have students role-play a group of town inhabitants talking.
>
> A group role-plays how the laser has changed their lives in the twenty-first century.

Nichols and Williams have some advice for those who use role-playing:

> Select situations that have more than one acceptable solution.
>
> Remember the teacher has the role of "producer" and may stop the scene at any time if students seem to be getting too personal or if physical activity becomes too rough.
>
> Stress the post-discussion. It is very important.
>
> One thing is absolutely imperative. The teacher must refrain from stating conclusions, moralizing, or putting the stamp of approval or disapproval on any part of the action or during the discussion. All ideas, points of view, and expressions must be accepted.
>
> Teacher insight comes with participation, planning, practice, and evaluation.(40)

As students become familiar with role-playing, most will learn to perform easily in a group and will establish a feeling of fellowship. They will come to respect each other's expressions and will grow in an understanding of the different ways in which people react to situations. As they develop self-discipline, their fears and anxieties will tend to diminish.

Role-playing naturally develops into dramatic activities where actions and dialogue are prescribed and students interpret the characters. They may write their own plays or use those in books or magazines. A video tape recorder can tape a play so that students may evaluate their performances or show the play to other school groups. Dramatic presentations allow students to express themselves, to contribute to a group activity, to develop self-confidence, and to "try out" other personalities and behaviors. Each student in the class should have some part in the staging of the play unless it is the special project of a small group.

Another creative teaching strategy for groups is the use of educational games. Many of these are commercially produced. (See Appendix V for selected references.) Some computer-assisted instruction consists of games which will interest teachers who have computers available. Nonsimulation games like checkers, chess, math bingo, password in Spanish, etc., have educative value. Many media centers keep such games and encourage students to use them. Electronic games have recently been added to some media centers.

Students may also construct games. These materials might be used: a game board or manila file folder marked in the game design with some colored space or otherwise specially designated spaces; place markers, such as bottle caps painted different colors; a die that players roll and move ahead the indicated number of spaces; a packet of colored question cards or pictures; a packet of problem cards. In the beginning the learner objectives should be stated, as, "After playing the game the student will be able to . . .." Prepare an evaluation in the form of a paper-and-pencil test or plan to assess progress by observation. Complete the construction of materials, prepare the rules of the game, and then try out the game with a small group. Evaluate the game and revise systematically. Let the class choose which of several games to donate to the media center.

A simulation game is a model of a real situation in the real world. It has several values for the learning process. Though simulation has not been found to increase cognitive knowledge, it has high motivation value, especially for culturally different students, because it is concrete, dramatic, and brings the world spinning into the classroom. The simulation game can also expand humanistic and societal awareness, encourage social interaction, and influence attitudes. Other values of this teaching method are that it tends to reinforce democratic processes, emphasize behavior rather than memorization, result in more integrated and realistic views of the subject matter, reach nonverbal students, foster student involvement, and develop self-confidence and leadership.

To achieve these values simulations should be coordinated with the curriculum. The students should clearly perceive the goal and should understand that they must reach it through their own efforts. A situation is identified that matches one in the community, national, or international environment. A goal is specified, and four or five students are given the roles to play. Basic rules and a time sequence govern the actions of the players. Within that framework students use their imaginations and their background of information and experience to express themselves in conversations, decisions, and the selection of courses of action to reach the goal. In this way students carry out real-life controversies vicariously and see the results of their decisions as they attempt to solve problems.

Here is one example of a simulation. A class is studying urban problems and the conflict arising from the needs of expanding industry. The simulation is developed: A federal government official, an army engineer, and the town mayor, all proponents of a dam to provide more power for needed industry, meet with the opponents, including the head of an environmental protection group and a representative of the taxpayers. In view of the various concerns, how shall this problem be solved in the best interests of the community?

A simulation game should not become too time-consuming, should be interesting but also educational and carefully structured. The following is one way for teacher and/or students to proceed:

1. Identify the concepts and/or skills to be learned.
2. Decide on some situation and write a description of it.
3. State the problem in writing.
4. State the objectives.
5. Write the directions for the students, identifying roles, number of group meetings, who may contact others (if that is relevant), when the group may meet, etc.
6. Explain how to complete any necessary forms.
7. Indicate time limits.
8. Plan post-discussion.

The media specialist provides much direction to students and teachers in identifying various aspects of the simulated problem, indicating sources of information, and assisting in evaluating and organizing the data.

The media specialist's expertise is utilized also in assessing the value of commercial simulation and other games. Features to be examined are the grade, age, and ability level for which the games are suitable, how they can be used effectively, their design quality, adaptability, flexibility, validation, and potential for developing social awareness.

The experience of teachers who have used simulation games indicates that they may be employed effectively to provide a change of pace. Simulations may be used anywhere in a unit or course of study where they fit into the sequence of the subject content, and are especially useful where reinforcement is desirable. Wherever they are used, the class should be carefully prepared, the participant's manual explained, directions given for forms or computations, and the time element made clear. The teacher may play the game with several students first, and they may introduce the game to the class. After a simulation game is used, the cognitive outcomes may be measured by teacher-made tests. Many of the outcomes are in the affective area, and there are still no adequate measures of these.

Two other teaching techniques that have a highly motivating effect on students and are characterized by much student involvement are the discovery and inquiry methods. According to Massialas and Zevin, discovery is primarily applicable to the initiatory phases of inquiry, and there is a great deal of overlapping between the two processes.(37). Therefore, they will be treated together here.

Discovery and inquiry provide the opportunity for students to identify problems, gather and organize information, analyze, synthesize, reach decisions, and evaluate outcomes. These methods can be used by one teacher continuously or intermittently. The teacher role shifts from the traditional one of presenting information to that of motivating, planning, guiding, and evaluating. The tone in the classroom is established by the teacher, who shows respect for the personal dignity of students, listens to their opinions, and gives them time to find a variety of possible answers for consideration and evaluation. The teacher role includes:

Helping students to identify problems of interest to them which can serve as a focal point for an inquiry activity.

Providing guidance as students formulate hypotheses.

Introducing the problem but not serving as a primary source of information.

Requesting the media specialist to review or teach media skills.

Planning with the media specialist the probable scope of the study and providing for adequate primary source material.

116

Having question-and-answer sessions with students. The teacher leads the students to ask questions and seek their own answers. A free flow of ideas is encouraged.

Encouraging diverse answers and listening to varying points of view.

Summarizing, recapitulating, asking for clarification.

Challenging and prodding students to explore and test new alternatives.

The teacher role is demanding and often quite frustrating, because it is so different from the customary role. Young believes that some teachers are neither emotionally nor psychologically suited to discovery or inquiry teaching. (63) Massialas and Zevin describe a discovery project on the evolution of man. A student raised the question, "Why were no apes or monkeys or ancient men found in Australia?" During the following discussion these were the teacher's contributions interspersed at various times:

"Why do you think they were not found there?"
"What can you say about Australia if no remains of primitives were found there?"
"Is that all you can get out of this idea?"
"What does that show us?"
"Why?"
"Why do you think that?"
"Does that interpretation sound reasonable?"(37)

The teacher later summarized what the students had found and asked a question that led to further investigation.

Since in discovery and inquiry students are conducting their own learning, there is much research, field work, and laboratory work, as well as small group discussion. The media specialist works with individual students and groups as they explore alternatives and seek solutions. Students are not given answers, but are directed to source materials to find the answers. One problem is in locating information which does not spell out the answers. Contemporary eye-witness accounts of events, diaries, letters, etc., give students the opportunity to formulate answers. When teachers elect to use discovery or inquiry methods, the media specialist should make a special effort to assemble a collection of primary source material.

Students who have been involved in these methods of study will develop self-direction in learning, will analyze data more critically, feel more secure in suggesting ideas, and have more respect for the ideas of others than formerly. (See Appendix VI for selected references on Inquiry and Discovery Methods.)

Another teaching strategy which also takes the center of the stage away from the teacher is small group work. The leadership role is not abdicated, but expressed in a non-directive way. The groups are allowed to work out their own problems as much as possible and rely upon the teacher only as a last resort. Students who are not accustomed to working in small groups may bring pressure upon the teacher to return to an autocratic role, so that it takes deter-mination to continue to exemplify an encouraging, facilitating, guiding mode. The structure of an overall plan provided by the teacher is the framework, but within it there is ample room for students' interests and ideas. There are certain guidelines planned with the class so that all will know the limitations and rules.

Schumsky states some problems with this method of in-struction: "How to encourage children's initiative and maintain teacher initiative, how to be in control without overcontrolling, how to plan subject matter and allow children to participate, how to encourage children to be strong and yet remain a strong teacher."(45) Certain deci-sions must be made. What core of subject matter should be studied by the class as a whole? What part should be small group work? What part should be designated as work for individual students?

Amidon suggests how to prepare the class for group work:

Try a limited kind of group work first.

Prepare yourself psychologically.

Have the class participate in setting up procedures.

Develop a climate in which experimental activities may be attempted.

Try a short-term project and observe student reactions.

At first check progress after every group meeting.

Train students in leadership and follower roles by having the class make a list of the functions of each. (See Appendix VII for Suggestions for Group Leadership.)

Divide the class into groups by choice, random selection, or an indicated interest. Use heterogeneous groups. (3)

The main thing is not to be discouraged if things don't go as planned the first time group work is attempted. Teacher attitude is the most important determinant of success. One must have the ability to maintain an experimental focus, to evaluate, modify goals, and try again. Those who have been accustomed to having restrictive rules that prescribe only one type of student behavior must start group work slowly. (Selected references on small group work are available in Appendix VIII.)

Another way to put spark into teaching is to make a habit of using community resources. These resources consist of speakers, field trips, and volunteers. The media specialist can help identify speakers who have contributions to offer for the subject a class is studying. A continuing program of speakers might be organized, with two or more speakers scheduled each week making presentations on subjects chosen by the students. The media specialist can make available a collection of materials on the chosen subjects. Also, there are places in the community which have educative value for a class visit. These are found in industry, community service agencies, cultural events, governmental operations, to suggest only a few. The media specialist can suggest background preparation for the class before a visit and help students to locate related materials.

Volunteers from the community can function as tutors, assistants in routine processes, and teachers of minicourses in their specialties. Three or four sessions of a minicourse on a topic related to a unit of study can be planned to provide extended knowledge for students (with the advice and consent of the school principal, of course, as when any interaction with the community is planned). Some volunteers have long years of experience, and also training, in various areas. This is a resource that should be utilized.

One instructional strategy which has the potential of energizing students is introducing them to the production of non-print materials, including the use of closed circuit television. The services of the media specialist are invaluable in this activity. The processes involved are discussed in detail in a later chapter, but the possibility is mentioned here as an option that should have high priority.

An exciting technique particularly useful for the social studies classroom is oral history, "the process of recapturing the past through the recollections of those who have lived through it."(38) This activity is especially effective if the accounts gathered can be issued in some form so that students have the satisfaction of knowing others see their work. Students using cassette tape recorders interview the older

120

people in the community. The material is transcribed for use in a publication. Many students are impressed with the "senior citizens," who enjoy the contacts too. Anyone interested in this activity may profit from the experiences of others by consulting the selected references in Appendix IX. Mehaffy and Sitton report that one teacher who organized an oral history project stated: "What is important is what happened to everybody involved with us—the students who do the work on the project, the people they talk to, and all the people who are touched by the project in various ways. It affects us all. It changes us."(38)

Another instructional strategy that has been developed, especially in the last ten years, is the application of computer technology to education. Two well-known computer-based systems are Computer Managed Instruction (CMI) and Computer Assisted Instruction (CAI). CAI provides the student with an entire course of study or large portions of it at a computer terminal. CMI concerns management rather than instruction, and its main purpose is test-scoring, diagnosis, prescription, and reporting. Using curriculum units designed by an instructional specialist, students work with different off-line media as prescribed. The computer analyzes and evaluates their work and makes the next assignment. Some advocates of computer-based instruction are now proposing the use of a combined CAI and CMI system. Studies have been made on both systems purporting to show cost-effectiveness and greater student achievement. Also reference is made to the fact that the systems are decreasing in price and are emphasizing improved software (learning materials).

Computer technology in instruction will not be discussed in more detail here for two reasons: first, it is outside the scope of this chapter, since the strategy does not originate from teacher creativity but from an extrinsic source; and second, very few school districts have the financial resources to provide the required computer services.

Even when computer services are available, some teachers do not think this technology should be applied to instruction because it does not address the affective area of learning, attitudes, values, feelings, and sensitivities. They believe that a vital factor in learning is the interactive relationship between teacher and student. Others point out, however, that that rapport sometimes did not exist before computers came on the scene. Proponents of computer-based instruction believe that the computer takes the burden of routine and technical tasks off the teacher and allows more time for the teacher-student relationship.

And so on with the pros and cons. In the atmosphere of economic and other resource shortages that seems likely to prevail in the 1980's who knows whether or not to believe the projection of a recent magazine article, which stated that by 1982 "5 million private computers will be in people's homes and available to students . . . while in schools computers will be more common than carousel slide projectors, movie projectors and tape recorders."(35)

It should be noted however, that micro-computers already in use in a few schools and even in private homes indicate that they can facilitate learning in many remarkable ways. Children as young as 3 or 4 years of age are able to interact creatively with "smart" computers, developing their own programs and games. The technology is in place, and teachers and media specialists would do well to explore a future in which an "Apple" evokes the home computer rather than the red fruit gift for the teacher!

In addition to the general teaching strategies described above, there are many types of unrelated teaching activities which may be used once or occasionally to relieve the routine and bring variety into the classroom. The media specialist can assist in originating, planning, and carrying out many of these ideas and others like them. Many of these may seem more suited to use with elementary students, others with secondary, and still others with either. To list some of them briefly:

Puppets used in many ways can help to present stories, teach skills, or instruct in good human relations and attitudes.

Mobiles at many levels of sophistication and complexity are interesting, and construction gives practice in many concepts.

Children enjoy making laminated folders with illustrations and questions and comments about favorite books.

Presentation of shadow plays is popular, and, similarly, cutout characters (from thick paper) can be shown on the "stage" of an overhead projector.

Scenes from stories can be given dimension when constructed in a box with small hole for viewing.

Individual activity cards may be used to specify an activity related to a particular affective or cognitive need. Each child can choose his own or have one assigned.

With appropriate adjustment of content level, either elementary or secondary students will like the challenge of trying to interpret an era through the use of its contemporary music.

Students will find it interesting to develop art projects related to science.

Design a graphically interesting and attractive bulletin board where students can post anything they want to share. Art and "shop" departments can be involved in this one.

Unusual and interesting pictures not relating to specific classroom activity can be the subject of a discussion, a contest.

Collages may be used to interpret a novel.

A period of history can be brought to life by means of a book of fiction set in the period.

A once-in-a-while brainstorming session, in which each person in the room (including teacher) tosses in ideas on a particular subject in quick succession, with no ideas criticized.

Charades, or student impersonation of book characters or authors.

Student interpretation of story titles in dance.

Choral speaking with puppet shows, shadow plays, pantomimes.

The combination of literature, oral expression, reading, art and music is brought about when the class chooses a story, divides up parts for reading it aloud, background music to play while recording it, and accompanies it with a filmstrip drawn on blank filmstrip by each child, to illustrate the part he or she reads.

Interest is stimulated by the correlation of art and literature, such as a reading of Eugene Field's *Little Boy Blue* with the famous Blue Boy portrait.

Authors can be communicated with by phone, utilizing the telephone company's special loudspeaker so that the whole class may listen and ask questions at the same time.

Closed circuit television can be used to teach media skills, to present scenes from books, to give original or puppet plays, etc.

Dioramas can be constructed in box theaters so that movement can be controlled from underneath by the use of magnets.

Popular songs can be used to study poetry, as the themes of the lyrics, the emotions being expressed, are compared with those of particular poems.

Science students can prepare kits containing materials for carrying out scientific experiments and present them to the library media center for circulation with a book on the subject.

Students in a psychology class may be asked to choose some fiction which illustrates particular psychological principles, psychological disturbances, etc.

Students may be asked to list terms used in medical ads, such as disinfectants, germicides, antiseptics, find the correct definitions, and engage in critical analysis of the words in advertisements.

Chemical experiments can be very well demonstrated and seen by a larger group when shown from the stage of an overhead projector, using flat-bottomed Petri dishes.

Creative teaching activities should be evaluated:

Did the activity contribute to the development of concepts?
Did student attitude improve?
Were some basic skills learned?
Did students learn to work better together?
Did critical thinking skills improve?
Did students appear to become more independent, more responsible?
Did students become more accepting of differences in others?
Did students learn more about different ways of using the media center?
Did student self-image improve?
Did students become more interested in learning?

There is one concern which many teachers feel needs discussion: student behavior. You may fear that if you relax a rigid control and introduce creative strategies the classroom will become chaotic. It has already been pointed out that appealing to student interests and bringing variety to the classroom routine may itself obviate some behavior problems. In addition, the following suggestions are offered:

Be fair. This is a teacher trait highly prized by students.
Be honest but tactful.
Be consistent. Inconsistency confuses students.
Know students as individuals.

FIGURE 4
## A FORMULA FOR CREATIVITY
Torrance gives the following formula for creativity:(55)

(The examples are suggested by the writers.)

S   SUBSTITUTE
Substitute small group work for lectures.

C   COMBINE
Combine social studies, mathematics, language, arts, and science instruction in a unit on Consumer Economics.

A   ADD
Add role-playing to the study of the United Nations.
ADAPT
Adapt a study of the causes of World War II to a simulation game.

M   MAGNIFY
Get video tape of a class play shown to all classes on closed circuit television.
MINIFY
Use an imaginary trip around the world for students to study places they might visit.
MODIFY
Instead of only one speaker on a subject, use two with opposing views.

P   PUT TO OTHER USES
Instead of using the 8mm camera for class work, let a group use it to record scenes around the school to make a documentary of school life to present at a PTA meeting.

E   ELIMINATE
Eliminate half of your talking in the classroom.
ELABORATE
Elaborate your plan for more student involvement.

R   REARRANGE
Rearrange your schedule to allow time for role-playing.
REVERSE
Reverse your policy of letting only above-average students participate in the student tutoring program and let some under-achievers serve as tutors.

Find behavior to praise.

Correct students in private.

Use humor. Laugh with students.

Be open and accessible.

Seek and use student ideas.

Observe the results of your behavior and modify it as needed.

Make flexible plans which are subject to modification.

Help the class identify common goals.

Tolerate some disorder, creative disorder if you will, the kind that results from student divergent thinking, originality, and exploration of ideas.

Plan guidelines *with the class* to define unacceptable behavior and to set limits.(8)

Creative teaching can be applied to every facet of the curriculum. If you have faith that it will brighten dull classrooms, if you are interested and enthusiastic, and if you have determination and perseverance, you will find that your students no longer will be "creeping like snails unwillingly to school."

TEACHER'S RESERVATION: The chapter is filled with many good ideas for the classroom teacher. There are many useful ideas for exceptional and college-bound students. The chapter, however, presents a utopia—not practical for elementary and average students. Not enough emphasis is placed on the basic skills. Very few media specialists have time for planning as outlined in the chapter.

Although the chapter offers many good suggestions, more emphasis should be placed on the learning level of the average student. We need to create an atmosphere for learning that does not present an impossible challenge.

WRITERS' RESPONSE: Again, the need for increased media center staff is noted. Teachers can effect this change if they will continue to make principals aware of the need.

We know that there is no agreed-upon definition of "average" students that enables teachers to identify them clearly. But it is a known fact that many "average" students will respond to creative teaching. We have offered many different suggestions that have *worked* in developing and *applying* creativity to the teaching of *all* youngsters. It will be necessary to adapt these suggestions not only to different ability levels, but also to different learning styles.

In response to "lack of emphasis on basic skills" we point out that Chapter 10 deals with reading as a skill. The activities in this chapter are designed to *exercise* basic skills rather than to introduce them. Teaching is, after all, a great "mix-and-match" game of combining content, skills, and activities to meet the needs of students. We hope the suggestions in the chapter will contribute to a teacher's success in planning.

Challenge there must be! Too often we underestimate youngsters and expect too little. We agree with Browning: "A man's reach should exceed his grasp, or what's a heaven for?

### BIBLIOGRAPHY

1. Abt, Clark C. and Gabriel D. Ofiesh. "Simulation and Games in Curriculum Development." (Audio tape). Englewood Cliffs, New Jersey, Educational Technology Publications, 1971.
2. Alcorn, Marvin D., James S. Kinder, and Jim R. Schynert. *Better Teaching in Secondary Schools.* New York, Holt, Rinehart, Winston, 1970.
3. Amidon, Paul S. "Self-directed Group Work." (Audio tape) Minneapolis, Paul S. Amidon and Associates, n.d.
4. Anderson, Paul. "Independent Study: Emerson Junior-Senior High School." *Illinois Libraries*, 2:41-43,

Winter, 1969.

5. Ball, Howard G. "What's in a Game?" *Elementary School Journal*, 77:42-49, September, 1976.

6. Bedwell, Lance E. "Developing Environmental Education Games." *American Biology Teacher*, 39:176-77;192, March, 1977.

7. Brodbelt, Samuel. "Simulation in the Social Studies: an Overview." *Social Education*, 33:176-78, February, 1969.

8. Brevard Inservice Teaching Center. *Developing Classroom Climate: Creating Personal Teacher-Pupil Relations* (Discipline). Cocoa, Florida, The Center, 1973.

9. Brown, L. Lakota. 'Name One Creative Thing You've Done Lately." *English Journal*, 56:1158-59, November, 1967.

10. Buehring, G. R. "Creativity." *Instructor*, 78:93, August, 1968.

11. Caldinge, James. "Teaching and Teaching Methods." *Education Digest*, 41:10-13, April, 1976.

12. Carin, Arthur A. and Robert B. Sund. *Teaching Science Through Discovery*, 3rd ed. Columbus, Ohio, Charles E. Merrill Publishing Company, 1975.

13. Center for Understanding Media. *Doing the Media: Portfolio of Activities, Ideas and Resources*, ed. by K. Laybourne and F. Clanciolo. American Library Association, 1979.

14. Chambers, Dewey W. "Signposts for Creative Teaching." *The Instructor*, 78:57, October, 1968.

15. Clark, Leonard H. *Teaching Social Studies in Secondary Schools*. New York, Macmillan, 1973.

16. Cyphert, Frederick R., Earl W. Harmer, Jr., and Anthony C. Riccio. *Teaching in the American Secondary School; Selected Readings*. New York, McGraw-Hill, 1964.

17. Dirks, Anne. "Dial a Style of Teaching." *Today's Education*, 65:82-84, January, 1976.

129

18. Dodge, Dorothy. *Simulation*. (Kit: 3 cassettes, 2 games, booklets) Minneapolis, Paul S. Amidon and Associates, 1970.
19. Dunn, Rita and Kenneth Dunn. "Seeing, Hearing, Moving, Touching, Learning Packages." *Teacher*, 94:48-51, May, 1977.
20. Evans, William H., ed. *The Creative Teacher*. New York, Bantam Books, 1971.
21. Flescher, Irwin. *Children in the Learning Factory*. Philadelphia, Chelton Book Company, 1972.
22. Frazier, Alexander. *Adventuring, Mastering, Associating: New Strategies for Teaching Children*. Washington, D.C., Association for Supervision and Curriculum Development, 1976.
23. Gardner, C. Hugh. "Making the Most of Your Listening Stations." *Learning Resources*, 2:20-22, May, 1975.
24. Gasche, Robert T. "Yes, They Can Make Slides, Use a Dry Mount Press, and More." *Audiovisual Instruction*, 21:60-61, March, 1976.
25. Glatthorn, Allan A. "Learning in the Small Group." Abington, Pennsylvania, Abington High School, n.d.
26. Gordon, Anitra. "Clicking With Kids." *Learning Resources*, 2:8-10, April, 1975.
27. Hatfield, Frances and Irene Gullette. "Individualized Learning in the Flexible School." *American Libraries*, 1:169-70, February, 1970.
28. Heller, Melvin P. "Education and Innovation." (5 audiotapes) Chicago, Instructional Dynamics Incorporated, 1970.
29. Joyce, Bruce R. "Learning Strategies for Learning Centers." *Educational Leadership*, 32:388-91, March, 1975.
30. Kagan, Jerome, ed. *Creativity and Learning*. Boston, Houghton Mifflin, 1967.
31. Kohl, Herbert. "Creativity and a Sense of Powerlessness." *Teacher* 92:20+, February, 1975.
32. Kohl, Herbert. "Creativity in the Curriculum." *Teach-*

*er*, 92:14 + , March, 1975.
33. Kohl, Herbert. "Planning the Unexpected." *Teacher*, 94:12 + , May, 1977.
34. "Learning Sensibilities; Interview with Barry Farnlarn." *Learning Today*, 8:46-53, Fall, 1975.
35. "Living: Pushbutton Power." *Time*, 111:46-49, February 20, 1978.
36. McClosky, Mildred G. *Teaching Strategies and Classroom Realities*. Englewood Cliffs, New Jersey, Prentice-Hall, 1971.
37. Massialas, Byron G. and Jack Zevin. *Creative Encounters in the Classroom: Teaching and Learning Through Inquiry*. New York, John Wiley and Sons, 1967.
38. Mehaffy, George L. and Thad Sitton. "Oral History Tells It's Own Story: the Loblolly Project." *Social Education*, 68:231-35, November/December, 1977.
39. Miller, Rosalind. "Why Can't I Create a Learning Center?" *School Media Quarterly*, 3:215-18, Spring, 1975.
40. Nichols, Mildred and Lois Williams. *Learning About Role-playing for Children and Teachers*. Washington, Association for Childhood Education, International, 1960.
41. Nieburger, Gayle D. "The Library and the English Program." *English Journal*, 64:83-85, February, 1975.
42. Peters, Wm. H. "The Open Classroom and Creative Teaching." *High School Journal*, 59:112-21, December, 1975.
43. Piltz, Albert and Robert Sund, *Creative Teaching of Science in the Elementary School*. Boston, Allyn and Bacon, 1968.
44. Polette, Nancy. *Developing Methods of Inquiry: A Source Book for Elementary Media Personnel*. Metuchen, New Jersey, Scarecrow Press, 1973.
45. Schumsky, Abraham. *Creative Teaching in the Elementary School*. New York, Appleton-Century-Crofts, 1965.
46. Shephard, Dorothy D. "We Meet the Question and

Answer Hang-up in a Library Orientation Telecast."
*Illinois Libraries*, 53:507-12, September, 1971.
47. Skeel, Dorothy J. and Joseph G. Decaroli, "The Role of
the Teacher in an Inquiry-centered Classroom." *Social
Education*, 33:547-50, May, 1969.
48. Smith, James A. *Creative Teaching of the Language
Arts in the Elementary School*. Boston, Allyn and
Bacon, 1973.
49. South Carolina State Department of Education. *Learning Centers; Children Alive*. Columbia, South
Carolina, The Department, 1973.
50. Strouse, Elva. "Let's Create." *Learning Today*,
11:66-69 Summer-Fall, 1978.
51. Sullivan, John J. and Calvin W. Taylor. *Learning and
Creativity with Special Emphasis on Science*.
Washington National Science Teachers Association,
1967.
52. Taggart, Dorothy T. "Innovative Programs in Kansas
Media Centers." *Audiovisual Instruction*, 22:22-24,
November, 1977.
53. Tapper, Nancy. "Independent Study: Lawrence High
School." *New Jersey Libraries*, 2:39-40, Winter, 1969.
54. Taylor, Kenneth D. "Creative Inquiry and Instructional Media." *School Media Quarterly*, 1:18-36, Fall,
1972.
55. Torrance, E. Paul. *Encouraging Creativity in the
Classroom*. Dubuque, Iowa, William C. Brown Company, 1970.
56. Vacca, Jo Anne L. and Richard T. Vacca. "Learning
Stations: How to in the Middle Grades." *Journal of
Reading*, 19:563-67, April, 1976.
57. Voight, Ralph Claude. *Invitation to Learning; the
Learning Center Handbook*. Washington, D.C.,
Acropolis Books, 1971.
58. Vollbrecht, John, "Will Future Media Centers be Built
Around Computers?" *Audiovisual Instruction*, 19:42-

44, May, 1974.

59. Van Haden, Herbert J. *Educational Innovator's Guide.* Worthington, Ohio, Charles A. Jones Publishing Company, 1974.

60. Ward, Andd. "Student-Produced Media Through Organized Chaos." *Audiovisual Instruction,* 19:16-18, October, 1974.

61. Wickenden, Hermione H. "Sunday School Independent Study Programs and Their Implications for Library Services and Resources." (Thesis) Southern Connecticut State College, 1969.

62. Wittner, Joe and Robert D. Myrick. *Facilitative Teaching: Theory and Practice.* Pacific Palisades, California, Goodyear Publishing Company, 1974.

63. Young, Virgil M. *Inquiry Teaching in Perspective.* Englewood Cliffs, New Jersey, Educational Technology Publications, 1969.

64. Zeloney, Leslie D. *How to Use Simulations* (How-To-Do-It Series). Washington, D.C., National Council for the Social Studies, 1973.

65. Zodikoff, David. *Comprehensive Teaching Models in Social Studies Education.* Dubuque, Iowa, Kendall/Hunt Publishing Company, 1973.

# 6

## "The Process of the Selection of Media to be Used in Instruction is Important, and I Need to Know Acceptable Procedures."

If they were asked if they think that teachers should be involved in the selection of media, most teachers would probably say "Yes." They might also say "Yes, but...."—either "Yes, but I don't have time," or "Yes, but I thought that was the responsibility of the media specialist." In the traditional school library the librarian often assumed the sole responsibility for selection of library materials. The teachers might be asked for suggestions, and sometimes they responded and sometimes they didn't. Often no specific criteria for selection were used. If a book dealt with a subject covered in the curriculum and was on the proper grade level, it was selected for purchase.

Now more and more materials are being produced that implement specific instructional objectives, and it is necessary for the selection process to become more refined. Now, before selecting materials, teachers need to formulate objectives for various study units or courses, and develop a program that implements these objectives and specifies teaching strategies for particular student learning needs and patterns. Some teachers keep a card file of all available materials, tapes, filmstrips, textbooks, etc., filed according to objectives. New materials are added as they are acquired, and those that are out-of-date or no longer useful are withdrawn.

The individual teacher's selection process is a component of the school or districtwide plan. Some districts allow principals of the individual schools the option of devising a plan. Others have definite procedures that must be followed. Very large and/or sophisticated school districts have a highly organized procedure. For instance, the school district of Montgomery County, Maryland, has an Evaluation and Selection Division in the Educational Media and Technology Department in the office of Associate Superintendent for Instructional Services. (8) The staff of this division consists of ten full-time people with a variety of duties, including maintaining files of professional reviews, maintaining records of evaluations, securing materials for review, disseminating information about current evaluations, providing workshops for media evaluators, and other tasks. The division has issued a handbook, *Evaluation and Selection of Instructional Materials and Equipment,* which contains the district selection policy. The number of the staff and the careful organization of this division is an indication of the importance the administration attaches to the media selection process.

Even a small school district should devise a plan that assures a wise choice from the mass of instructional media available. The basic feature of the procedure is a media selection policy. The formulation of this policy is usually coordinated by the district media director or supervisor working with a committee composed of media specialists, teachers, administrators, and parents. Some school districts add students to this committee. After the policy is developed, it is approved by the superintendent and the district governing body, and all schools in the district are expected to abide by it.

135

Such a policy usually contains the following features:

A statement that the legal responsibility for the selection and purchase of instructional materials is vested in the governing body of the school district and delegated to the professional personnel.

An outline of the educational philosophy and objectives of the school district and of the media program.

Some media policies include *The School Library Bill of Rights for the School Media Program* issued by American Association of School Librarians. (See Appendix X.)

The general criteria for selecting media with special attention to sensitive or controversial areas.

The selection aids most frequently used.

A statement that no child will be required to use material that he or his parents believe is objectionable.

The procedure to be followed if any material is challenged, including a copy of the complaint form that must be completed by the challenger.

A statement that the superintendent will appoint a committee to reevaluate and report upon the challenged material.

A statement of the policy toward gifts of books or other materials, on replacement of out-of-date or worn books, about the purchase of multiple copies of the same items, and concerning free or unsolicited material.

An excellent statement on policy-making with regard to instructional media is available from the American Association of School Librarians.

Before beginning to evaluate and choose materials media specialists and teachers need certain general information, of which Gillespie and Spirt give an excellent summary:

Knowledge of the community, including ethnic and religious backgrounds, general economic status, occupations, cultural and recreational interests, educational levels, and libraries or other cultural resources.

Knowledge of students, their abilities, activities, interests, reading interests, personal, social, and emotional problems, and level of sophistication.

Knowledge of the curriculum. The teachers will know this in their own areas, but the media specialist needs to become more knowledgeable about the overall curriculum, to know teaching methods and how media are used.

Knowledge of media. Teachers should "keep up" with the media in their own fields. Both teachers and media specialists should read reviews of new media, evaluate firsthand where possible, and know the advantages and disadvantages of media in various formats. There should be an emphasis on teachers being familiar with the media center's holdings of materials in their fields.

Knowledge of bibliographic and reviewing tools. Emphasis should be placed on the importance of teachers being familiar with those useful in their fields. (See Appendix XI-XII.)

Knowledge of the budget, including the allotments for the current year and the coming year or years, and knowledge of possible additional federal, state or local funds.(7)

Recognizing the need for this knowledge, a teacher might do some self-questioning:

Do I assume responsibility with the media specialist for

137

the selection of instructional materials?

Do I know the media center's holdings in the subject area or areas that I teach?

Am I knowledgeable about the interests of the students I teach?

Do I relate the material I am examining to a certain instructional objective and to a specific learning need or learning pattern?

Am I familiar with standard bibliographic tools?

Have I conferred individually with the media specialist before a materials order is completed?

Have I given the media specialist copies of courses of study, guides, outlines, textbooks?

Have I offered to test materials in my classroom?

Do I confer with my instructional supervisor or consultant about the selection of materials?

Do I consider for selection the supplementary resources recommended in textbooks?

Do I give the media specialist information about my students' needs, interests, abilities, goals, reading levels?

Do I use student help in evaluating and testing new materials before selection?

Do I read the reviews of new materials in professional journals?

Do I examine materials if possible before recommending them for purchase? Do I request that materials be ordered for examination purposes?

Do I take enough time to evaluate materials on the basis of established criteria or just scan them casually?

The media specialist should assume part of the responsibility for the participation of teachers in the selection process. Workshops on selection should be offered, selection aids should be publicized, and teachers should be alerted when new media come on the market. Before an order for materials is completed opportunities should be given to every teacher to discuss with the media specialist suggested items for a specific learning need, to formulate objectives, and to develop specifications.

The great quantity and variety of materials available today makes it essential that all the faculty contribute to the selection.

The types of media to be evaluated that are used most are books, magazines, non-print materials, curriculum packages, equipment, free materials, charts, maps, globes, flat pictures, and study prints.

There are many good lists of criteria for evaluating books, but a simplified "refresher" list follows:

CRITERIA FOR FICTION AND NONFICTION

*Style of writing*
Fast moving?
Good sentence structure?
Literary quality?
Good choice of words?
Readable?

*Descriptions*
Vivid word pictures?
Too brief?
Too wordy?
Dull?

*Vocabulary*
Suitable for age?

*Technical quality*
Durable?
Attractive?
Appropriate, useful, well-executed illustrations?

*Projected use*
Curriculum area?
Topic?
Cocurricular activity?


## ADDITIONAL CRITERIA FOR FICTION

*Story*
Clear discrimination between fact and fancy?
Logical development of plot?
Of interest to age group?
Free of racial, religious, ethnic and sexual bias and stereotyping?

*Theme*
Worthy?
Appealing to age group?
Well developed?
Expands students' view of life?

*Characters*
True to life?
Developed with individual human qualities?

*Dialogue*
Too little?
Too much?
Suited to character?


## ADDITIONAL CRITERIA FOR NONFICTION

*Purpose*
How well accomplished?
For whom intended?

*Author*
Well qualified?
Unbiased?

*Content*
Authoritative?
Accurate?
Suitable for age?
Up-to-date?
Clearly presented?
Sources of information listed?
Organization contributes to understanding?
Provision of learning aids, summaries, exercises,
   activities?
Free of racial, religious, ethnic, and sexual bias and
   stereotyping?
Table of contents and index adequate?
Useful appendixes?

It is best, of course, to be able to make a "hands on"
evaluation of books with enough time to examine them
thoroughly. Since this is not always possible, it is helpful to
know the reputable, professionally prepared selection aids,
especially those in the relevant subject area. (Consult the list
in the Appendix XI-A–C.) It is risky to select a book from a
publisher's catalog without evaluating it oneself or finding a
favorable review.

Most important for today's instructional program is an excellent periodical collection to provide current information.
Most media centers stock the back issues of news and informational periodicals only as far back as the media specialist
and teachers deem necessary. Most high-school libraries
have turned to the purchase of periodicals on microfilm in
addition to the paper edition. This takes care of the
availability of back issues, without a storage problem.

In the selection of periodicals care must be taken to pro-

141

vide for all areas of the curriculum with, in addition, recreational types of periodicals. Much reliance is placed upon selection from lists professionally compiled. One such list is *Periodicals for School Libraries: A Guide to Magazines, Newspapers, and Periodical Indexes* issued by the American Library Association. Another acceptable list is the *Dobler World Directory of Youth Periodicals* by Lavinia C. Dobler, published by the Citation Press. Besides selecting periodicals for the average students, the gifted students and also those with reading disabilities must not be overlooked.

Sometimes not enough effort is directed to the professional selection of non-print materials, and the producers' catalogs become the principal selection source—a *very* risky practice. In addition to judging content, great attention must be paid to technical matters such as compatibility of materials with equipment. There are not as many good selection guides to non-print materials as there are for books. (See Appendix XII.) More time will probably be needed to examine and assess these materials. Most producers will send non-print materials to the school for examination and evaluation, and this is much more to the point than glancing at these materials in exhibits. However, this is a good way to identify items to request to be sent to the school for review.

Criteria for the evaluation of non-print materials are listed in the *Educational Research Service Report* published by the Educational Research Service, Incorporated. The criteria for charts, maps, globes, flat pictures, and study prints, films, filmstrips, cartridge films, slides, transparencies, and tape and phonograph records are given here in detail because they are often disregarded in the selection process. (6)

# CHARTS

|  | Yes | No | NA |
|---|---|---|---|

I. Is the content of this material well organized and well balanced? _____

   A. Is the material presented logically and clearly? _____

   B. Does the material achieve its stated purpose? _____

   C. Does the chart aid conceptualization of subject matter? _____

   D. Is the content presented as clearly and simply as possible for the level intended? _____

   E. Is material arranged in logical sequence? _____

   F. Are charts presented in a series? _____

   G. Is the scale or size such that comparisons can be made between or among charts? _____

   H. Are symbolizations adequately explained? _____

II. Is the technical quality of this material acceptable? _____

   A. Is printed material sharply and clearly defined? _____

   B. Are the media used durable and opaque? _____

   C. Is some provision made for display? _____

      1. Are the charts provided with wall attachments? _____

      2. Are the charts mounted on a tripod or other floor display holder? _____

      3. Is the holder easy to manipulate?

      4. Does the holder take only a reasonable amount of space?

© Educational Research Service, Inc., 1976, pp. 51–56. *Procedures for Textbook and Instructional Materials Selection* by Linda Kunder, based on materials originally provided by the Board of Education of Carroll County, Maryland.

# FILMS, FILMSTRIPS, CARTRIDGE FILMS, SLIDES, AND TRANSPARENCIES

|  | Yes | No | NA |
|---|---|---|---|

I. Is the content of this material well organized and well balanced?

   A. Have the principles of learning been followed in developing the material, e.g., reinforcement—transfer?

   B. Is the material presented logically and clearly?

   C. Is the sequence developed adequately?

   D. Are data sufficiently comprehensive to be useful?

   E. Is the content appropriate for this type of presentation?

   F. Is the material imaginative when imagination is really needed?

   G. Is the quality of the script or commentary satisfactory?

   H. Is the music or background satisfactory?

   I. Are the titles, labels, or captions appropriate?

   J. Is all material essential?

II. Is the technical quality of this material acceptable?

   A. Is the visual image satisfactory?

      1. Is the photography clear and artistic?

      2. Does it have enough close-ups?

      3. Are printed items adequate in size?

   B. Is the quality of sound clear and intelligible?

   C. Is color used effectively?

   D. Are sound and visual image synchronized?

© Educational Research Service, Inc., 1976, pp. 51–56. *Procedures for Textbook and Instructional Materials Selection* by Linda Kunder, based on materials originally provided by the Board of Education of Carroll County, Maryland.

# GLOBES

|  | Yes | No | NA |
|---|---|---|---|

I. Is the content of this material well organized and well balanced?

   A. Is the material presented logically and clearly?

   B. Does the material achieve its stated purpose?

   C. Are latitude and longitude lines or indicators provided?

   D. Are color symbolizations pleasing but distinctive in quality?

   E. If raised-relief techniques are used, is vertical exaggeration excessive?

II. Is the technical quality of this material acceptable?

   A. Will materials used in the construction of the globe resist denting and breakage?

   B. Are jointures on globes smooth and relatively unnoticeable?

      1. Are map segments well registered?

      2. Are places where parts of a globe are jointed in construction prominent?

   C. Is the base firm and heavy enough to resist tipping in use?

   D. Will connections of movable parts wear well?

   E. Is there an axis provided for the globe?

   F. Is a place provided for the storage of an axis pin if it is removable?

   G. Is the surface soil-resistant and cleanable?

   H. Is the surface made to be marked upon?

# MAPS

|                                                                                                                              | Yes | No | NA |
|------------------------------------------------------------------------------------------------------------------------------|-----|----|----|

I. Is the content of this material well organized and well balanced?

  A. Is the material presented logically and clearly?

  B. Does the material achieve its stated purpose?

  C. Is the projection suitable for use at the level intended?

  D. Is the projection suitable for the content to be shown?

  E. Is the map scale suitable for the purpose intended?

  F. Is the legend adequately and clearly presented?

  G. Are color symbolizations pleasing but distinctive in quality?

  H. If raised-relief technique is used, is vertical exaggeration in good proportion?

  I. Are latitude and longitude clearly delineated?

  J. Are contents dated when this is a significant factor in their utilization?

  K. Are the contents developed on a comparable basis if the map is part of a series?

  L. Is the detail appropriate to the intended use?

II. Is the technical quality of this material acceptable?

  A. Is the durability of the material upon which the map is reproduced adequate for the purposes intended?

    1. Is the map constructed so it will not curl along the edges?

    2. Is the map constructed of a material that will not crack, split, or tear easily?

  B. Are printed materials acceptable in terms of legibility and placement?

  C. Is the mounting device durable?

  D. Is the mounting device appropriate for the intended use?

  E. Is the surface washable?

  F. Is the surface as nonreflecting as possible?

  G. Can marking devices be used on the surface?

© Educational Research Service, Inc., 1976, pp. 51–56. *Procedures for Textbook and Instructional Materials Selection* by Linda Kunder, based on materials originally provided by the Board of Education of Carroll County, Maryland.

146

# TAPE AND PHONOGRAPH RECORDS

I. Is the content of this material well organized and well balanced?

   A. Have the principles of learning been followed in developing the material, e.g., reinforcement—transfer?

   B. Is the material presented logically and clearly?

   C. Does the material achieve its stated purpose?

   D. Is the content appropriate for presentation in recorded form?

   E. Does the material complement printed and visual teaching resources in the same subject area?

   F. Is the quality of the script or commentary satisfactory?

II. Is the technical quality of this material acceptable?

   A. Is the recording clearly labeled? (Title, number indicating playing sequence, and speed.)

   B. Is the type of material used for the record or tape durable?

   C. Is the quality of sound satisfactory?

     1. Are the speakers' or actors' voices clear and understandable?

     2. Is the music free from distortion?

# FLAT PICTURES AND STUDY PRINTS

|  | Yes | No | NA |
|---|---|---|---|

I. Is the content of this material well organized and well
   balanced?

   A. Is the material presented logically and clearly?

   B. Does the material achieve its stated purpose?

   C. Do the colors used (include black and white) contribute to learning?

   D. Is the size commensurate with the purpose for which it is intended?

   E. Has the composition been planned to illustrate or emphasize the intended purpose?

   F. Is explanatory material provided?

   G. Are the captions a good interpretation of the material yet not distracting?

   H. Is there a recognizable sequence if the picture is a part of a series?

   I. Is the material such that it will not be out of style too quickly?

II. Is the technical quality of this material acceptable?

   A. Is the definition sharp and clear?

   B. Are the color reproductions accurately registered?

   C. Is the base material durable and opaque?

   D. Is the surface as nonreflecting as possible?

   E. Is the material constructed so as not to curl, split, or tear easily?

© Educational Research Service, Inc., 1976, pp. 51–57. *Procedures for Textbook and Instructional Materials Selection* by Linda Kunder, based on materials originally provided by the Board of Education of Carroll County, Maryland.

148

Another type of instructional material which needs to be most carefully evaluated before selection is the curriculum package, or instructional unit. Features to be considered were listed in a brochure entitled *Selecting New Aids to Teaching* published by the Association for Supervision and Curriculum Development: (12)

Objectives of the unit: those of the producer as well as yours

Relevance and validity of unit's content

Compliance of unit with principles of human growth and development

Time and space (organizational) considerations

Personnel factors

Community factors

Cost analysis of the unit

Instructional and curricular factors

Evaluation procedures

Dissemination

Implementation

The above is only part of the complete guidelines, which includes initial probing of proposed unit, developing a plan of action, accomplishing the plan, decision, revision, and recycling. A caution is given: "Yet, *in most instances*, the process of making decisions about instructional units suffers because of oversimplified and inadequate procedures."

It might seem that the selection of equipment should be left to the principal and district media director or the school media specialist. But although teachers may not need to know about all the technical aspects they do have a role to play simply because they use equipment. Gillespie lists specific criteria for the evaluation of audio, visual, and audio-visual equipment:(8)

CRITERIA FOR AMPLIFIER, LISTENING STATION, RECORD PLAYER, TAPE RECORDER, CAMERA, MICROSCOPES, PROJECTORS, TELEVISIONS, AND OFFICE PRACTICE MACHINES
(Reprinted with the permission of the Department of Instructional Resources of the Montgomery County Public Schools)

I. Is the equipment portable?
   A. Is it reasonably light in weight in comparison with others?
   B. Is it compact?

II. Is the equipment sturdy and attractive?
   A. Does the material of which the equipment is constructed appear durable?
      1. Is the equipment well constructed?
      2. Is the material of which the equipment is constructed easily damaged or broken?
   B. Are the control features durable and reliable?

III. Is the equipment easy to operate?
   A. Are the controls accessible and plainly marked?
   B. Is there a minimum number of operating controls?

IV. Does this equipment consistently meet desirable performance standards in terms of its specific function?
   A. Is tonal quality true?
   B. Is volume range adequate and well defined?
   C. Is image sharply defined?
   D. Is light supply adequate?
   E. Is magnification of projection adequate?
   F. Are sound and visual image synchronized?

V. Are adaptations easy to perform?

A. Are adaptors included within the equipment or its container?

B. Is the equipment compatible for use with other types of equipment?

VI. Is the equipment easy to maintain and repair?
   A. Can minor adjustments be made simply and quickly when needed?
   B. Is it easy to remove parts likely to need repairs?
   C. Are the parts standard and easily available for replacement?

VII. Is the distributor dependable? (Evaluator, omit this section.)
   A. Does the distributor have a proper credit rating?
   B. Are the distributor and manufacturer faithful to their agreements?
   C. Are repair and emergency service facilities readily available?
   D. Are adequate stocks of spare parts maintained locally?

VIII. In comparison with the cost of similar equipment, is the price reasonable?

Almost every media center has a vertical file of pamphlets, leaflets, brochures, etc. Most of this material has probably been secured free from business establishments, embassies of foreign countries, various health service organizations, conservation groups, state and federal government offices, and other such sources. Since this material at times has undesirable advertising and propaganda, the teacher should collaborate with the media specialist to make certain that items are worthwhile. The following considerations will help in making a wise selection:

1. Identify the instructional objectives which the material will implement.

2. Decide whether the concepts presented and the vocabulary used are too difficult for the students who will be studying the subject covered.

3. Scan the material for propaganda or excessive advertising.

4. Determine whether opinions are stated as facts.

5. Note whether only one side of a two-sided issue is presented.

6. Be sure that the information given is up-to-date.

7. Check the quality of the illustrations, and whether they add clarity to the content.

8. Determine the usefulness of any supplementary teaching aids which might be included.

In summary, the teachers in a school building have an important role to play in partnership with the media specialist in the selection of all media, print and non-print materials and equipment. This responsibility includes: Being really familiar with the holdings of the media center in their subject area or areas; Maintaining as a goal the development of an excellent collection of materials geared to the curriculum and the special needs, interests, and ability levels of the students; Selecting only the media which have been personally evaluated or have been favorably reviewed in a recognized professional publication.

TEACHER'S RESERVATION: This chapter is a thorough treatment of the process of selecting media to be used in instruction. The authors not only enumerate the steps in devising a media selection policy, but also provide criteria for evaluation. Even though the media selection policy is not particularly relevant to the classroom teacher, the lists of criteria for evaluation of media are especially useful.

The authors appropriately point out the importance of teacher participation in media selection. It is unlikely, however, that the average classroom teacher will have time to carry out every responsibility described. Most teachers will find the strength of this chapter to be its usefulness as a reference when evaluating a book, film, or record.

WRITERS' RESPONSE: The media selection policy for a school or a school district should be considered relevant to individual teachers. Often policy is determined at the highest levels of administration, and teachers are uninformed or unaware of the reasons for policy decisions because of poor lines of communication. It is our contention, however, that teachers should be involved in setting the media selection policy and should follow the policy in making recommendations for media acquisition.

We are glad that the lists of criteria for selection are useful to teachers. Proper selection of materials is an extremely important part of a teacher's job.

### BIBLIOGRAPHY

1. *Aids to Media Selection for Students and Teachers*, compiled by Kathryn J. Moses and Lois B. Watt. Washington, U.S. Department of Health, Education, and Welfare, 1976.
2. Belland, John C. "Why Develop Materials at the School

Level?" *High School Journal*, 50:327–31, May, 1976.
3. Branscombe, F. R. "Challenges and Changes; the Resource Guidelines for Canadian Schools." *Canadian Library Journal*, 36:296–300, August, 1978.
4. Darling, Richard. "Review and Evaluation Control." *Drexel Library Quarterly*, 5:104–09, April, 1969.
5. Davies, Ruth Ann. *The School Library Media Center; A Force for Educational Excellence.* New York, R. R. Bowker Company, 1974.
6. *Educational Research Service Report; Procedures for Textbook and Instructional Materials Selection,* study conducted and reported by Linda H. Kunder. Arlington, Virginia, Educational Research Service, Inc., 1976.
7. Gillespie, John T. and Diana L. Spirt. *Creating a School Media Program.* New York, R. R. Bowker, 1975.
8. Gillespie, John T. *A Model School District Media Program; Montgomery as a Case Study.* Chicago, American Library Association, 1977.
9. Hicks, Warren B. and Alma M. Tillin. *Developing Multi-Media Libraries.* New York, R. R. Bowker, 1970.
10. Komoski, P. K. "Realities of Choosing and Using Instructional Materials." *Educational Leadership*, 36:46–48 + , October, 1978.
11. Limbacher, James L. *A Reference Guide to Audiovisual Information.* New York, R. R. Bowker, 1972.
12. Miller, Richard J. *Selecting New Aids to Teaching.* Washington, D. C., Association for Supervision and Curriculum Development, n.d.
13. Niedermeyer, F. C. and M. H. Moncrief. "Guidelines for Selecting Effective Instructional Products." *Elementary School Journal*, 76:127–31, December, 1975.
14. Sabol, J. W. "Selecting Instructional Materials."

*English Journal*, 66:9–14, January, 1977.
15. Scuorzo, Herbert F. *The Practical Audio-visual Handbook for Teachers*. West Nyack, New York, Parker Publishing Company, 1967.
16. Shapiro, Lillian. "Quality for Popularity? Selection Criteria for Young Adults." *School Library Journal*, 25:2, November, 1978.
17. Wittich, Walter Arno. *Instructional Technology*. New York, Harper & Row, 1973.

# PART III
## MEETING STUDENTS' SPECIAL NEEDS

# 7

## "I Could Use Help In Developing Ways To Foster Desirable Student Attitudes And Values."

Education plays a dual role in our society. It serves as an agent of socialization, helping to mold society, and also functions as a mirror reflecting current trends or concerns in the culture. It is not surprising that a major issue in our society today is the responsibility of the public schools for morals education. In a recent Gallup Poll (1975) four out of five adults surveyed favored morals instruction in public schools.(23) A year later 69 percent stated that the schools share part of the responsibility for the moral behavior of young people.(1) At a time when crime rates are at an all-time high, when vandalism has become a pastime and corruption in government and business an everyday occurrence, the public is demanding to know what the schools are doing (or not doing) to foster moral development in young people.

At the same time, society continues to condone "moral relativity." Everyone has a right to his own standards, his own ethics or lack of them. Society continues to value individualism. "Doing your own thing" is a way of life for adults as well as for young people. The schools—or, more precisely, the teachers—are caught in a dilemma. The great majority of the citizenry seems to want education to foster moral development, but there is no agreement as to what *specific* moral values should be taught.

The approach of many educators has been "value clarification" techniques, in which students are given opportunity to express their values and to make value decisions without any judgments being imposed. The value clarification approach teaches students the valuing process, a strategy for dealing with value conflicts. (See Figure 5.) The value clarification approach offers many interesting and worthwhile opportunities and activities to teachers. These exercises stimulate youngsters to think about values and require them to practice decision-making skills in light of their stated beliefs. This approach gives students freedom to explore value concepts without being judged or criticized for their choices.

Opponents of the value clarification technique consider that the lack of value judgments is its greatest weakness. They believe that this moral neutrality implies to students that all values are equally valid, and that thereby teachers are putting themselves in a position of condoning or affirming questionable values. Critics argue also that individuals do *not* have complete freedom of choice, but must conform to the values of the society. They declare that value clarification techniques violate a student's right to privacy because of the intensely personal nature of the approach. Objecting to the inexact nature of value clarification, they contend that values instruction in this manner cannot be evaluated to determine whether it is helping or harming students and therefore should not be utilized.

FIGURE 5
STEPS IN THE VALUING PROCESS

CHOOSING:
  (1) freely
  (2) from alternatives
  (3) after thoughtful consideration of the
      consequences of each alternative

PRIZING:
  (4) cherishing, being happy with the
      choice
  (5) willing to affirm the choice
      publicly

ACTING:
  (6) doing something with the choice
  (7) repeatedly, in some pattern of life(25)

Many opponents of the value clarification approach are students of Lawrence Kohlberg's theories. Kohlberg determined through many years of study and research that there are six stages of moral development, and that these are universal in all societies. He supported the teaching of *moral reasoning*, the goal of which is to assist students as they advance from one level of moral development to the next.

The six stages of moral development described by Kohlberg are summarized as follows:

Stage (1).
Response to punishment, little
    awareness of accepted norms.

Stage (2).
   Concerns with self-benefit; some
   awareness of reciprocity.

Stage (3).
   Conformity; desire for acceptance.

Stage (4).
   Respect for authority; understanding of need
   for social order.

Stage (5).
   Contract fulfillment; awareness of duty.

Stage (6).
   Response to conscience; respect for individual
   rights and dignity.(15)

Kohlberg's followers recommend the teaching of moral reasoning by means of moral dilemmas. In the use of moral dilemmas students are confronted with hypothetical/authentic situations in which they must choose an action and justify it. The discussion that accompanies such decisions gives students an opportunity to perceive higher levels of moral reasoning and to begin to judge their own decisions and actions in view of that understanding. For example, a consideration of John Dean's role in the Watergate affair would give ample opportunities for discussions of moral obligations.

A particularly significant element of Kohlberg's work is his belief that educators *are obligated* to teach such basic values as justice, equality, and freedom. This is in contrast to the moral neutrality inherent in value clarification techniques. Kohlberg's followers stress the role of the school in socialization and argue that failure of the schools to instill these societal values will be the undoing of our society as we know it.

Still other educators believe that the issue of whether or not to teach values is a moot question. They maintain that teachers teach values constantly—in the choices they make, in their interactions with students and fellow-teachers, through body language or facial expressions, and in countless other ways. Some educators argue that the education system itself teaches values—and not necessarily "good" ones. Etzioni declares that the real question is how our schools "can be *restructured* to make them sources of ethical experiences rather than, as they too often are, training grounds for cheating, intolerance, or coping with bureaucratic or arbitrary authority."(14)

In his book *Helping Students Think and Value* Jack Fraenkel contends that the teaching of values is inevitable.(15) He argues that since the teaching of values cannot be avoided, teachers must make certain that it is not haphazardly done. They must make some deliberate, conscious choices about which societal values will be taught so that it is not left to chance. He is in agreement with Kohlberg that these choices should be in keeping with the social values on which our country was founded. Fraenkel states further that morals education consists of two elements: development of the student's moral reasoning capacity and development of the student's ego strength. "The development of the student's moral reasoning increases his ability to make distinctively moral judgments," while the development of ego strength "increases his ability to apply his judgmental capacities to guide and criticize his own actions."(15) Many educators share this point of view, and materials in the area of morals education often stress development of a healthy self-concept.

How to tackle these challenges in one's own teaching on a day-to-day basis? The teacher who concedes the inevitability of "teaching" some values and agrees that the schools are obligated to help develop ethical and moral behavior in students is faced with several decisions:

163

1. Deciding how to help students identify their own values so that they can make satisfactory decisions when they face value conflicts.

2. Devising ways to help students raise the level of moral development at which they are functioning.

3. Determining which values to teach, selected from among those that represent widely accepted moral standards, and which, to the extent possible, are common to all cultural groups in our multicultural society. Of course, attitudes toward values as well as toward values education will vary from one community to another, and it is very important that community feelings in these matters be taken into consideration and that parents be involved in the process.

4. Delineating the teaching strategies that are best utilized in terms of individual students.

There is little doubt that a combination of techniques will serve most effectively. In the realm of personal values, where there is bound to be a wide range of accepted beliefs and behaviors, value clarification techniques will be most suitable. In the area of social values that are worth preserving, moral dilemma exercises and open discussion (decision-making/justification) may be most helpful.

The variety of activities and techniques to support various strategies affords many options. There are countless materials and resources available to assist the aware teacher in providing a rich, diversified program. But of all the strategies none is as significant as the example the teacher himself provides to students. "Preaching" moral admonitions is generally a waste of breath. Students learn by imitating, and demonstrating value concepts is much more influential than merely talking about them. The *most* effective method for instilling value concepts is by allowing students to experience them. Therefore the classroom environment is of primary importance.

A starting point in implementing values education is to define with students what constitutes a value. There are seven criteria for determining a value (see Figure 5). These include "choosing, prizing, and acting on" one's beliefs. Students must begin to analyze their choices and decisions in terms of these seven criteria. As they become aware of their behavior and the values it represents, they can begin to weigh and evaluate their choices in light of accepted societal values. They can then begin to build their own value systems.

Values instruction requires careful planning of goals and objectives, just as any good teaching does (see Chapter 4). Contrary to common belief, there are ways to plan values education which is meaningful to students personally and which can also be evaluated in terms of outcomes. Allen and Foreman (2) specify five considerations that should determine the selection of objectives in values instruction:

1. Objectives should be stated in behavioral terms. Vague, "high-minded" objectives should be avoided. Evaluation of values must be based on overt behaviors.
2. Objectives should be stated in a way that allows for evaluation with a limited amount of time and money. Prolonged observation should not be a necessity.
3. Objectives should be stated in measurable terms. These provide a basic structure to which activities and enrichments are added.
4. The fewest objectives possible for achieving the desired goals should be selected.
5. Objectives (skills learned) should be useful to students. Input from students in developing the objectives is desirable.

Examples of such objectives might include:

Students will develop a personal ranking system for classifying various careers or vocations according to overall worthiness.

Students will describe characteristics of friends that are desirable and those that are undesirable.

Students will demonstrate tolerance of others by dramatizing situations in which understanding of opposing views is necessary.

Allen and Foreman categorize values instruction objectives in three ways:

1. "Humanistic values" are represented in objectives determining desirable human interactions, such as learning to take turns or learning leadership techniques.
2. "Democratic values" are fostered by objectives that provide for the success and survival of the democratic process. Student participation in planning class activities or in forming a representative council would enhance skills as well as attitudes.
3. "Personal valuing skills" are inherent in objectives that force students to discover and analyze their own values.(2)

Ranking exercises in which students must identify priorities force students to claim specific values. These various categories of objectives can be implemented through a variety of procedures and resources. The following possible procedures and accompanying examples will demonstrate the many options open to you. It should be noted that in any of the following exercises the teacher must refrain from imposing values, but remain objective and open to students' ideas.

1. Simulations
   labor/management conflicts

international confrontations
town meeting
a mock trial

2. Role-playing
   the generation gap in families
   historical incidents involving value conflicts
   influence of peer pressures on teenagers
   proper lunchroom manners

3. Open-ended stories
   hypothetical situations for which no outcome is
   provided so that students can resolve the issue

4. Values continuum
   ranking on a scale personal feelings about a
   specific issue such as capital punishment
   ranking certain behaviors according to their
   appropriateness for specific situations
   evaluating solutions to societal problems

5. Value auction
   forcing students to make choices of careers
   leisure activities
   spiritual values
   material possessions

6. Moral dilemmas
   open-ended, hypothetical situations involving
   value conflicts
   speculating about real moral dilemmas in history
   and the consequences involved.

It is imperative in selecting activities in values education
that they be appropriate to the needs of students. The media
specialist can assist in setting objectives, in selecting activities and materials, and in evaluating outcomes. By supply-

ing specific titles or providing catalogs to study, the media specialist can guide selections. For example, *Deciding* is published by the College Entrance Examination Board for middle or junior high-school students.(11) *Decisions and Outcomes* is published for high-school students.(12) The Center for Humanities produces many sound-slide programs of exceptional quality dealing with specific issues for mature students.(5) DUSO (*Developing Understanding of Self and Others*) is prepared by American Guidance Service for elementary school children.(13) The emphasis in the DUSO kits is on self-concept and a respect for individuality. These are only a few examples of the many materials available, and the media specialist can identify many other resources.

The efforts of the media specialist will reinforce what the teacher is trying to achieve in the classroom, especially if there has been mutual discussion and cooperative planning in advance. The media specialist comes in contact with virtually every student in the school and can assess student behavior realistically, foster group values effectively, help to interpret community attitudes, and contribute to identifying desirable values to teach and develop. The issue of books and other materials stolen from the media center is an example of a ready-made opportunity for values education. The media specialist can point out to students both individually and in groups that the materials in the media center belong to everyone, and stress the rights of the whole group that are being infringed upon. The media specialist may perhaps work through the student council, encouraging student leaders to take the initiative in finding solutions to such problems, and representative parent groups may be asked to assist in formulating solutions and policies.

The ways in which the media program contributes to affective values education and development of positive attitudes are many and varied. The media specialist can

1. Provide for development of positive self-concepts by
    displaying student work and giving recognition to
        student achievements
    providing an environment in the media center which
        fosters positive attitudes
    exemplifying fairness, integrity and justice in deal-
        ing with students

2. Promote responsible behavior by
    encouraging self-directed study and research
    assigning meaningful jobs to students in the media
        center
    seeking student opinions regarding materials acqui-
        sitions
    seeking student ideas for solving such problems as
        book loss, vandalism

3. Demonstrate desirable values by
    encouraging respect for rights of others in the use of
        resources and materials in the center
    encouraging respect for competency and efficiency
    demonstrating open-minded consideration of issues
    providing models of moral behavior through reading
        materials

4. Assess student behavior
    through observation
    in group interaction

Perhaps the most pertinent problem for a teacher is how
to include values instruction in the specific subject areas
being taught. Fortunately, almost any subject matter or
content lends itself to the teaching of values. Harmin, Kirschenbaum, and Simon have written a book which gives
examples of value clarification exercises in many different

subject areas. They point out that content can be taught on three levels:

1. Content can be taught as factual information.
2. Content can be explored to determine concepts and generalizations.
3. Content and concepts can be related to the student's own life to give personal meaning (value) to the information learned.(16)

An example from their book is in the subject area of art. On the factual level the students would learn to stretch a canvas, to use a palette knife, to mix colors, and to identify warm colors as opposed to cool colors. On the concept level they would explore the function of perspective and learn how light and shadow are used in painting. On the values level they would be asked to paint a still life from objects they feel represent the best/worst in our culture. The values level is dependent upon the factual level and the concept level; but the students are not merely acquiring information, they are applying it in a meaningful way to their own lives.

The media specialist can be particularly helpful in translating content into the values level of instruction. In many cases teaching at the values level will require independent reading assignments or other research activities. A broad knowledge of the materials available in the media center will enable the media specialist to make helpful recommendations as the teaching plans develop.

The moral dilemma as a teaching technique also lends itself to content application. In every subject area there are individuals who have faced real moral dilemmas; there are issues that present moral dilemmas; and there are situations that lend themselves to structured hypothetical dilemmas. Working through such a dilemma and applying the decision-making process afford students vital experience in moral reasoning. The possibilities for such experiences are endless.

In literature there are countless examples to analyze, such as the characters in *Silas Marner*, the betrayal of Caesar by Brutus in Shakespeare's *Julius Caesar*, or Scarlett O'Hara's manipulating of people to gain security for herself.

In history there are possibilities for real, contrived, or speculative dilemmas that students must solve. Historical figures such as Martin Luther, Henry VIII, Neville Chamberlain, members of the French underground, German citizens who befriended or who betrayed Jewish neighbors, Quakers who operated the Underground Railroad, Harriet Tubman, or, more recently, William Calley are examples representing ready-made real-life dilemmas that students can debate and evaluate.

In science there are any number of people who have faced intense moral conflict, most dramatically biological and atomic scientists. Even in athletics there are excellent examples of authentic moral dilemmas with which students must deal. The withdrawal of participants from the Olympics as a protest against specific conditions or policies in participating nations is only one example.

A moral dilemma can be presented through a film, a reading, role-playing, an open-ended story, or in any number of other ways. It should involve a main character who has to make a major decision. Students must decide what this character will do. Discussion should follow four steps: confronting or defining the dilemma; considering alternatives and stating tentative positions; examining the reasons for decisions made; and reflecting on individual positions. In all discussions the reasoning process should be emphasized. If students have difficulty working through a dilemma, they can be assigned individually or in small groups specific tasks to accomplish. One might be asked to list all the reasons *for* one alternative action; another group would list all the reasons *against* it. Students could then

171

select the two best reasons from each list and discuss the merits of each before making a final decision.

Another good exercise in connection with a moral dilemma is to use a values continuum. Students may begin by considering each alternative individually and rating it on the continuum. Ultimately they should be able to choose a most acceptable and least acceptable solution and give reasons to justify their choices. Any activities that require students to rate or prioritize their values (or alternatives) are excellent, but students should justify their decisions in the light of accepted societal values.

It could well be that in using moral dilemmas the aid of the media specialist should be enlisted to refresh students on various media skills, such as use of reference materials, critical reading and thinking skills, interpreting charts and graphs, or predicting outcomes based on factual data. Discussion with the media specialist in advance can help determine which media skills will be exercised and what help students need with these skills. One area that deserves major emphasis is criteria for evaluation of media. The schools need to help students evaluate critically the movies, television shows, radio programs, recordings, and advertisements which they spend so much time viewing and listening to, and from which so many of their attitudes and values are derived.

It cannot be overemphasized that the environment in which students interact is the *most important influence* on the values they ultimately claim for themselves. Schools at their best are democratic societies in microcosm. They provide a setting in which students can experience the meaning of our democratic ideals—one in which justice and fair play dominate, in which people care about each other, and in which they can experience at first hand a society that encourages and supports ethical values(27). It is a primary responsibility of teachers, media specialists, and all other staff members to create this kind of environment in every school.

TEACHER'S RESERVATION: In order for the school media center to have impact in values education most students would have to be more keenly attuned to it. This is usually not the case. Moral development is influenced by many factors, all of which are not controllable or even apparent. Students are most likely to develop or clarify values through real-life situations.

Two authors in the field of values education were not cited: Oliver and Shaver's jurisprudential model and Hunt and Metcalf's value analysis. These approaches need to be given consideration. Kohlberg's theories may be questionable, and therefore should be considered carefully. As a teaching tool, value clarification exercises are excellent— but not as an end in themselves.

WRITERS' RESPONSE: Getting students attuned to the media center is directly related to the frequency with which the center is used. The more students are involved in media center programs and in the variety of learning activities, the more they will see the reality of their learning, the universalization of their conflicts and choices, reflected and reinforced there.

There are probably many creditable authors we have not cited, since the central purpose of the chapter is not a review of the literature on values education, but rather how the media center program can contribute to it. The writers cited the theorist—Kohlberg—whose writings support their own experience and belief that the schools and teachers have been vested by the society with the responsibility for pointing out to students that all values are not created equal and emphasizing those espoused by the majority and inherent and implicit in their country's foundation documents.

BIBLIOGRAPHY

1. *Admittance to the Moral Domain... where schools have feared to tread.* Curriculum Report, No. 2. National Association of Secondary School Principals, December, 1976.
2. Allen, Sally J., and Dale I. Foreman. "Can Values Be Evaluated?" *Today's Education* 66:66–67, January–February, 1977.
3. Braverman, Miriam. "Wanted: Youth Advocate Librarians." *Education Digest*, 44:23–26, May, 1979.
4. Callard, Ester D. "Developing Socially Valued Behavior in Young Children." *Education Digest*, 44:8–11, May, 1979.
5. *Catalog of New Audio-Visual Programs for Human Development: Society and Mankind.* The Center for Humanities, White Plains, New York, 1979.
6. Cianciolo, Patricia Jean. "Children's Literature Can Affect Coping Behavior" in *The Special Child in the Library.* Chicago, American Library Association, 1976.
7. Clark, Leonard H. *Teaching Social Studies in Secondary Schools.* New York, Macmillan, 1973.
8. Clark, Todd, ed. "Whose Job Is Values Education?" *Social Education*, 41:405–06, May 1977.
9. Davies, Ruth Ann. *The School Library Media Center: A Force for Educational Excellence.* New York, R. R. Bowker, 1974.
10. Davison, Susan E. "But You Can't Do That! That's Not Fair!" *Today's Education*, 66:68–69, January–February, 1977.
11. *Deciding.* New York, College Entrance Examination Board, 1971.
12. *Decisions and Outcomes.* New York, College Entrance Examination Board, 1973.
13. *Developing Understanding of Self and Others.* Circle Pines, Minnesota, American Guidance Service, 1970.

174

14. Etzioni, Amitai. "Can Schools Teach Kids Values?" *Today's Education*, 66:29–36, September-October, 1977.
15. Fraenkel, Jack R. *Helping Students Think and Value*. Englewood Cliffs, New Jersey, Prentice-Hall, 1973.
16. Harmin, Merrill, Howard Kirschenbaum, and Sidney B. Simon. *Clarifying Values Through Subject Matter*. Minneapolis, Winston Press, 1973.
17. Kirschenbaum, Howard. "In Support of Values Clarification." *Social Education*, 41:398–401, May, 1977.
18. Kurfman, Dana G., ed. *Developing Decision-Making Skills*. Arlington, Virginia, National Council for the Social Studies, 1977.
19. Lockwood, Alan L. "What's Wrong with Value Clarification." *Social Education*, 41:399–401, May, 1977.
20. McClosky, Mildred G. *Teaching Strategies and Classroom Realities*. Englewood Cliffs, New Jersey, Prentice-Hall, 1971.
21. McGough, Kris. "Values Clarification: Your Job or Mine?" *Social Education*, 41:404–06, May, 1977.
22. Miles, Benny. "How An Elementary Teacher Does It." *Today's Education*, 66:76–77, January-February, 1977.
23. Nicholson, Shirley. "Teaching Morals and Values." *Professional Report*, Croft-NEI Publications, January, 1977.
24. Raths, Louis E., Merrill Harmin, and Sidney B. Simon. *Values and Teaching*. Columbus, Ohio, Charles E. Merrill Publishing Company, 1966.
25. Simon, Sidney B., Leland W. Howe, and Howard Kirschenbaum. *Values Clarification: A Handbook of Practical Strategies for Teachers and Students*. New York, Hart, 1972.
26. Skeel, Dorothy. "What Values Are Most Important?" *Today's Education*, 66:63–64, January-February, 1977.

27. Tyler, Robert W. "The School and Character Development." *Today's Education*, 66:72–73, January-February, 1977.
28. Van Sickle, Ronald L. "Experiential Concreteness and the Presentation of Value Dilemmas to Slow Learning Students." *Social Education*, 42:64–67, January, 1978.

# 8

## "I Need Assistance In Finding Ways To Challenge The Gifted Student And To Motivate The Slow Learner."

Finding ways to motivate and to challenge students is a never-ending quest for teachers. There are myriad numbers of variables in a classroom situation, and any one of them can cause problems in getting students involved and eliciting from them their best efforts. Home environment, the nature of materials in use, physical feelings, student attitudes, previous successes or failures, peer pressures, all influence the student's response to learning. It is not surprising that many teachers have moments of real pessimism.

One solution to the problem of getting and holding student attention and participation lies in individualized instruction. But it can be discouraging to try to individualize instruction for a large class. Many conditions—class size, teacher time, lack of diverse materials, among others—work against successful individualization. Successful individualization depends upon careful classroom management and making every teacher-student encounter productive. Whenever possible, housekeeping or record-keeping chores should be left to aides, or even to students. If paid aides can not be employed, volunteer assistance should be sought. An organized team of assistants can assume many time-consuming tasks, enabling teachers to devote maximum time to working individually with students. Grouping students to accomplish a variety of assignments provides opportunities for individuals to contribute their particular skills or expertise to a group endeavor. However, each student needs personal, individual interaction with the teacher. Conference time should be scheduled for each student on a regular basis, perhaps weekly, to keep abreast of student progress.

It is a good idea to keep a work folder for each student, in which all papers and assignments can be assembled for easy checking. Students can profit from checking and correcting their own work. They will learn also from checking each other's work from time to time. If true individualized teaching is in force, each student will be working toward his own set of objectives. Evaluation on the basis of clearly understood objectives is meaningful to the student in a way that group testing can never be.

Many of the hurdles in individualizing instruction can be eliminated by a true teaching partnership between teacher and media specialist. The quality of instruction and the probability of successful individualization are greatly enhanced by the teacher/media specialist team. The media center becomes the learning laboratory, providing, as no single classroom in the school can, the diverse resources needed. Gifted, slow, or in-between students can benefit immensely from tailored instruction made possible by the teacher's cooperative planning with the media staff.

CHALLENGING THE GIFTED STUDENT

There is growing demand by concerned citizens that immediate attention be given to the educational needs and opportunities of gifted students. It is not only the parents of

178

such children who complain that their potential has been neglected, but thoughtful leaders who recognize that future leadership in research, in government, in business, and in the arts will come primarily from those whose various types of giftedness have been sufficiently developed to allow them to make significant contributions to the society. It is also beginning to be fully understood that very talented children whose talents are not developed along constructive lines very often turn those talents to destructive ends. Some experts believe that as many as 20 percent of all high-school dropouts are gifted youngsters who became bored, disillusioned, and disgusted with school. Of the gifted who remain in school, many are known to have emotional or behavioral problems, and large numbers of them work far below their capability. Social and emotional development does not necessarily correlate with intellectual growth, especially in highly gifted children. Even in the best of situations disruptive behavior can result from feelings of frustration, alienation, and loneliness. Where no organized efforts are made to provide appropriately for them, gifted students can develop serious problems of maladjustment. The president of the Texas Association for the Mentally Retarded has stated that the association *frequently* finds extremely gifted individuals among its youngsters.(39)

Success in meeting the needs of gifted students is hampered by at least two major problems: the difficulty in identifying gifted children early enough, and the lack of public and financial support for special programs for the gifted. Government spending at the federal level for these programs is about 1 percent of that spent on special programs for the handicapped—$6.5 million for the gifted as compared with $600 million for the handicapped. Yet experts say that 4 to 5 percent of the student population is comprised of gifted children. By no means are all of them found in the upper social and economic levels of society. Yet one reason for lack of funding is a fear of elitism, a misinterpretation of "all men are created equal," which produces something very like a fear of admitting that some children have more aptitudes than others. Tragically, many gifted children, especially those from poor, lower-class, or minority culture families are never properly identified, and never exposed to a climate of expectation or a learning environment that allows them to develop their full potential.

Because of the failure of school districts to designate funds for gifted programs, most teachers are in school systems where the task of identifying gifted students and planning for their needs falls to the individual teachers. Concerned teachers can do a great deal, even in this less-than-ideal situation, to rescue at least a few of the gifted children who cross their paths.

There are many good books on gifted and talented children, and any number of lists of characteristics of gifted children that can be used as guidelines in recognizing them. All teachers and all media specialists should raise their own consciousness and awareness concerning the several areas in which giftedness can be demonstrated. There is intellectual or academic aptitude; there is creativity, unusual leadership ability, talent in the visual or performing arts and in psychomotor ability. I.Q. scores, performance on standardized tests, and observation by teachers, parents, and other adults who work with the children in various settings are all used to establish that children are gifted. Often a child will appear to be gifted by some criteria and not by others. In general, the gifted child is "able to deal with abstract concepts earlier than others of his own age, formulate critical judgments, make inferences, and perceive unusual relationships." His rate of reading and inquiring leaps ahead of that of his peers, and his "sense of humor and irony are usually more fully developed."(3) It should be noted also, however, that withdrawal, indifference, or downright misbehavior can also be cited as fairly common characteristics of gifted children who for one reason or another have "turned in on themselves" instead of developing outward. Every teacher needs to be alert to these signals as well as to the more positive characteristics.

Among these positive characteristics commonly observed in talented and gifted children are that they

learn quickly
like order and structure
are very inquisitive
read extensively
are very creative and inventive
have a long attention span
dislike drill and repetition
prefer independent study and projects
exhibit versatility
have many interests and enjoy many hobbies
demonstrate leadership ability
demonstrate artistic ability
are unusually articulate in expressing themselves.

Obviously, gifted students will manifest their giftedness and diverse talents and personalities in different ways, and not all of them will exhibit all of the above characteristics. But these criteria can be effectively applied in various combinations to help identify gifted children in the classroom.

Education for all students is basically the process of learning *how* to learn, and this is doubly true for gifted students. The teacher serves as a guide, a counselor, to the gifted student, but strongly encourages self-directed learning. Mastering skills—study skills, research skills—and learning to apply them are key elements in this. Both in the classroom and in the media center this kind of student needs access to a wealth of information in a variety of forms so that his own interests can motivate him and lead him from one project to another. This is why, more perhaps than with any other kind of student, the teacher who is trying to plan for the gifted student will want to, *must*, work very closely with the media specialist. It will, in fact, take the best joint efforts of every faculty member in the school who impacts the gifted student's learning in any way to provide all the development opportunity he needs.

The following principles are probably basic to all planning of learning experiences for gifted and talented students:

1. Instruction must be individually tailored to the student's needs and interests.
2. Independent and self-directed learning is essential.
3. Flexibility and variety are necessary to prevent boredom, and repetition and drill are to be avoided.
4. Problem-solving and inquiry are modes of learning that exercise essential skills.

Basic to the process of self-directed learning are research skills, critical thinking skills, communication skills, and skills in the use of media of all kinds. Gifted students like to do projects that have a beginning, a middle, and an end—and a *product*. They like to see things fit together and to share their discoveries and conclusions with others.

There are major differences of opinion regarding the best type of program for gifted students and/or for developing giftedness. There are some who believe that *accelerated* study which allows the student to move ahead of his age mates, to tackle more advanced materials and skills, and to explore more complex ideas is a good idea. Others stress that an *expanded* program, an add-on curriculum type of honors program, allows the gifted student to enlarge his interests wherever he is on the education ladder, and to explore subjects of his choosing in great depth and breadth without the

182

disorientation of the time-honored solution for the extraordinarily able—moving them ahead of their age mates. Most formalized programs of instruction for gifted and talented students will operate along one or the other of these lines, sometimes combining attributes of both.

Some good school systems have vested one particular teacher in each building with responsibility for carrying out planning for the gifted program. In one such school system a large proportion of the building leaders are, quite appropriately, the school library media specialists. In these schools two hours of special time during the week, not necessarily consecutive, are devoted to a "pull-out" program for talented and gifted, of whom as many as fifty have been identified in a single school. Seminars led by outside specialists in areas of student interest, field trips, special research projects, and structured discussions of ideas and particular books are among the extra added attractions that keep Talented and Gifted (TAG) program participants interested under the guidance of the school library media specialist. Research skills, including outlining, compiling bibliographies, footnoting, note-taking, and literature searching are taught to each student as needed, and supervision and assistance are provided for the production of print and nonprint materials.

Whatever the methodologies utilized, and wherever the primary responsibility rests, whether with a specially assigned teacher or, as more usually, with the classroom teacher, any program for the talented and gifted will rely heavily on the media center for media and upon the media specialist for assistance with every aspect of each individual program: selection of materials, planning activities, counseling and guidance, and skills instruction. Figure 6 outlines some areas of complementary responsibility for teacher and media specialist in guiding the gifted through a range of learning experiences.

FIGURE 6
RESPONSIBILITIES IN GUIDING THE GIFTED

| *Teacher* | *Library Media Specialist* |
|---|---|
| *Flexibility of Procedures* | |
| 1. Provide opportunities for independent use of the media center. | 1. Grant special privileges in the use of materials and facilities. |
| 2. Allow students time in the media center for browsing and reading. | 2. Act as consultant to individuals and groups in planning reading objectives. |
| 3. Have students participate in the planning of reading objectives and other learning goals. | 3. Plan with teacher for independent research projects for individuals or small groups. |
| 4. Organize class for individual or small group work. | 4. Suggest readings related to parallel class work, current events, etc. |
| 5. Plan for diversity and balance in reading assignments. | 5. Provide wide variety of selection aids in collection. |
| 6. Help students gain familiarity with a variety of selection aids. | |
| *Opportunities for Response* | |
| 1. Make opportunities for students to discuss their reading. Permit liberal questioning. Design analysis of literary works. Expect students to judge style. | 1. Provide discussion sessions on various readings periodically. |
| 2. Encourage written and artistic reactions to, or interpretations of, reading selections. | 2. Display student work in media center. |
| 3. Encourage non-print productions for presentation in class to summarize reading or research. | 3. Assist students in production of non-print materials. |

184

### Developing Critical Reading, Viewing, and Listening Skills

1. Encourage use of a wide variety of materials.

2. Give assignments that develop organizing, generalizing, and analyzing skills.

3. Expect students to evaluate the literary quality of similar writings.

1. Provide a varied collection of materials.

2. Seek student aid in evaluating films, filmstrips, recordings, periodicals, and other materials.

3. Assist students in scientific method of inquiry.

4. Encourage development of the skill of critical analysis.

### Developing Research Skills

1. Help students build skills in note-taking, outlining, compiling bibliographies.

2. Work with students in learning to scan materials for significant information.

3. Assign students to locate reference books on a variety of subjects.

1. Call teacher's attention to students who have specific weaknesses in this area.

2. Plan cooperative classroom instruction with teacher to assist students in developing skills.

3. Assist teacher in assembling a collection of various materials on assigned topic(s).

4. Encourage use of other libraries in the community.

### Building Lifetime Reading Habits and Personal Libraries

1. Be a reader yourself. Know what students are reading. Share excerpts from your reading with them. Let them know how much you enjoy it.

2. Get students to think about books they want to own and to purchase for themselves.

1. Be a reader yourself. Know the books you are encouraging students to read.

2. Have a paperback "store." Have a paperback bin for "leave one, take one" sharing. Build a model home library reflecting different interests.

Guiding gifted students in the selection of reading materials requires a more-than-casual acquaintance with the student and frequent exchanges of information between teacher and media specialist as a useful aid in counseling.

Sometimes gifted children tend to perform exceptionally well in just one area and virtually ignore others. They may become expert in a relatively narrow subject to the exclusion of others, and will then need to be reminded that some diversity is in order. Teachers and media specialists working as a team can try to broaden the range of interests. Many media specialists have check-out records that may reveal a lopsided reading pattern, and this can be discussed with the child's teacher. As specific topics are studied and talked about in class, these can be shared with the media specialist, who can then recommend some special "spin-off" topics and materials tailored to the interests of a particular gifted student.

The teacher who has identified a gifted student in class should plan with the media specialist to give careful reading guidance to him or her. Gifted students often do not need much external motivation to read. Most of them read quite voraciously, but they do require guidance. For instance, they need to be reminded that the quality, not the quantity, of their reading is the important thing. Comprehension, interpretation, and application—response to what is read—is more important than the numbers of books read, whether for study or for pure recreation. Response, in the form of modified thinking and perhaps changed behavior, is the essence of self-directed learning.

There are a number of proven techniques that a teacher and/or media specialist can employ in helping students to read critically. *Bloom's Taxonomy* can be of great help in planning activities that lead students from recognition and recall to the higher levels of analysis, synthesis, and evaluation. Gifted and talented students should be able to move rapidly beyond the mere recall of information and be expected to see relationships, understand and perceive new

186

concepts, make comparisons, analyze ideas, apply knowledge, draw conclusions, and, ultimately, make valid judgments. Obviously, even the most talented student must be *taught* to do these things, but the quick grasp of possibilities characteristic of such students and their delight in "seeing," is tremendously gratifying.

Help with selection of reading materials is especially critical for gifted students. Such guidance really begins with decisions about acquisitions. While the ultimate responsibility for these decisions lies with the media specialist, teacher and students should be brought into the process.

A suitable collection in the media center for use by gifted students(8)

1. Contains both print and non-print materials on a wide range of subjects.
2. Provides a variety of approaches within each subject area.
3. Provides many and varied reference materials.
4. Contains bibliographies.
5. Contains magazines and periodicals of a scientific and industrial nature.
6. Provides interdisciplinary materials.
7. Offers many problem-solving books.
8. Contains histories and biographies, particularly in the area of science.
9. Offers materials dealing with the applications of science in medicine, war, technology, etc.
10. Provides a good range of weekly news magazines.
11. Contains many books and other materials dealing with a great variety of hobbies and sports.
12. Contains high-quality books of fiction and poetry.

In order to use the media center effectively gifted students must feel perfectly at home there and possess a knowledge of its physical layout even greater than that of average users; of the cataloging and shelving systems, and skill in using vertical and other files; of the *Readers' Guide to Periodical Literature* and other reference tools; of how to operate equipment such as the filmstrip projector, microfilm reader, tape player, video tape recorder, computers, and other such hardware; and of techniques and equipment for producing non-print materials.

Ways in which teacher and media specialist can complement each other in the work with gifted and talented students are perhaps best explained with concrete examples.

SPECIAL ASSIGNMENTS TO ENCOURAGE CREATIVITY

Creative writing helps to establish creative thinking patterns and should be encouraged in gifted children. Writing original plays or stories based on actual people or events is an exciting assignment, and one that is adaptable to a wide age range. Of course, authenticity regarding historical events or persons requires some research in the media center. The media specialist can advise on selection of persons or events to be highlighted and ensure that there is plenty of interesting material available on the chosen subjects.

Students of almost any grade, from upper elementary on up, can video-tape productions for which they have written the script. Development of non-print materials for use in class presentations can provide talented children with learning experiences of many kinds. A sound-slide program can present the solution to a problem debated in science class. A sound filmstrip can illustrate the molecular structure of several elements. Transparencies and overlays can enable a student to trace the history of the labor movement or to demonstrate correct diagramming of compound/complex sentences. Assignments of this nature capitalize on a student's creative and artistic abilities while demanding research and organization skills as well.

Another interesting activity for older students is the rewriting of a story into script form. Students may select their stories, and may elect to enact their scripts and videotape them. Again, the role of the media center and staff is evident, with the media specialist assisting the teacher by giving both substantive and technical help to the student.

Another good project, especially for the musically gifted student, is the selection of appropriate background music to go with certain poems or stories, music that conveys mood and enhances the message. A student with dramatic reading ability might team with a musically talented student to produce some tapes of readings against background music. These might be played in public service time on the local radio station. Several pieces of music can be spliced together to represent mood changes in the poem or story. The media center's record or tape collection may be the starting point for students working on such an assignment. Also, taping and recording equipment, splicing equipment, and, of course, technical assistance are available from the media specialist.

## SMALL GROUP ACTIVITIES

There are many kinds of small group activities that are suitable, or may be adapted with some variations, for gifted students, which rely upon the team efforts of teacher and library media specialist.

Brainstorming—lively creative discussion with no holds barred—is in itself a stimulating learning activity, which may lead to the use of leadership and organizational skills, research, the use of surveys and sampling techniques, evaluation skills, and others. Students might, for example, brainstorm ideas for a class slogan, and may want to search for similar slogans adopted by groups in the past. They can brainstorm new uses for a specific object. They can brainstorm new inventions or products. Such a session could be

189

followed, for example, by investigation of the procedure required to obtain a patent on an invention, utilizing the assistance and resources of the media specialist.

Group projects like the publication of a class newspaper or school magazine also require exercise of a variety of skills. Such a project could produce a highly creative work and the students learn a great deal about planning, organizing, meeting deadlines. It could also inspire special studies in the media center, such as analysis of the propaganda techniques used in local papers, or untruth and stereotyping in magazine advertisements.(23)

Students might also research and publish a newspaper for a given day and a certain event and place they are studying. For example, they might choose to publish a newspaper for the day after Lincoln was shot, complete with advertisements, local notices, and the like. Two small groups might publish two newspapers for the same day—one from a northern city, one from the South.

Debating issues requires the use of many kinds of skills. Two small groups of gifted students might each be given a particular viewpoint to research on a particular issue. The media specialist would need to be alerted to the topics and would assist both sides to present their points of view.

Another satisfactory group activity for gifted students is the design of a model city. Students will need to analyze all the elements of city life in order to make provisions for the needs of the population that is to live in the model city. Such a project will require research, problem-solving, organization of ideas, and writing and media skills for the final presentation. It will help students to think about urban problems such as transportation, energy conservation, the job market, food supplies, housing, schools, the political system, and so forth.(23) And it is quite evident that the media specialist will need to work closely with both teacher and students in planning and carrying out this project.

Hypothetical problem-solving appeals to many gifted students. Individually or in small groups, they may be assigned a hypothetical situation that poses a problem they must resolve. Having made a decision, they must justify it. Another small group of students then evaluates the solution and gives a justification for their evaluation.

Students will enjoy and learn a good deal from interviewing celebrities, either real or role-played by a classmate. Students would write out in advance appropriate questions to ask an author, athlete, statesman, or someone in the news. Older students might like to hold a mock press conference with the President, especially shortly after observing the real thing on TV.

Variations on traditional book reports that highlight critical reading are always welcomed by gifted students, individually or in groups. One student might be asked to read variations of folk tales—similar stories from different cultures—and report on the differences in explanations of such phenomena as the origin of the world, night and day, etc. The report might be made with transparencies or with the help of slides or tape. Another student might read several biographies of one person as a project, and report to the class on differences in them of fact and interpretation. Another student might take as a project taping excerpts of writings by different authors, using those with distinctive styles. The media specialist's help with this will be invaluable. Then, the class, or others of a small group of able students might be asked to identify the writers and give reasons for their identification. This leads to a discussion of the components of style led by a student, the teacher, or perhaps the media specialist.

Any of the small group or individual activities described as examples—and of course hundreds more—can be adapted and can serve as springboards to other projects. The value of group projects is that they require group planning, execution, and evaluation. Responsibility lies with the students. Leadership and organization skills must be exercised.

We have already mentioned in Chapter 5 the possibility and value of cross-age tutoring. Although tutoring should not be limited to gifted children, they can profit greatly from it, especially if they are matched with low/average tutees from a lower grade. Gifted students may sometimes show a tendency toward arrogance—they understand so quickly, why doesn't everyone? It can be good for them to have the experience of explaining ideas or procedures simply and clearly, working through to the answers the hard way, as most people have to! Matching students, handling attitudes of superiority or impatience, and supervising tutoring sessions can take time, but generally the results are worth the effort, and valid learning takes place for all students involved.

The media center offers available space, support materials, and a good environment for tutoring sessions. Specific arrangements with the media specialist made well in advance should result in good additional supervision and resource support for the objectives to be accomplished.

Field Trips and Community Resources

Many school districts now have so many regulations and restrictions regarding field trips requiring transportation that some teachers have virtually ruled them out as possibilities. This is regrettable, because field trips can afford some exciting learning experiences if they are properly planned and organized. Whatever the obstacle to be overcome, the field trip is a real opportunity for gifted students to relate what they are learning to the world outside—the world of government, of science, and of business. Field trips got something of a bad name because of the image, from simpler times, of a whole class dragging through a routine visit to the zoo or local dairy that had little direct relationship to a project or classroom activity. The media specialist can be of tremendous help in planning a field trip for a small group of students. By consulting the community resource file, teacher and media specialist can identify agencies, institutions, or businesses that might welcome a visit, and careful advance arrangements can be made. Some media specialists have compiled kits for particular trips which include transportation options, instructions for students, questions to be asked, and some follow-up activities to reinforce the learning experience.

Another use for the community resource file is to identify community members who are willing to work with gifted students in a one-to-one relationship. Such "mentors" may advise students about specific projects, encourage a particular interest, or suggest activities to develop a particular skill or talent. They may share a hobby with a student. The relationships exist on an ongoing basis, and the mentor keeps in touch with the teacher as well as with the student. In many cases the media specialist can assist in matching mentor to student and suggest support materials and equipment to facilitate their work together.

INDEPENDENT STUDY

Independent study has proven to be a successful solution for providing individualization for many students of every age. The degree to which a student is involved in designing his own study and assuming responsibility for it depends a good deal upon his level of maturity. Close supervision is more necessary for some students than for others. Gifted students can profit immensely from independent study.

The media center will be the primary resource for the student, and the decision regarding the topic for study and the mode of investigation should certainly involve the media specialist. Before assignments are made final consideration must be given to the availability of materials and the adequacy of working space and facilities. There should be a meeting of the minds between the teacher and the media specialist as to the type and degree of assistance given to students.

Figure 7 presents a checklist for evaluating independent study assignments:

## FIGURE 7
### CHECKLIST FOR INDEPENDENT STUDY ASSIGNMENTS

Is the learner's role active rather than passive?

Are objectives clear to students?

Are students encouraged to explore and investigate individually?

Is the climate one that encourages questions?

Are students required to respond at various cognitive levels? Are they expected to analyze or evaluate information?

Are students given opportunities to express themselves creatively?

Are opportunities provided for students to organize their own learning?

Are students growing in self-assurance?

Does the media specialist understand the objectives?

Is the media specialist involved in planning and implementing the assignments?

Are the necessary materials and resources available in the media center?

Do students have adequate access to the media center and to a variety of resources there?

194

To sum up what has been said about cooperative efforts between teacher and media specialist in working with gifted and talented students, here are two lists of responsibilities that may prove useful.

## THE CLASSROOM TEACHER
—Recognizes giftedness in students, whatever its form.
—Individualizes instruction as much as possible.
—Encourages creativity and self-directed learning.
—Guides students in the development of balanced reading habits by: encouraging personal reading; giving diverse reading assignments; recognizing quality rather than quantity; introducing students to selection and evaluation aids.
—Stresses development of critical thinking skills.
—Provides variety and flexibility in teaching techniques.
—Encourages students to undertake independent work.
—Stimulates use of a variety of media in addition to print.
—Plans cooperatively with the media specialist regarding
    needed acquisitions
    topics assigned to students
    materials expected to be in heavy demand
    skills students need to exercise
    abilities and interests of students working in center
    dates or times for space and resource requirements.
—Insists that gifted students develop their own intellectual resources rather than relying on the teacher's.

## THE MEDIA SPECIALIST
—Helps identify giftedness in students.
—Gives guidance in selection of reading matter that provides for progression of reading experiences.
—Becomes sufficiently acquainted with individual students to learn about interests, motivations, aspirations, and abilities.
—Provides a comprehensive collection of media and

teaches how to use it effectively.

—Permits flexible use of the materials and facilities.

—Assists in planning student projects and activities.

—Provides a pleasant, cordial, and stimulating atmosphere that invites students to inquire, discover, and learn.

—Confers often with classroom and subject area teachers and all special teachers (counselors, reading, etc.).

—Keeps current on materials which enhance potentials for independent work in the media center.

—Gives technical assistance to students and teachers in utilizing production facilities.

—Provides a forum and setting for student projects, presentations, discussions.

## Motivating the Slow Learner

The term "slow learner" is so inclusive, and therefore so vague, that it has virtually a different meaning for everyone who uses it. Some educators use the term to refer to students whose learning problems have a specific cause, such as retardation, poor visual perception, learning disability such as dyslexia, or some other handicap that impedes classroom success. Others use the term to designate only low-achievers who lack any identifiable disability. Still others understand the term to include all low-achievers, with or without a specifically identified disability. Since we address the subject of selecting instructional strategies for mentally and physically handicapped students in Chapter 9, the discussion of slow learners in this chapter will deal with those low-achievers in regular classrooms who are considered able to meet the minimum requirements of the regular curriculum. Some of them may have emotional or attitudinal problems; some below average IQ's; others, difficulties due to cultural background. Some of these students may be mainstreamed from special programs in which they participate periodically. All of them will need special attention and assistance.

To identify the slow learner more specifically, consider some of the characteristics observable in such students.

A slow learner may be one whose physical development and coordination are lagging. This student usually has a short attention span, and often has great difficulty in mastering reading and math skills. He is easily distracted in class. Most slow-learning children are painfully conscious of their deficiencies and inadequacies, though they may hide their concern. They have great need of experiencing success in some area.

Many slow learners come from homes where they may not have been read to as young children or become familiar with books, magazines, or even much adult conversation. They may have experienced a great deal, but it often has not been put into any sequence or context for them and bears little relationship to the ordered world of the classroom. Their world, before school and outside of school, is *different*, often insecure, crisis-ridden, and even painful. Many such children have very limited capacity for verbal expression of their thoughts and feelings or even ability to give things their proper names.

There is an enormous complexity in the causes of slow learning, and the characteristics of the slow learner may baffle and frustrate. An apparent slow learner may even be a gifted child with problems! In most cases, however, the condition is accompanied by a poor self-concept and a serious lack of motivation, which may be both causes of low achievement and the results of it. In any case, there are few teachers who don't have some of these children in the classroom.

Slow learners all too often fall into the "vicious cycle" of poor reading ability, leading to poor learning ability, which results in poor achievement, with resultant poor behavior. This cycle must somehow be broken. With as many different types of media and as many different techniques as possible the teacher must somehow intervene to effect a change in the slow learner's self-concept or in his learning style, in his study habits or in his attitudes toward learning. Somewhere in the cycle of failure there is a way to interrupt the process. The student must realize some success that enhances his self-respect and thereby motivates him to aim for greater achievement. Easier said than done? Probably. But there *are* ways to succeed in motivating slow learners. This section of the present chapter will highlight some successful techniques.

There are certain basic principles of instruction for slow learners that should be kept constantly in mind:

1. Individualized instruction allows teachers to capitalize on students' interests, talents, abilities.
2. Even small successes can bolster a student's self-image.
3. Class activities that relate to the student's world help him understand the usefulness of what he is learning.
4. A relaxed, nonthreatening learning environment induces response and participation.
5. Action-based learning is most appropriate for reluctant learners.
6. Prompt, tangible rewards encourage effort and involvement.

These principles of instruction, coupled with creative techniques and innovative use of materials, can provide rewarding experiences in teaching slow learners.

One teacher met with success by making use of video tape recording equipment. Her class of slow learners was divided into small groups, with each group assigned the task of creating a TV production. The group had to pick a topic and research it, prepare graphics, write and edit a script, record a practice run-through, evaluate the practice tape, and produce a final tape acceptable to the instructor. The

198

students were exercising academic skills while learning a new skill they saw as marketable. Because they chose their own topics, they took real interest in the project. The results were phenomenally good. Enthusiasm spread. One interesting side effect was that the students sometimes sought "expert advice" from faculty members on the topics they were exploring. "Many teachers, who had formerly viewed these students as troublesome or completely lacking in ability, reevaluated their opinions....Again, self-image for the student changed as teacher expectations changed."(12)

If video tape recorder (VTR) equipment is part of your school's equipment, it probably is, and should be, housed in the media center. Consult the media specialist about its availability and plan for specific student projects. The media specialist can assist in instructing students in the proper use of the equipment and give them technical advice as they plan their productions. These projects can be adapted to any subject area and to a wide range of age groups. Similar projects may be completed with less expensive equipment; for example, home movie cameras could be used. For younger students the use of regular photographs illustrating an audio tape might constitute an exciting project.

A dedicated biology teacher succeeded in reaching slow learners by using a variety of media. In order to prepare students for actual observation of marine life, the teacher had the class begin the study by examining preserved specimens from his collection. Students then expanded their knowledge by viewing films and filmstrips which illustrated many types of marine life. The media specialist helped the teacher collect books from the school media center and also from the public library which expanded upon the subject. The terminating activity was a field trip to a biology lab where students could observe living forms of the sea life they had studied.(29)

One sure way to turn slow learners *off* is to present them with materials that are too difficult. Careful selection is important. Media specialists are trained to match students to appropriate materials. Teachers and media specialists need to communicate frequently about subject areas under discussion, ability levels of students, interest levels of students, and so forth. Several guidelines to selection of materials for slow learners are available and include these points:

Questions about sentence structure—
    Are they simple sentences with no more than 10–15 words?
    Are there many dependent clauses? compound sentences? (Avoid these.)
    Are simple verb tenses (past and present) used?
    Is the language concrete?
    Is the text readable? Personal references (pronouns, mother, father) make a text more readable.

Questions about the content—
    Is the material too preachy?
    Are there frequent repetitions of words?
    Is the reader involved? Does the material relate closely to the student's experiences?
    Is the material humorous?
    Is it tuned to current topics of interest?(10)

An important factor to consider in selecting reading materials for slow learners is relevancy of content. Reading assignments should have meaning easily grasped by the student, relating to his interests, concerns, and maturity level. Media centers should have an extensive collection of high-interest, low-vocabulary materials. Teachers and media specialists should collaborate on the acquisition of such materials and consideration of the use of specific titles.

The need to present slow learners with successful classroom experiences is universally stressed by educators. The media center provides many opportunities for such experiences. Training in the operating of A-V equipment gives the student a useful role he can fill successfully. Responsibility for organizing and managing the stock of A-V equipment or specific facilities of the media center can also give these students confidence and motivation. Other tasks that can be completed successfully by such students include check-out duties, shelving of books, assisting in inventories, repairing damaged materials, and so forth. Make an effort to suggest specific students to media specialists for these responsibilities, giving consideration to students' personalities, interests, schedules, or extracurricular activities.

Contract teaching offers a possible solution to the problem of motivating slow learners. It not only provides a means of individualizing instruction, since the contract can be tailored to the student's abilities and interests, but helps ensure success for the student. Because the student participates in designing the contract, he feels that it is attainable and reasonable. He is freed from the anxiety of competing for grades in knowing he is judged *not* in relation to what his classmates can do but on the basis of *his own* achievement as compared to promised performance in the contract.(24) While the teacher dictates broad content areas, the student can select specific content details to research, projects to pursue, methods of presentation, etc. It is important that all contract assignments be real work, not just busy work. The media specialist needs to be involved in planning activities geared to students' abilities and interests and also in planning assignments to assure the availability of appropriate materials related to the subject matter. The quality of work should be stressed with slow learners to emphasize that good work is expected from them. Teacher expectation has a major influence on the student's self-concept.

Slow learners should be given opportunities for independent work whenever possible. The assignments should not be lengthy or complex. But self-reliance is enhanced when students work independently, and therefore slow learners need such opportunities when they are feasible. Creative writing is one possible assignment for independent work, provided careful parameters are set. Devising games or simulations, creating crossword puzzles, problem-solving of "real-life" situations, computing specific budget needs are all examples of appropriate independent work that can be fun and stimulating for slow learners.

A major advantage of independent work is that assignments can be related to a student's special interests, making the work appealing as well as instructive. A student will learn more about research skills when applying them to some aspect of his favorite sport than to some political or literary topic. Budgeting his own (imaginary) funds may mean more to the student than analyzing the national budget. Using map skills to chart and plan a vacation trip real or imaginary, will be more motivating than just locating cities on blank maps. Calculating distance covered and time involved in walking to and from school may provide a student with valid reasons for purchasing a bike or car. Such realistic use of skills gives more incentive to a writing assignment than arguing points for or against nuclear-powered energy. Discovering the cause of pollution in a nearby lake or river will be more relevant than reading about pollution in Lake Erie.

All students need to see relevance in what they are being asked to learn or to do, but for the unmotivated slow learner relevance is especially important. It is unrealistic, and indeed unfair, to expect a slow learner to exert effort to learn something he sees as totally useless and irrelevant to him. Part of the teacher's responsibility, of course, is to expand the student's understanding of what information, ideas, or skills are relevant to him and in what way. But the student wants to arrive at this judgment for himself in terms of his own interests and ambitions.

Another term for relevance in studies is "reality-centered learning."(30) This means using the realities of the student's life—the real world of his experiences—as the organizing structure of his learning experiences. Students select topics of study that relate to their own concerns. Topics might include sensationalism and propaganda techniques used in stories about teen idols; incidences of teen-age alcoholism; pollution in recreational areas; government involvement in antismoking campaigns; competency-based education; population control; censorship in movies, television, and printed materials. Obviously topics must be suitable for the maturity level as well as the ability level of the students. The significance of reality-centered education is that students, regardless of age level, will choose topics of study that seem important to them. In choosing topics, students should be encouraged to consult fully with the media specialist. The steps involved in such a study require that students (1) identify the problem; (2) collect pertinent information regarding the issue; (3) list possible solutions to the problem; (4) evaluate these in terms of feasibility and effectiveness; (5) plan a strategy for action in tackling the problem. The students should take the study further if possible by (6) taking action; and then (7) evaluating the effectiveness of the action taken. (30)

If the method of study outlined above seems beyond the realm of possibility for your students, there is an alternative approach that still allows for student input. Given a topic of study, the students can write what they already know about the topic, followed by lists of questions about the subject they wish to pursue. In this manner they will cover mandated topics of study, but can investigate the subject from their own chosen vantage point.

Effective learning activities for slow learners must include a variety of media. Textbook-centered teaching is often deadly dull to slow learners, in part because many of them have come to see the textbook as an impenetrable obstacle. Many slow learners are youngsters whose mode of learning is simply different from the usual mode of teaching. They may need primarily auditory or visual input rather than relying principally on the written word. Collections of multimedia materials that allow variation in teaching techniques in a broad range of content or topic areas can be built in collaboration with the media specialist. Where materials are nonexistent or prohibitively expensive, teachers can work with the media specialist to create suitable materials for student use, or, better still, enlist student assistance in creating these materials. Slow learners become more interested in a project if they contribute to it by taping a reading selection or specific work instructions, by drawing illustrations, by printing or typing work sheets, or by making transparencies or slides. And certainly their sense of self-worth is improved when their efforts are clearly important.

Another factor to consider in working with slow learners is the need for repetition, reinforcement of concepts and methods. Repeating the same activities or procedures over and over again will *not* necessarily facilitate learning. But *reinforcement* of learning through *varied* activities is a must. If students have worked today on multiplication facts, they may apply those facts tomorrow by working up a materials order (perhaps with the help of the media specialist). Another day they may work word problems that require multiplication, and those same word problems may include vocabulary terms students have previously defined. If students have read a story about forest rangers in class, they may want to survey the card catalog and vertical file in the media center to see what other information is available about rangers. Consultation with the media specialist can be helpful in planning follow-up activity for some of the reading selections in the basal readers. Reinforcement of learning through varied approaches and formats is most effectively achieved through the use of varied media.

For the slow learner with particularly poor response, crafts projects or other activities involving the arts may provide needed motivation. Research indicates a significant correlation between learning ability and hand/eye coordination, visual perception and other motor abilities. Projects that develop various kinds of muscle coordination may enhance the child's learning ability as well. And such activities are generally motivating in themselves. If they also set the stage for applying academic skills in some related study, the value of the activity is manifold. Added to these benefits is the fact that craft projects offer the student an opportunity for success and self-satisfaction. It takes only a little imagination to find ways to correlate crafts or other arts projects to the basic curriculum in almost any subject area. Activities that allow the slow learner to build on prior learning experiences demonstrate to him that he has acquired knowledge upon which he can now expand, and help him to gain confidence in his own ability. Picture collections, record albums, specialized periodicals, books on various crafts, and a rich assortment of other resources in the media center can stimulate a variety of activities or projects of this nature.

Teaching the slow learner requires careful planning and preparation. Activities must be within the realm of possibilty for achievement *as he sees it* if the student is to be motivated to participate with enthusiasm. The goal is integration of activities so that one experience positively reinforces another. Fragmentation of learning experiences in which reading has no relation to science, and math no relation to social studies, serves only to confuse and frustrate the slow learner. It is difficult for teachers in departmentalized situations to achieve complete integration. In this case the role of the media specialist in helping to *correlate* the efforts of several teachers in several subjects is truly vital. The resources of the media center and the services of the media specialist are invaluable to all teachers in preparing an integrated curriculum for slow learners.

Figure 8 presents a summary of the techniques teachers may employ in planning for slow learners and the skills the media specialist can contribute as a support resource person. Perhaps it will help to summarize the three R's of education for slow learners as *Recognition* of individuality and potential, *Reinforcement* of previous learning, and *Reward* at every successful step.

TEACHER'S RESERVATION: On first reading, the role of the media specialist as described by the authors seemed somewhat contrived. After the second reading it made more sense. Media specialists are not strong curriculum persons, but they should be highly resourceful people and, as such, very helpful to teachers as they plan activities. The activity suggestions in this chapter are very appropriate and cover a wide range of ideas. The description of the ideal collection for gifted students bothered me. How do the characteristics of such a collection differ from those for other students?

WRITERS' RESPONSE: The reader's first reaction probably stemmed from the fact that few teachers have had experience with media specialists as coplanners in curriculum. Unfortunately, it is not often that media specialists have the opportunity to participate with teachers in detailed planning. Their role in this area has not yet been fully realized. But it is past time for the potential to be recognized.

The question about the collection of materials for gifted children is well taken. Perhaps the difference is rather a matter of degree than of substance. Materials for gifted youngsters should cover a wider range, be more challenging, have more depth than the majority of materials presented to other students.

BIBLIOGRAPHY

1. Anderson, Paul. "Independent Study: Emerson Junior-Senior High School." *Illinois Libraries*, 2:41–43, Winter, 1969.

# FIGURE 8
## TECHNIQUES AND BEHAVIORS
## FOR WORKING WITH SLOW LEARNERS

| | TEACHER | MEDIA SPECIALIST |
|---|---|---|
| *Working With Students* | Get to know the student personally.<br>Be warm and friendly, yet firm.<br>Accentuate the positive aspects of the student's personality and abilities.<br>Provide students many opportunities to achieve success. | Get to know the students personally.<br>Provide a friendly environment in the media center.<br>Provide flexible policy that assures individualization of services.<br>Whenever possible, liberalize loan policies to allow for lending of periodicals and A-V materials and equipment.<br>Seek student opinions regarding appropriate acquisitions. |
| *Planning for Individualized Instruction* | Gear learning experiences to the talents and interests of students.<br>Allow students input in planning activities.<br>Allow students to work independently as much as possible.<br>Employ a variety of teaching/learning modes in instruction.<br>Draw on a variety of media in lesson activities.<br>Allow plenty of time for completion of tasks.<br>Reinforce learning experiences through varied activities and applications.<br>Aid students in strengthening attention span by gradually increasing length of tasks.<br>Stress quality of performance not quantity. | Provide wide range of high-interest, low-vocabulary materials and a wide range of non-print materials on variety of subjects.<br>Provide variety of equipment for student use, such as film and cameras, recorders, phonographs, etc.<br>Provide wide range of concrete, "hands on" materials for student manipulation.<br>Display items of special interest to students.<br>Provide "read aloud" story hour for students, perhaps "serialized" over several days.<br>Prepare (or supervise) recordings of stories appealing to students and provide read-along materials for them to look at as they listen.<br>Develop media skills lessons geared to the needs of slow learners.<br>Provide multi-media interest centers that reinforce classroom learning.<br>Plan special projects with individual students. |
| *Working with Staff* | Assist media specialist in developing collection of high-interest, low-vocabulary materials on a wide range of subjects.<br>Suggest variety of materials to media specialist for acquisition.<br>Prepare activity-folders, kits, tapes as supplementary materials to be used in media center.<br>Seek assistance from media specialist in planning integrated learning experiences.<br>Recommend students to media specialist for responsibilities in the media center. | Seek teacher assistance in selecting acquisitions.<br>Consult teachers when choosing students for jobs in media center.<br>Provide materials or suggestions to assist teachers in correlating activities in different subject areas.<br>Be knowledgeable about reading levels and appropriate usage of materials. |

207

2. Barbe, Walter B. and Joseph S. Renzulli, eds. *Psychology and Education of the Gifted*, 2d ed. New York, Irvington Publishers, 1975.

3. Baskin, Barbara and Karen H. Harris. "Gifted Children and the Elementary School Librarian—Theory into Practice" in *The Special Child in the Library*. Chicago, American Library Association, 1976.

4. Batchelor, Lillian. "Setting a Reading Climate for the Gifted" in *The Special Child in the Library*. Chicago, American Library Association, 1976.

5. Beechhold, Henry F. *The Creative Classroom*. New York, Charles Scribner's Sons, 1971.

6. Bell, Jo Ann. "The Technical-Vocational Student and the Library." *Southeastern Librarian*, 20:241, Winter, 1970.

7. Berkman, Cele. "Field Trips—Much More Than A Day's Outing." *Christian Science Monitor*, September 5, 1978.

8. Beswick, Norman. "The School Library and the Highly Gifted Child" in *The Special Child in the Library*. Chicago, American Library Association, 1976.

9. Bigaj, James J. "A Reading Program for Gifted Children in the Primary Grades" in *The Special Child in the Library*. Chicago, American Library Association, 1976.

10. Boutwell, William. "Motivating the Slow Learner" in *The Special Child in the Library*. Chicago, American Library Association, 1976.

11. *Challenge: A Handbook for Parents of Gifted and Talented Students*. Greenville, South Carolina, Greenville County Schools, 1978.

12. Cohen, Judith. "Geniuses at Work" in *The Special Child in the Library*. Chicago, American Library Association, 1976.

13. Cyr, Helen W. "Why Not the Instant Media Center?"

*School Libraries*, 20:21–23, Spring, 1971.

14. "Dear Principal, Dear Librarian: A Dialogue on the Heart of the Matter." *Wilson Library Bulletin*, 48:54–57, September, 1973.

15. Feldhusen, John F. and Margaret B. Kalloff. "A Three-Stage Model for Gifted Education." *Education Digest*, 44:15–18, January, 1979.

16. Flescher, Irwin. *Children in the Learning Factory*. Philadelphia, Chelton Book Company, 1972.

17. Frary, Mildred P. "School Library Services to the Disadvantaged Student." *Library Trends*, 20:405–15, October, 1971.

18. Gallagher, James J. *Teaching the Gifted*, 2d ed. Boston, Allyn & Bacon, 1975.

19. *How to Enhance Individuality in Learning*. Dayton, Ohio, National Association of Secondary School Principals and /I/D/E/A/, n.d.

20. Hawkins, Francis P. *Involving Students in Questioning*. Boston, Allyn & Bacon, 1976.

21. "Independent Study." Curriculum Report, No. 11. National Association of Secondary School Principals, May, 1967.

22. *Information Aid: Gifted Students: Identification Techniques and Program Organization*. Arlington, Virginia, Educational Research Service, 1975.

23. Kaplan, Sandra N. *Providing Programs for the Gifted and Talented: A Handbook*. Reston, Virginia, Council for Exceptional Children, 1977.

24. Kennemore, Florence and Mary Ann Wickwire. "Planning for Educational Initiative." *School Libraries*, 20:16–20, Spring, 1972.

25. Kirschenbaum, Robert. "Who are the Gifted and Why are They Different?" *Education Digest*, 45:34–35, November, 1979.

26. Klong, Mary P. "The Role of the Media Center in the Education of Disadvantaged Children." *Southeastern*

*Librarian*, 20:158–65, Fall, 1970.

27. Martinson, Ruth. *The Identification of the Gifted and Talented*. Reston, Virginia, Council for Exceptional Children, 1975.

28. Mavrogenes, Nancy A. and Nancy D. Galea. "Cross-Age Tutoring: Why and How." *Education Digest*, 44:17–20, April, 1979.

29. McClosky, Mildred G. *Teaching Strategies and Classroom Realities*. Englewood Cliffs, New Jersey, Prentice-Hall, 1971.

30. Ruchlis, Hy and Belle Sharefkin. *Reality-Centered Learning*. New York, Citation Press, 1975.

31. Sattley, Helen R. "Reading Guidance for the Gifted Child" in *The Special Child in the Library*. Chicago, American Library Association, 1976.

32. Schmidt, Alfred. *Craft Projects for Slow Learners*. New York, John Day, 1968.

33. Schumsky, Abraham. *Creative Teaching in the Elementary School*. New York, Appleton-Century-Crofts, 1965.

34. Shipp, Randy. "How Teachers Can Spot and Help the Gifted." *Christian Science Monitor*, January 29, 1979.

35. Sisk, Dorothy. *Teaching Gifted Children*. Columbia, South Carolina, State Department of Education, 1976.

36. Stevens, Nathaniel O. "Geniuses from the Ghetto." *Christian Science Monitor*, September 5, 1978.

37. Syphers, Dorothy. *Gifted and Talented Children: Practical Programming for Teachers and Principals*. Arlington, Virginia, Council for Exceptional Children, 1972.

38. Tapper, Nancy. "Independent Study: Lawrence High School." *New Jersey Libraries*, 2:39–40, Winter, 1969.

39. Tomasson, Verna. "Gifted Children in a Bind." *Education Digest*, 39:32–35, February, 1974.

40. Torrance, E. Paul. *Encouraging Creativity in the Classroom*. Dubuque, Iowa, William C. Brown Company, 1970.

41. Torricelli, Betty. "Curriculum Change—A Catalyst of Library Development." *New Jersey Libraries*, 2:48–50, Fall, 1969.
42. Walker, H. Thomas. "Media Services for Gifted Learners." *School Media Quarterly*, 6:253–54, 259–63, Summer, 1978.
43. Wehmeyer, Lillian B. "Independent Study" in *The School Librarian as Educator*. Littleton, Colorado, Libraries Unlimited, 1976.
44. Wickendon, Hermione H. "Secondary School Independent Study Programs and Their Implications for Library Services and Resources." (Thesis). Southern Connecticut State College, 1969.
45. Zimmer, Robert. "Gifted Pupils at Disadvantage." *Greenville (S.C.) News-Piedmont*, March 26, 1978.

# 9

"One Of The Most Difficult Things I Have To Do Is To Select Appropriate Materials And Instructional Strategies For Mentally And Physically Handicapped Students."

Since the passage of the Education for All Handicapped Children Act of 1975 (Public Law 94-142) teachers have been justifiably concerned about the implementation of the law and its impact on their classrooms. According to PL 94-142, after September 1, 1978, all handicapped children aged three to eighteen must be provided opportunity for a free appropriate public education. After September, 1980, the age range will extend to twenty-one-year-olds. The purpose of the law is to achieve "mainstreaming" into regular classrooms of special education children previously taught in segregated special classrooms or centers, if at all. To the maximum extent possible handicapped children are now to be educated with children who are not handicapped. Segregated classes will be continued for those youngsters whose needs are such that their education in a regular classroom cannot be satisfactorily achieved. But large numbers of handicapped children will now be placed in regular classrooms for all or part of the school day to make sure that they are in the "mainstream" of public education.

The philosophy of "mainstreaming" stems from the belief that *every* individual is unique and the concept of normalization, which is also the goal of mainstreaming. Evidence indicates that, in the main, segregated, special education children do not learn any more or progress any better in separate, special classes than they do in regular classrooms. Indeed, the evidence indicates that special education youngsters develop a much more positive self-concept and demonstrate greater self-reliance when they are part of a regular classroom. Acceptance of handicapped children by other youngsters is likewise facilitated, and all the children benefit from the interaction.(60)

But what of the teacher in whose classroom these changes are taking place? How do the changes affect the regular classroom teacher? What are the implications of the law? Consider, if you will, the field of "special education" and what it includes. Who are the youngsters coming now into regular classrooms? There are as many as nine or ten categories of "exceptional" children whose learning capabilities or physical conditions separate them from other children. Among these are the visually impaired, the hearing impaired, the mentally retarded, orthopedically or neurologically impaired youngsters, children with specific learning disabilities, those with behavioral or emotional disorders, those with speech handicaps, and children with multiple handicaps. Some educators also include in the category of exceptional or atypical students those who have cultural or linguistic handicaps. And finally, the category of exceptional children also includes the gifted and talented, though they are not classified as handicapped under PL 94-142. This represents a very heterogeneous group of students, whose range of special needs is enormous and often seems overwhelming to the classroom teacher, who feels unprepared and incapable of meeting these diverse needs.

213

PL 94-142 requires that handicapped students have access to free public education in the least restrictive environment possible in light of their specific needs. It further states that every handicapped child must have an individualized education program (IEP) designed specifically for him by his teacher(s) and parents or guardian. This program of instruction must be completely individualized, defining the student's present level of achievement, stating desired long-term educational goals, and setting forth realistic short-term instructional objectives. The IEP is reviewed periodically and revised as necessary.

Obviously, implementation of PL 94-142 is placing increased demands on many teachers who, often without any special training for work with handicapped students, are faced with the responsibility for teaching them. Many teachers have reacted with resentment and frustration. They fear that implementation of the law may result in educational neglect for the majority of the students, since meeting the needs of one handicapped student can drain 50 percent of a teacher's time and energy away from the others. How are teachers to meet these new responsibilities when their time and energy resources are already seriously stretched?

Many solutions to the problems can come only with increased aid, either through more funding or more volunteer assistance. Meanwhile, work with resource teachers (special education teacher/consultants), media specialists, and parents of handicapped children can help in the transition period to offer the exceptional children some exciting educational experiences that fulfill their individual needs. The solution lies, as always, in individualized teaching.

As we have said before, individualized teaching demands diligent classroom management. Good use must be made of every scrap of time, talent, and material. Volunteer assistance from parents or other community members is invaluable, especially if school funds do not permit paid aides. Learning packages, learning centers, activity folders, independent assignments in the class or in the media center engage the student in study geared to his needs while freeing the teacher to concentrate on students one at a time. Pairing of students to work together should match students so that they complement the strengths and weaknesses of one another. A definite time each day or each week set aside for checking student folders enables the teacher to keep abreast of individual progress. Likewise, a designated time for daily or weekly conferences allows the teacher to give individual attention where it is most needed. Careful planning of class activities to integrate learning experiences and reinforce concepts and skills will enable the teacher to meet the needs of students individually and collectively.

Getting to know the student and understand his particular problems is the initial step in working with a handicapped child. With assistance from a resource teacher, the classroom teacher evaluates the student's level of achievement and his potential. The resource teacher and the parents of the student should work with the teacher to develop realistic instructional objectives for the handicapped child. The media specialist can then assist in planning appropriate activities and selecting materials to ensure maximum opportunity for success. Since different handicapped children may be limited to the use of one or more types of media, selection is highly significant. The media specialist provides flexibility in instructional strategies, not only because of a wide knowledge of existing media and materials, but also because of skill in adapting or modifying materials and expertise in producing varied instructional aids.

Day-to-day contacts with the media specialist will be needed for cooperative planning. The media specialist can provide an ongoing system for informing teachers about the availability of special education materials from various sources. For example, the Bureau of Education for Handicapped Children (U.S. Department of Education) has

215

established the National Center on Educational Media and Materials for the Handicapped (NCEMMH). There are also thirteen Area Learning Resource Centers, four Associated Special Offices, and thirteen Regional Resource Centers. The function of these centers is to give leadership in the development and dissemination of media, materials, and technological instructional aids designed for handicapped students. The centers will also provide training programs and materials for teachers, as well as production assistance to those developing new materials for use with handicapped youngsters. The national center is developing a National Instructional Materials Information System (NIMIS), a computer-based retrieval system to assist teachers and parents in locating appropriate materials for specific needs. The media specialist in the school is prepared to fill a liaison role between teachers and information centers such as NCEMMH.

Media specialists are continually receiving information about new materials and programs available to educators. If cued by the teacher, the media specialist will be alert to information about media programs for atypical students. Project "ME" is an example of a program designed for use with handicapped children.(52) The system enables a child to interact motorically, tactically, and verbally with a life-size projected image. This program is especially useful with children who have specific learning disabilities or emotional disorders. Information about the program is available from Media for the Exceptional. (See Appendix XIII for complete address.)

Very often commercially developed materials are not available for the specific combination of needs of particular children. Media specialists can assist teachers in producing instructional materials to fit the needs of the children they teach. In deciding to develop original teaching components or materials for students, these criteria of valid materials should be kept in mind:

Content and activities should be appropriate for the

student's chronological age as well as developmental age.

Activities must enable the student to attain specific instructional objectives.

Activities should provide a reasonable sequence of development, including: progress from three-dimensional concrete reality, through photographic and pictorial representation, to understanding of abstract symbols; present progressive increments of tasks in very small steps; repeat learned skills through varied tasks for reinforcement; exercise accumulated skills.

Instructional mode of the materials developed should be appropriate to student's learning style.

Programs should be designed for flexible, independent use.

Content and activities should maximize student's learning potential and minimize his handicap(s).

Handicapped adults often express the need for experiences and relationships that make them feel more human. The need is equally great among handicapped young people. All school personnel should project a genuine acceptance of handicapped students. Simple gestures mean as much as elaborate ones. Whatever is done to help the handicapped student build and develop his assets directly affects his ability to accept his impairment. Guidance needs to be available, even to young students, in assessing vocational and career options. The media center should have a collection of materials on careers and vocational opportunities for the handicapped. If it isn't there, it can be obtained.

Handicapped youngsters are no different from others in their need for success and self-confidence. Class assignments or small group activities designed to highlight the special skills of each student help build self-esteem and peer esteem. Those students who can successfully fill jobs in the media center, the school office, the cafeteria, or school store should be encouraged to do so. It is wise to capitalize on the artistic

217

ability of students, especially the handicapped, to provide lesson illustrations that may well enhance the attractiveness of the classroom.

It is of primary importance that the teacher of handicapped children communicate frequently and objectively with the parents of these children. Each can be of assistance to the other in understanding the needs, feelings, and abilities of the handicapped child. Teachers should assist the media specialist in informing parents of special programs or materials that may be used at home, and about organizations that may provide services to handicapped children. The media specialist in your school may already have begun a newsletter to parents of handicapped students in the school; many have done so. Useful publications that should be brought to parents' attention include *Help for Parents of Handicapped Children—an Annotated Bibliography* and the journal published by the Council for Exceptional Children. (See Appendix XIII for a full listing with sources and addresses.)

Figure 9 outlines a variety of helpful services that teachers should be able to expect from the media specialist in support of their work with exceptional children. This list identifies general services that facilitate the educational process for any handicapped child. However, the diversity of conditions that exist under the label "handicapped" or "exceptional" necessitates more discussion by categories if specific suggestions for teaching strategies are to be truly usable. Although some suggestions offered in the following paragraphs may be effective in a variety of circumstances, the strategies highlighted have been selected because of their appropriate application to specific conditions.

VISUALLY IMPAIRED

Students classified as visually impaired range from the totally blind to those who have limited, partial sight, but

218

are legally blind. The visually impaired, who have partial sight, may be able to read large print or to discern large, simple outline drawings. Other visually impaired students may rely totally on braille or on recorded materials. The teacher must be completely aware of the *degree* of a student's impairment and know what specific recommendations have been made for the student by a vision specialist. The first consideration is for the student's comfort and well-being in class. Special equipment or materials needed, such as magnifiers or large-print books, should be in ready supply. Careful attention must be given to lighting, seating arrangements, and acoustical conditions for the partially sighted student. For example, he should not be seated facing into the light. Surfaces that might cause a glare should be covered. Visual instructional aids used in the classroom should be simple in design with distinct color contrasts. Print should be bold, colors bright and clear. The student will need frequent rest from using his eyes to prevent strain or fatigue. Class activities should be carefully structured to provide variety, alternating reading or writing assignments with activities that rely on listening or on verbal interaction.

As a teacher, you will need to work closely with the media specialist to make appropriate materials available for visually impaired students. Blind students learn to rely heavily on the senses that are not impaired, particularly on hearing and touching, to gain information. Learning experiences for these students need to be geared in that direction. Tape recorder players and phonographs, readily available in the media center, should be actively used in classrooms as well. The media center usually provides a typewriter and work space for students. Visually impaired students should be given ample time to make use of this service. Three-dimensional objects and other realia (such as scientific models of human organs, stuffed and mounted animals, historical artifacts, physical relief maps and globes) should be exhibited and available for examination both in the classroom and in the media center.(8) The effectiveness of such exhibits is enhanced by recorded verbal descriptions or explanations made available to the student. Educational radio and sound recordings of speeches, plays, stories, or poems heighten the blind student's feeling of participation in classroom experiences. Teachers should plan acquisitions with the media specialist to ensure a varied, well-rounded collection of sound materials. Talking books, available from the Library of Congress through state agencies, provide students with exposure to a variety of materials.

A school media center will need a significant collection of large-print books for the partially sighted. This collection should be varied, covering a broad range of subject matter and special interests. All material or equipment to be used by the partially sighted is easily identified if it is color-coded and conspicuously located. Sectional or organizational signs in large print facilitate use of the media center by students with partial vision. If such signs are not in use in the media center, a class may want to provide them as a class project.

FIGURE 9

## GENERAL SERVICES OF THE MEDIA SPECIALIST FOR HANDICAPPED STUDENTS

Services to Students

1. Creates an accepting, friendly climate in the media center.
2. Provides specialized materials in an environment free of barriers that restrict use.
3. Serves as liaison between the student and a variety of outside sources of specialized materials.
4. Develops or adapts lessons on media skills that adjust to the specific handicaps of students.
5. Identifies parent or student volunteer tutors.
6. Provides collection of materials on vocations and careers for the handicapped.
7. Maintains a card file on handicapped students identifying each one's reading level, special interests, favorite authors, etc. Develops a recommended reading list for each student.

8. Exhibits in the media center art works, personal collections, finished models done by handicapped students.
9. Enlists assistance of handicapped students whenever possible in completing tasks in the media center.
10. Makes materials and equipment physically accessible or provides necessary assistance.

### Services to Teachers

1. Schedules conferences with teachers to discuss needs of specific students.
2. Informs teachers of new programs and materials for the handicapped as they become available.
3. Publicizes sources of specialized materials and organizations that provide services.
4. Organizes in-service programs to help teachers improve skills needed with handicapped students.
5. Designs and implements an efficient delivery system for circulation of media center materials.
6. Consults teachers regarding their recommendations for acquisition of materials.
7. Maintains materials and equipment in good repair and ready for use.
8. Plans learning activities with the teacher.

### Services to Parents

1. Publicizes sources of specialized materials and organizations that provide special services.
2. Provides copies of laws and regulations regarding the rights of the handicapped.
3. Recommends reading materials that may help parents.
4. Encourages involvement of parents in the media center programs and elsewhere in the school.
5. Seeks parental recommendations regarding acquisition of materials.
6. Holds periodic conferences with parents to discuss their observations as to children's developing interests and skills, reinforcement of school experiences and the like.

A student committee conferring with the media specialist may make specific decisions about location and design of signs before the work begins.

Braille materials augment the collection of sound materials for students who do not see at all. Since braille materials require a substantial amount of storage space, only a standard collection of materials is usually justified in public school media centers. Reference materials and other widely used sources that will stay in circulation should comprise the collection. Less widely used materials should be stored on tape cassettes. Twin Vision materials present the text both in print and in braille.(26) The visually impaired student can follow along as the material is read aloud, and the two sensory modes of learning reinforce each other.

Teachers may want to rely on a "buddy system," which means that a sighted student reads textbook selections to a visually impaired classmate, copies information off the blackboard or other visual aids, assists the student in the media center, and in general "sees" for his partner. Twin Vision materials can be effectively used by a visually impaired student either with his "buddy" or with a teacher or aide.

Teachers should give visually impaired students many opportunities to recite orally in class. Likewise, these students need frequent access to the media center to use the great variety of non-print media housed there. (A reference list of sources of specialized material is provided in Appendix XIII.)

Teachers and media specialists should work together to produce tape cassettes for visually impaired students. Stories or reading selections used widely and repeatedly should be taped so that the visually impaired student can have access to the selections. Since blind students cannot see facial expressions and gestures, effort must be made to convey moods and feelings in the voice. Students who read expressively may assist in making such recordings.

## The Hearing Impaired

The hearing-impaired student presents a serious problem to the teacher who relies heavily on oral communication in the classroom. These students are visual learners, for the most part, and the "talking-teacher" learning of most classrooms simply will not suffice. Hearing-impaired students in a regular classroom may have partial hearing with use of a hearing aid, or they may be able to lip-read. The degree of concentration needed to hear and comprehend is intense and exhausting, and these students must have visual instructional aids to support their learning experiences. It will be a challenge to find ways to help hearing-impaired students "see" information that other students hear. Again, a clear knowledge of the student's handicap—the degree of the hearing loss and the expertise of the student in compensating skills—is necessary. Conferences with parents, special education teacher/consultants, hearing specialists, and guidance counselors are all in order. The deaf student who relies on lip reading inevitably misses a great deal, and often misunderstands what is being said. In all likelihood, the hearing-impaired student is well acquainted with failure. His self-image may be quite distorted, and his behavior (whether aggressive or withdrawn) a problem. You will need to know these things at the outset.

Again, the "buddy system" can ease a deaf student's misgivings and facilitate his entry into the classroom. With a classmate he can rely on to assist him in getting correct information, the hearing-impaired student will feel more confident and at ease. If a hearing student in the class is skilled in sign language, he should be asked to translate in class. Learning sign language may, in fact, be a good project for several members of a class.

For the hearing-impaired student who relies on lip reading there are several considerations that will improve communication with him. Be alert to any conditions or objects that hinder his view of a speaker (teacher or any other). Light or reflection that causes glare, classroom equipment, even fellow students can prevent him from having direct face-to-face contact with someone who is speaking. If this happens, even momentarily, he loses information that may be vital to his understanding. Writing on the board while talking is a sure way to destroy communication with the hearing-impaired. On the other hand, use of an overhead projector allows continual face-to-face contact with students while reinforcing oral statements with writings or drawings.

Hearing-impaired students are frequently very adept in subjects like mathematics, where exactness and precision are required. Teachers can build the self-esteem of such students by assigning them tasks involving the skills at which they excel and by calling attention to their achievements. Showing concern for their welfare also contributes to the feelings of self-worth of these students. Frequent breaks are needed from the intense effort involved in lip-reading. Noisy distractions that may interfere with a student's reliance on a hearing aid must be avoided. Working out a system of signals for the hearing-impaired student for such things as tardy bells, lunch bells, fire drills, and regular activities in class can take some worries out of the day. A signal takes only an instant of time and doesn't leave him confused when there is sudden change. A similar service to hearing-impaired students is the generous use of signs, in the classroom, in the halls, in the media center. The more these students can rely on themselves, the better they are able to adjust.

There is an impressive variety of visual instructional aids available for use with hearing-impaired youngsters and an almost infinite variety of ways to use them. Posters, charts, transparencies, diagrams, board illustrations, pictures, films, filmstrips, printed materials of all kinds are among the instructional aids available. These visual aids need to be used carefully and precisely, however, to avoid confusing the hearing-impaired student. If, in talking to the class about the duties of congressmen, one is holding up a diagram of how a bill becomes a law, it becomes very difficult for the lip-reading student to reinforce the lip reading with the visual cues. Discussion outlines and study guides that provide vocabulary terms are helpful to this student and should be available prior to and during class activities as much as possible. Class discussions with a number of people

224

taking part are particularly frustrating to a hearing-impaired student. By the time he identifies the speaker, he has probably lost out on what is being said and cannot follow the train of thought. Students need to be aware of the necessity to cue the deaf student and to make a special effort to include him in small group conversations.

Specialized materials for deaf students are becoming increasingly available. Captioned films and filmstrips enable hearing-impaired students to "see" what the other students hear. If professionally produced captioned materials are not available, the existing collection of films and filmstrips in the media center can be made useful by preparing written scripts or study guides to accompany them. Teachers and media specialists will need to work cooperatively to compile scripts or study guides for an extensive collection. With concerted effort it can be accomplished over a period of time. Assisting in the project may be a good activity for students as well. It is an excellent exercise in the use of listening skills and in summarizing. (See Appendix XIII for sources of captioned films and similar materials.)

More and more television stations are providing sign-language interpretation of news programs for the deaf. Teachers should encourage deaf students to "listen" to the news and report back to class. Schools may provide a similar service for regularly scheduled announcements over the P.A. system or for schoolwide assembly programs.

Use of visual aids is important to hearing-impaired students, but it is equally important for these students to learn to *communicate* their thoughts and ideas visually. One teacher was highly successful with a group of deaf children when she provided each of them with a camera and film. They were given freedom to photograph everywhere. The pictures they took became resource material for class activities. Motivation was improved, their ability to express feelings improved, they became more self-confident, and more successful, at transferring learning from one area to

225

another. They showed increased understanding of a sense of time as they began sequencing the photographs they had taken. Their ability to memorize began to improve.(59) There is no guarantee of such dramatic results with one or two hearing-impaired students in a regular class, but these students should be encouraged to express their ideas and report on what they have learned through self-produced visuals. The media specialist can give excellent technical assistance in the production of transparencies, the use of photography, production of filmstrips, and the use of VTR (video tape recorder) equipment if available in the school. Using their vision to gain information is only one side of the coin; they can learn to use it to communicate, and that can open a whole new world!

## ORTHOPEDICALLY AND NEUROLOGICALLY IMPAIRED

Handicapped children with orthopedic or neurological impairments will have the same range of skills, abilities, and learning styles as other students. The same variety of teaching techniques and strategies that are planned for all students will apply with these youngsters as well. The area of greatest concern for teachers of orthopedically and neurologically impaired students is the affective domain of learning. These students may feel very little sense of self-worth. They may have been very protected and may not have a great deal of self-confidence. Their outlook for the future may be clouded and pessimistic. The greatest challenge to a teacher will be in finding ways to strengthen their confidence. It is essential to be realistic in dealing with them about their assets and their liabilities, and not to restrict them any further than does the handicap itself. They must be challenged to stretch their skills and abilities, to accept responsibilities, to exercise leadership; and they need to be given responsibilities and expected to perform. Most of these students will be able to operate A-V equipment, to monitor class activities, to take leadership in small group activities. With help from the media specialist, they can use the variety of media and equipment in the media center. They can design and develop sound-slide productions or give oral reports illustrated with self-made transparencies. For most of these students the major limitation is a lack of faith in themselves. The best course for the teacher is to treat them like any other students, except when physical limitations make involvement impossible.

Obviously there are certain things that can be done to make school life a little easier for these youngsters. For students with crutches and leg braces "buddy system" assignments to take care of carrying books or opening doors, can ease anxiety. Storing materials and equipment where they are easily accessible to students in wheelchairs is an important consideration. In the classroom, in the media center, in laboratories, perimeter shelving around the walls of the room is more accessible for students in wheelchairs. Space considerations are also important. In the media center the aisles between stacks should be wide enough to give the wheelchair student room to negotiate. Storage of standard reference materials and frequently used equipment in the media center should be low enough for the student to reach from his chair. Locker assignments should be suitable.

There are four basic rules to remember in working with orthopedically or neurologically impaired students:(42)

1. Treat these students like any others. Look for opportunities to bolster their self-esteem.
2. Find ways for them to be useful. Enable them to offer services to other people so that they may feel comfortable accepting services for themselves.
3. Accept them as they are so that they can accept themselves. Encourage them to extend their range of activities.
4. Emphasize to all students the right to be an individual.

Retarded children in public school classrooms will usually be mildly or moderately retarded, *i.e.* educable. These children may have identifying physical traits. Some of them may have multiple handicaps. Certainly they will need a great deal of attention and special concern. They are not doomed to failure, however. Often we tend to stereotype retarded students in terms of traits requiring institutionalization. In actual fact, retarded students placed in public school classrooms are very much like the slow learners that teachers have become accustomed to. They can accomplish a great deal if the objectives set for them are realistic and if teaching techniques are matched to their learning styles.

The learning characteristics of retarded students dictate a very slow-moving, carefully structured learning program. A retarded student has a limited attention span. He is usually very literal-minded. Retention is poor. The retarded student needs to learn through a variety of modalities. Learning activities should involve varied sensory experiences. The pace of learning is slow, but it must be steady. Learning activities should be structured to provide a carefully sequenced accumulation of skills and a gradually expanded capacity for understanding.

The need for repetition cannot be overstressed. But repetition needs to be cloaked in a variety of activities to prevent boredom. For example, for word drills flash cards may be followed by pictures the students must identify, using the words orally. Then students may be asked to find the words in books. Later they may be asked to group the words in categories. Students may be given small objects to manipulate, then asked to match them to word cards or to number cards. After several exercises with these objects, they may be asked to group the objects according to their likenesses and differences. This kind of activity can become

228

increasingly complex as the students improve in skill, gradually working toward more abstract ideas.

The reading program for retarded students should differ not so much in the nature of the material as in the *pace* of the program. Vocabulary development should be very gradual. Students should read, discuss, and reread. Teachers should require a great deal of oral reading, followed by oral review of content and drill on new words. Retarded students need to learn good reading habits, and they should be encouraged to build personal libraries as other students are. They should have time for browsing in the media center as often as possible, with careful guidance given to book selection. Books chosen for retarded children need to present stories that are within the experience of the readers. Sentence structure, as well as vocabulary should be simple, and illustrations should be primary and uncluttered. Stories dealing positively with the doubts and insecurities plaguing these children can help them understand themselves. Textbooks for them should be well illustrated with pictures, drawings, simple charts and diagrams. For older students it is important that subject matter and the approach to the subject fit the student's chronological age. Paragraphs should be short, stressing a single point.

With retarded students, there is no substitute for the use of A-V materials. Films are particularly effective when they deal with concrete rather than abstract ideas. Use of a film is most effective as a summarizing tool. It is important that sound and action be precisely synchronized. Films not properly synchronized are too distracting and disturbing to retarded children to have any value, whatever their other qualities.(1)

Unfortunately, there has not been a great deal of activity in developing media specifically for the retarded, and often teachers find that materials on the appropriate ability level are unsuitable in other ways. It could be rewarding to work with the media specialist to create original materials that fit the needs of specific students. In designing such materials, it is well to avoid any figurative language that may confuse a literal-minded student. Vocabulary should employ words that have been stressed in class. Content and illustrations should complement experiences of the students and should be concrete in nature. A-V materials are effective when designed to exercise skills in perception, differentiation, visual scanning, retention, and others that are appropriate to the students. Use of flannel boards is particularly effective with younger retarded students, and with a little imagination can be used as a teaching tool in any subject area.

The following criteria should be applied to any lessons, teachings tools, or instructional strategies used with retarded children, whether they are commercially produced or teacher/media specialist developed. These criteria can be used to evaluate planned lessons and materials.

1. Lessons should be broken down into single steps, learned one at a time. Skills need to be reduced to as many independent steps as possible and learned in sequence.
2. Repeat often. Repetition to the point of overlearning is essential.
3. Allow plenty of time for the completion of assigned tasks.
4. Assign work units that are brief and realistic.
5. Verbal instructions should be simple and precise. They should be accompanied by demonstration. *Show* the students how to accomplish the task.
6. Arouse the students' interest so that they feel a desire to learn.
7. Plan for reinforcement through interdisciplinary teaching.
8. Provide a variety of activities. Students should experience information in as many ways as possible. They need to hear it, say it, see it, write it, illustrate

it, demonstrate it, touch it, even smell it, or taste it if possible.

In classes with a wide range of abilities represented children can work together and help each other. Ways can be found for the retarded child to achieve success and gain the respect of the other students. Let the slow students answer opening questions that are simple in nature, then rely on the other students to fill in more complicated details as the lesson progresses. Keep prepared with a supply of activity folders and simple interest centers to help slow students who need more time for drill. Above all, be aware of the retarded child's need for acceptance and for dignity. Have faith in him, and demonstrate that faith until he can begin to internalize it. Always encourage him to expand his knowledge and never fail to reward his efforts.

## Emotionally Handicapped

Working with emotionally disturbed and socially maladjusted students presents perhaps the greatest challenge to teachers of all the various handicapped conditions they may encounter in students. The expression of emotional disturbance may be manifested in an infinite number of ways. The complete unpredictability of seriously disturbed youngsters makes dealing with them disconcerting. Of course, troubled students who need intense therapy will not be able to cope in regular classrooms. But emotionally handicapped youngsters with a broad range of problems will be enrolled in classes with other students.

Childhood and adolescence are normally unstable periods in our lives, periods when we must adjust rapidly to growth and change, both internal and external. Some emotional disturbance is expected in all youngsters from time to time. When the disturbance becomes the norm rather than a periodic deviance from the norm, the child has lost inner

231

control and becomes a victim of himself. Because of the unpredictable nature of emotionally disturbed behavior, it is difficult to define characteristics of maladjusted students. They will indulge in a variety of behaviors, depending on the nature of internal tensions and external circumstances. The following list of characteristics may help in identifying a student with an emotional disorder, though it is not definitive:(51)

1. Student daydreams almost incessantly, shows little interest in any school activities.
2. Student is extremely impulsive and/or hyperactive.
3. Student has very short attention span with poor ability to concentrate.
4. Student cannot tolerate frustration, seeks immediate gratification.
5. Student is destructive, displays hostility.
6. Student craves attention, is an exhibitionist.
7. Student is compulsively ritualistic.
8. Student is disturbed by, resistant to, change.
9. Student is burdened by excessive doubts, is indecisive.
10. Student is chronically fearful, displays severe anxiety.

Any student exhibiting several of these characteristics should be referred to the school psychologist or caseworker.

Emotionally disturbed students need to be in a warm, accepting atmosphere. Their greatest need is for security. Obviously teachers will need to explore ways to provide this kind of environment for these students. It should be emphasized, however, that *it is not the job of the teacher to solve the student's difficulty* or *to be his therapist.* The teacher's obligation is to try to disentangle the emotional disturbance from the learning situation so that the student can get on with the process of education. (47) The teacher *can* provide external controls, routine, and stability, which will give to the student a feeling of security. In a climate of security he can lay aside his anxieties and turn his attention to learning.

What are some techniques recommended to teachers in relating to emotionally disturbed youngsters? A regular routine the student can depend on is important. Consideration of space is almost equally important. The student should never feel hemmed in. He needs freedom of movement, but within clearly understood limitations. The emotionally disturbed student needs to feel loved and wanted. He needs a feeling of belonging. He needs a sense of purpose. Learning experiences planned for these students should be addressed to these needs, as well as to the need for skills and knowledge.

Emotionally disturbed students need a variety of activities. A varied schedule with frequent changes of pace helps them harness their restlessness. The use of varied media helps them keep their attention to the task before them. Their attention doesn't wander so frequently when the teacher repeatedly captures that attention through varied stimuli. Varied activities must have a central focus, however. Students need to be aware of the purpose, the objectives, of what they are asked to do.

The ultimate outcome of therapy for disturbed youngsters is to bring them into control of themselves, to free them from being dominated by their fears and anxieties. Educational experiences must support this effort. One technique used by many teachers is peer influence. Emotionally disturbed children crave the approval of their peers. A systematic withdrawal of peer attention (and therefore approval) when a disturbed student is disruptive will discourage such behavior. (54, 56) Approval and appreciation of acceptable behavior is likewise a powerful reinforcement. Emotionally disturbed students need the experience of belonging to a "normal" group in order to develop an image of acceptable, constructive social behavior. (56) The group itself can exert tremendous influence on the disturbed

233

youngster simply as it approves or disapproves the child's behavior.

The emotionally handicapped student needs the opportunity to learn responsible behavior. Demands made before he can handle them only exacerbate the disturbance. A gradual process that begins with inviting the student to take responsibility in very small ways allows him in time to shoulder larger responsibilities that are thrust on him. This process needs to be a part of all of his educational experiences.

Some research indicates that emotionally disturbed students suffer from language disabilities, an inability to communicate. Emphasis in the classroom needs to be on making communication pleasant, reading and writing skills developed through activities that are "painless." Other means of communication and expression should be explored. Artistic expression should be encouraged. The techniques of non-print media production are especially applicable as skills these students need to develop. Creating cartoons or caricatures, producing diagrams on transparencies, designing a logo for an important person or group, making a symbolic, historical time-line via frieze or collage, producing book jackets or newspaper ads, setting a poem to music are all examples of activities that encourage controlled expression or communication.

Bibliotherapy is a term applied to reading guidance or directed reading with emotionally disturbed persons. The value of bibliotherapy can be that students read about people with problems similar to theirs, who also have doubts, value conflicts, traumas. They can experience healthy adjustments vicariously. The media specialist in a school has knowledge, or knows where to get it, of books that might fit the needs of a particular child. But careful consultation with any therapist or psychologist on the case would be *essential* to avoid doing more harm than good. It might be that a particular child would be better served by being given stories or books of fact that have nothing whatever to

234

do with his own fears, fantasies, or other problems.

With younger students puppetry is especially effective. The same techniques (without the puppets) may also be applied to the study of literature with older students. Puppets (or literary characters) can provide youngsters a risk-free transference situation in which to explore and express feelings. The extent to which action is structured can vary. Students may enact a story exactly as written, or they may ad lib situations as they go. A good technique is to enact a play intact, then reenact it, giving students an opportunity to "freeze" action and discuss "what if" alternatives to a character's behavior or decision. The same procedure can apply in role-playing with older students.(62)

Behavior modification is a technique frequently used with disturbed youngsters, rewarding and reinforcing positive or acceptable behavior. A variation of this technique requires the disturbed student to observe himself, collecting data on his own behavior patterns. Then he is taught to be his own change agent by becoming aware of cues that precede undesirable behavior and altering the situation accordingly. Teachers should work with such techniques only with the advice and monitoring of the school psychologist. Whatever techniques or strategies are employed, it is well to remember that patient understanding, acceptance, and stability are the framework for creating an environment in which emotionally disturbed students can begin to develop inner control and security.

## Learning Disabled

Learning disabilities are disorders about which very little is known. Neither the causes of the disabilities nor specific therapies for them are understood or identifiable. They may be neurological in nature. They may be the result of brain damage at birth, of illness, or of an injury. Learning disabilities are distinguished from retardation in that they are isolated disabilities in children of otherwise normal or above normal intelligence, whereas retardation is a general condition of slow learning ability. Students with learning disabilities are generally bright youngsters for whom normal teaching techniques are simply ineffective. These are students whose learning styles require different ways of "programming" information into the storage centers of the brain.

Frequently learning-disabled students are identified as "bright kids who can't read."(49) Reading disability is common among these youngsters, but it is only one of many symptoms they may exhibit. Other characteristics of the learning disabled include:

1. Poor visual discrimination
2. Poor capability for retention of words
3. Poor auditory memory for words or word sounds
4. Persistent reversals of words, syllables, or letters in reading, writing, or speech
5. Poor memory for auditory or visual sequence
6. Weakly established handedness (left or right)
7. Clumsiness and poor hand control
8. Immature articulation
9. Poor recall for reproduction of simple geometric forms
10. Hyperactivity and distractibility

When students with these various problems are put into therapy situations, there is no clear-cut formula for determining what methods will help them. Some respond to psychotherapy, some to remediation, some to a combination. Some youngsters improve with visual-motor training, some respond to a combination of visual-motor training and remedial reading instruction. Some simply "grow out of it." Some never do. The point is that with these students every possible technique needs to be tried, multiple methods employed. Development of compensating skills should be encouraged. Exercises that develop visual perception, visual-motor coordination, differentiation, and retention should be stressed. Opportunities for excelling in areas such as art, drama, music, or sports should be expanded.

In selecting reading materials for learning-disabled students it is a good idea to consult both the media specialist and the special education teacher. Reading materials for these students need to be appealing to their interests as well as appropriate to their skills. The style should be straightforward, the action concentrated on one person or event without distracting, irrelevant details. Storybooks for young children need to have meaningful illustrations that help explain the text. Teachers need to be alert for discrepancies between text material and content of illustrations that may confuse the reader. Students should not be overwhelmed with too much detail at once.

Use of non-print media is effective with learning-disabled students. Sound or visual instructional aids that do not require reading skills are helpful to many of them. Action-oriented learning is effective. Breaking activities down into simple, manageable steps helps the student in mastering skills. Frequent repetition of skills through varied activities helps to reinforce learning. Use of tape recorders for note-taking, resorting to oral testing, reporting through use of non-print media are obvious ways around reading disability. Drill and repetition may help to overcome retention weaknesses. The strategies that are effective will be those that enable the student to recognize his own potential for success in learning.

To meet all the individual needs of every student in the classroom will be a demanding job. It is helpful to work with students who are grouped according to common needs. Handicapped youngsters with pressing needs make the demand for truly individualized instruction crucial. There is no formula to offer to teachers for organizing their time to achieve an individualized program. Every classroom is different; every group of youngsters, unique. It is a matter of determining what the instructional needs are of each student, what materials and activities will best meet those needs, and then organizing available time and effort so that as many students are reached at once as can profit from what is going on. Those that cannot profit from interaction during a particular activity must have meaningful independent work to do, whether at their desks, at interest centers, in the media center, or wherever. Assignments or activities that students engage independently at school or at home should reinforce what they learn when they *do* interact with you. It is equally important to have an effective system for monitoring the educational progress of each student so that activities can be planned according to progress. The more one can rely on help from aides, the better. Without aides, students must be organized to work with each other and check themselves objectively. The more you individualize the teaching, the easier it will become. With the media specialist as partner, the time to start is now.

TEACHER'S RESERVATION: I learned a lot from reading this chapter. I did not know that media specialists had so many resources available. This information is valuable for teachers. I think it should be noted that in the case of emotionally handicapped, learning-disabled, or retarded students the psychologist makes recommendations to regular classroom teachers as well as to resource teachers. These recommendations should be studied and implemented to the fullest extent possible. From reading this chapter I am convinced the media specialist could help tremendously in implementing these recommendations.

Trainable students will not be found in the mainstream. They are always placed in self-contained classes. The regular classroom teacher will usually be working with only the highly educable students. Students with a low level of educability are normally in self-contained classes, also.

Criteria for defining LD — determining the existence of a specific LD — is based on (1) whether a child does not achieve commensurate with his/her age and ability when provided with appropriate educational experiences, and (2) whether the child has a severe discrepancy between achievement and intellectual ability in one or more of seven areas relating to communication skills and mathematical abilities.

WRITERS' RESPONSE: We did not sufficiently stress the role of the psychologist in this chapter. The psychologist is a source of valuable information to teachers, and we do recommend that regular classroom teachers and media specialists, too, work closely with the consultants or specialists who can assist them in understanding the needs of any exceptional child.

In the research and study for this chapter the writers found references to both educable and trainable retarded students who were mainstreamed all or part of the school day. Since the law requires the least restrictive environment that also best meets the student's needs, it is conceivable that interpretations may vary widely from state to state or district to district. Teachers need to be aware of the policy in their own districts and knowledgeable about the techniques for working with the level of the exceptional children who will be placed in their classrooms.

In this chapter we attempted to describe characteristic or symptomatic behaviors of learning-disabled students which might be helpful to teachers in making referrals. We are glad to be able to include the additional information regarding identification criteria.

### BIBLIOGRAPHY

1. Aserlind, Leroy. "Audiovisual Instruction for the Mentally Retarded" in *The Special Child in the Library.*

Chicago, American Library Association, 1976.

2. Ayrault, Evelyn West. *Helping the Handicapped Teenager Mature.* New York, Associated Press, 1971.
3. Baskin, Barbara H. and Karen H. Harris, eds. *The Special Child in the Library.* Chicago, American Library Association, 1976.
4. Baskin, Barbara H. and Karen H. Harris. "Storytelling for the Young Mentally Retarded Child" in *The Special Child in the Library.* Chicago, American Library Association, 1976.
5. Bate, Sr. Doris. "The Hearing Impaired Child in the Library" in *The Special Child in the Library.* Chicago, American Library Association, 1976.
6. Bland, Elwood L. "Learning Resource Services for the Handicapped." *Exceptional Children*, 43:161–63, November, 1976.
7. Bond, Guy L. and Miles A. Tinker. *Reading Difficulties, Their Diagonosis and Correction.* New York, Appleton-Century-Crofts, 1957.
8. Brown, Jean. "Storytelling and the Blind Child" in *The Special Child in the Library.* Chicago, American Library Association, 1976.
9. Burklow, Mabel B. "Library Services to Mentally Retarded Children." *Southeastern Librarian*, 20:147–53, Fall, 1970.
10. Cohn, Lorynne, and Charles E. Nolan. "Learning Disabled Adolescents: Creating a Climate for Learning." *National Association of Secondary School Principals Bulletin*, 60:16–20, October, 1976.
11. Cain, Leo F. "Parent Groups: Their Role in a Better Life for the Handicapped." *Exceptional Children*, 42:432–37, May, 1976.
12. Cianciolo, Patricia Jean. "Children's Literature Can Affect Copying Behavior" in *The Special Child in the Library.* Chicago, American Library Association, 1976.

13. Cohen, Shirley. "Improving Attitudes Toward the Handicapped." *Education Digest*, 43:16–19, March, 1978.

14. Daniel, Winifred G. "School Library Service to the Visually Handicapped." *School Media Quarterly*, 3:347–48, Summer, 1975.

15. Dardig, Jill C. "A Visual Literary Program for Deaf Students." *Audiovisual Instruction*, 19:24 + , October, 1974.

16. *Directory of Organizations Interested in the Handicapped*. Washington, D. C., Committee for the Handicapped, n.d.

17. Dykman, Ruth Anne. "Elementary Music Education for the Handicapped." *Education Digest*, 44:34–35, May, 1979.

18. *Educating Children with Special Needs*. Arlington, Virginia, National School Public Relations Association, 1974.

19. "Education for the Handicapped." *Education Digest*, 43:12–15, March, 1978.

20. Ehlinger, Clifford J. and Gail Sullivan Flug. "Media Specialist and Special Educator — a Partnership That Works." *Audiovisual Instruction*, 21:20–22, December, 1976.

21. Ellingson, Careth and James Cass. *Directory of Facilities for the Learning Disabled and Handicapped*. New York, Harper & Row, 1972.

22. Gayne, Eve E. "Educating Delinquents: A Review of Research." *Journal of Special Education*, 11:13–21, Spring, 1977.

23. Gregory, George P. "Using the Newspaper in the Mainstreamed Classroom." *Social Education*, 43:140–43, February, 1979.

24. Harasymiw, Stefan T. "Teacher Attitudes Toward Handicapped Children and Regular Class Integration." *Journal of Special Education*, 10:393–99, Winter, 1976.

25. Hofmann, Ruth B. *How to Build Special Furniture and Equipment for Handicapped Children*. Springfield, Illinois, Charles C. Thomas, 1970.

26. Horn, William. "To See and to Touch" in *The Special Child in the Library*. Chicago, American Library Association, 1976.

27. Huston, Patrick. "Storytelling" in *The Special Child in the Library*. Chicago, American Library Association, 1976.

28. Hutcherson, Ruth. "Books That Help Children" in *The Special Child in the Library*. Chicago, American Library Association, 1976.

29. "In The Mainstream." *Instructor*, 87:132–34, January, 1978.

30. Jackson, William D. "Educational Media in Teaching The Deaf Child" in *The Special Child in the Library*. Chicago, American Library Association, 1976.

31. Johnson, Doris J. and Helmer Myklebust. *Learning Disabilities; Educational Principles and Practices*. New York, Grune and Stratton, 1967.

32. Johnson, Elizabeth and Thelma Merriwether. "Blind Children Learn to Relate." *American Libraries*, 1:168–69, February, 1970.

33. Kennedy, Eddie C. *Classroom Approaches to Remedial Reading*. Itasca, Illinois, F. E. Peacock Publishers, 1971.

34. Kirk, Edith C. "Designing Desirable Physical Conditions in Libraries for Visually Handicapped Children" in *The Special Child in the Library*. Chicago, American Library Association, 1976.

35. Klein, Nancy K. "Special Education: Implementation of New Rules." *Citizen Guide to Quality Eduation*. Cleveland, Citizens' Council for Ohio Schools, 1978.

36. Kroth, Roger. *Communicating with Parents of Exceptional Children*. Denver, Love Publishing Company, 1975.

242

37. Kroth, Roger and Gweneth B. Brown. "Welcome in the Parent." *School Media Quarterly*, 6:246–52, Summer, 1978.
38. Lilly, M. Stephen. "A Merger of Categories: Are We Finally Ready?" *Journal of Learning Disabilities*, February, 1977.
39. Luchow, Jed. "Selecting Picture Storybooks for Young Children With Learning Disabilities" in *The Special Child in the Library*. Chicago, American Library Association, 1976.
40. Mahoney, Michael J. and Kathryn Mahoney. "Self-control Techniques in the Mentally Retarded." *Exceptional Children*, 42:338–39, March, 1976.
41. Metcalf, Mary Jane. "Helping Hearing Impaired Students." *School Library Journal*, 25:27–29, January, 1979.
42. Mullen, Frances A. "The Crippled." *NEA Journal*, December, 1958.
43. Mullen, Frances and Miriam Peterson. "Special Education and the School Librarian" in *The Special Child in the Library*. Chicago, American Library Association, 1976.
44. National Park Service. *National Park Guide for the Handicapped*. Washington, D. C., U.S. Government Printing Office, 1971.
45. Newcomer, Phyllis. "Special Education Services for the 'Mildly Handicapped': Beyond a Diagnostic and Remedial Model." *Journal of Special Education* 11:153–64, Summer, 1977.
46. Norwood, Malcolm F. "Captioned Films for the Deaf." *Exceptional Children*, 43:164–66, November, 1976.
47. Redl, Fritz and Stanley Jacobson. "The Emotionally Disturbed." *NEA Journal*, December, 1958.
48. Reynolds, Maynard C. and Sylvia W. Rosen. "Special Education: Past, Present, and Future." *The Educational Forum*, 40:551–52, May, 1976.

243

49. Richardson, Sylvia O. *Learning Disabilities: An Introduction*. Pittsburgh, Association for Children With Learning Disabilities, n.d.

50. Robertson, Mary Lett, ed. "Idea Exchange: Making the Media Center Special to the Special Child." *School Media Quarterly*, 6:273–74, Summer, 1978.

51. Robertson, Patricia. "Impact of the Physical Environment on the Emotionally Disturbed and Socially Maladjusted Student" in *The Special Child in the Library*. Chicago, American Library Association, 1976.

52. Shaeffer, Florence, Morton Heilig, and Serwin Rubin. "Project 'ME': A New Approach to Media in the Education of Learning Disabled Children." *Journal of Learning Disability*, 7:76–86, February, 1974.

53. Simpson, Dorothy M. *Learning to Learn*. Columbus, Ohio, Charles E. Merrill Company, 1968.

54. Smith, Marion F. and Arthur J. Burks. *Teaching the Slow Learning Child*. New York, Harper, 1954.

55. "Special Feature on Learning Disabilities." *Today's Education*, 66:36–57, November-December, 1977.

56. Strain, Phillip S. "The Role of Peers in Modifying Classmates' Social Behavior." *Journal of Special Education*, 10:351–55, Winter, 1976.

27. Sutherland, Prudence A. "On The Need of the Severely Handicapped to Feel That They Are Human," in *The Special Child in the Library*. Chicago, American Library Association, 1976.

58. Swett, Sheila C. "Math As a Teaching Tool for the Learning Disabled." *Education Digest*, 44:38–40, January, 1979.

59. "Teaching the Deaf with Photography" in *The Special Child in the Library*. Chicago, American Library Association, 1976.

60. "Update on Education of the Handicapped." *Today's Education*, 67:60–62, September-October, 1978.

61. Velleman, Ruth. "Library Adaptations for the Handi-

capped" in *The Special Child in the Library.* Chicago, American Library Association, 1976.

62. Vidler, Virginia. "Use Puppets to Reach the Emotionally Disturbed" in *The Special Child in the Library.* Chicago, American Library Association, 1976.
63. Wearne, Carol. *Tips for Teachers: Recommendations for Teaching Children with Perceptual Problems.* Denver, Children's Hospital (reprinted by ACLD).
64. Wedemeyer, Avaril and Joyce Cejka. *Learning Games for Exceptional Children.* Denver, Love Publishing Company, 1971.
65. Winchell, James F. and Elizabeth A. Lawrence. "Short-term Memory: Curricular Implications for the Mentally Retarded." *Journal of Special Education,* 9:395–407, Winter, 1975.

# 10

## "SUPPORT AND SUGGESTIONS FOR SOLVING SPECIAL READING PROBLEMS ARE MY GREATEST NEED."

In the simplest terms nonreaders can be categorized as belonging to two groups: those who never mastered the skills of reading and those who have learned the mechanics of reading but lack interest in, or actively dislike, reading. The factors that contribute to the development of these two types are usually cited as socioeconomic, psychological, physical, and educational.

These factors present many problems beyond the control of teachers and media specialists. One course of action is to assume the responsibility for identifying as many problems in these areas as possible, and securing the specialized help needed.

Students with psychological disabilities should be referred to a psychologist or guidance counselor. The reports of these specialists should be reviewed and the suggested remedial steps followed. The same can be said for students who are handicapped by visual, hearing, or other physical conditions. For those with visual defects the media specialist can develop a collection of large-print books or secure the "talking books" from the state agency which circulates them. Those with hearing problems would benefit from

246

filmstrips with captions on each frame (See Chapter 9 for instructional strategies for the handicapped).

The teacher and the media specialist *can* do much to counteract both the socioeconomic and educational factors that cause lack of comprehension in reading and lack of motivation to read, which together account for the majority of reading problems. Kennedy has identified some of the educational factors:

Unsuitable learning environment
Failure to make reading purposeful
Inappropriate teaching methods
Undue pressure to learn mechanical skills
Inappropriate reading materials
Inadequate evaluation techniques(12)

Above all is the importance of motivation, reading stimulus and expectation from the home as well as from the teacher. Kennedy states that ". . . scant benefit will result from a program that does not develop a lasting appetite for reading. . . . Motivation thus becomes the first task in remedial reading instruction."

Motivation is defined as "an intrinsic desire to engage in activities that are essential in achieving a personal goal."(12) Carter and McGinnis agree that "the most important principle of successful remedial teaching is motivation."(3) This aspect of remedial, corrective, and also *developmental* reading demands that a strong media specialist role be recognized and utilized, requiring continuing communication and collaboration between teacher and media specialist. Suderman quotes McCracken as saying that "our students are over-taught and under-practiced."(28) Media specialists have traditionally implemented unilaterally many projects and practices to help students develop reading habits and expanded reading tastes. Teachers need to become more involved in these activities and media specialists more aware of reading skills and student difficulties with them so that both participate in planning projects that more adequately supplement and implement the skills teaching. In short, the reading/ classroom teachers and the media specialists in the school building need to see themselves as a reading development team with shared responsibilities for the development of lifetime reading habits.

How can you and the media specialist counteract the *educational* factors which cause students to develop problems and to lack a motivation to read? Those cited by Kennedy seem a good place to begin, and each factor will be followed by suggestions for teachers and contributions which media specialists can make:

### Unsuitable Learning Environment

*Preventive measures you can take:*
1. Have materials easily available.
2. Be patient and pleasant in giving extra individual help.
3. Be encouraging and optimistic about students' ability to learn.
4. Establish a rapport with the student, accept him as a person, understand and respect him.
5. Help students to accept reality. Carter and McGinnis suggest that the student should be "helped to know that he can do some things well, some only average, and some things he cannot do with any degree of success."(3)
6. Allot more time for reading for pleasure.
7. Coordinate reading lessons with other reading experiences.
8. Devise ways to foster the students' need to learn to read.
9. Find ways to bolster the students' self-concept.
10. Plan learning activities that assure success.

11. Promote the students' use of reading in the pursuit of creative activities.
12. Contribute input to faculty media committee as policies and practices are determined to foster a good learning environment in the media center.
13. Develop a flexible plan for the use of the media center by individuals, small groups, whole class.
14. Humanize the conditions in which teaching machines (a tachistoscope, for example) are used. Stimulate thinking and generate an interest in reading. Bring warmth and caring to the process.
15. Consider the whole child, his physical and emotional condition as well as his mental and social maturity.

*Preventive Measures by the Media Specialist:*
1. Provide an attractive, interesting media center environment with many eye-catching displays and projects. Coordinate these with students' interests and with instructional units.
2. Provide places for quiet reading.
3. Exhibit genuine interest in students and in their progress. Seek to know students as individuals.
4. Provide "helping jobs" in the media center at which students can be successful, such as stamping books, serving on A-V student staff, arranging bulletin boards, etc.
5. Capitalize on expressed student interests and provide materials and displays on these.
6. Make the media center freely accessible with a minimum of rules.
7. Organize media of all types so that students can easily locate the materials they need.
8. Provide individual help to students as needed. Stress the availability of assistance.
9. Secure specific information about the needs of certain students.

10. Have a significant role in the counseling program as a non-grade-giving faculty member.
11. Keep an interest file on students and teachers.
12. Display class projects in the media center.
13. Develop flexibility in borrowing rules to meet special needs.
14. Encourage student self-selection of books.
15. Help students find success and satisfaction as they use media.
16. Publicize the media resources so that all students realize that the media center has something for them.
17. Exhibit enthusiasm about reading and share personal reading interests with students.
18. Increase the time the media center is open before and after school.
19. Help identify those children who are having reading difficulties.

FAILURE TO MAKE READING PURPOSEFUL

*Preventive measures you can take:*
1. Introduce hobbies to be pursued by reading.
2. Encourage reading for pleasure.
3. For older students, use driver training, car, and sports manuals for instructional materials.
4. Canvass students for vocational interests and use materials on these vocations for instruction.
5. Allow students some self-selection of books.
6. Become familiar with literature written for and read by students.
7. Promote independent study and disciplined inquiry for some students.
8. Utilize other curriculum areas to provide practice for reading skills.
9. Help students develop goals and keep them informed

concerning progress in learning skills.

10. Motivate students to make frequent use of media resources in the classroom and in the media center.
11. Make sure that students know their weaknesses and the purposes for using certain materials or teaching machines.
12. Teach students the reading proficiencies needed in such subject areas as social studies, science, and mathematics.
13. Encourage students to participate in a program of reading to groups of primary children.
14. Take an inventory of students' interests by identifying favorite stories, radio and TV programs, comics, movies, games, songs, music, pets, and out-of-school activities.
15. Coordinate reading lessons with other subject area assignments.
16. Help students establish their own purposes for reading.

*Preventive measures by the media specialist:*

1. Encourage creative activities which require reading for information, e.g., a sound-slide sequence, a set of transparencies, a video or audio tape, a "write-on" filmstrip, an 8mm film, a chart, a map, etc.
2. Keep students and teachers informed concerning current films, television shows, art exhibits, concerts, and related books.
3. Develop a book review bulletin or a file of book reviews to which students contribute and which they recommend.
4. Put students' stories, which they have used as reading material, into book form with pockets and cards, and circulate them.
5. Teach media skills in connection with an immediate need.
6. Assist students who are engaged in independent study

251

of a topic of interest.
7. Urge teachers to let individuals and small groups use the media center frequently for study or reading.
8. Inform teachers concerning students' special reading interests as indicated by the books they select.
9. Teach students how to vary reading according to purpose of reading and the nature and difficulty of the material.
10. Teach the use of pictures, graphs, maps, and charts as the occasion arises.
11. Help students find the right book to help solve personal or developmental problems.
12. Devote extra time to helping students select the material they want or need.
13. Seek to develop and expand student interests and arouse intellectual curiosity.
14. Encourage students to read to small groups of primary children.
15. During the discussions of books the students have read ask questions to relate the books' content to the students' own experiences.

## Inappropriate Teaching Methods

*Preventive measures you can take:*
1. Provide much individual help.
2. Use materials geared to students' reading levels, abilities, and interests.
3. Use varied teaching methods such as visual, auditory, or phonic, a combination of these, or kinesthetic.
4. Teach the skill in which the student is deficient. Start at student's current level.
5. Involve students in planning and developing activities.
6. Use materials in many formats, print and non-print.
7. Make reading enjoyable, free from excessive pressure.

8. Make a special effort to arouse and sustain interest.
9. Evaluate frequently, and revise program as needed.
10. Provide many opportunities to apply reading skills.
11. Plan learning activities that ensure success.
12. Give students many experiences in using the media center.
13. Cooperate with the media specialist on teaching media skills as they are needed.
14. Keep the media specialist informed about student abilities, reading levels, interests, attitudes, needs.
15. Support the practice of kindergarten and first-grade children borrowing books from the media center to take home at the first of the school year as well as later.
16. Be sure the media specialist understands how children learn to read.
17. Plan for student use of teaching machines, check progress, develop follow-up activities.
18. Support and cooperate with a plan for students to read to small groups.
19. Become familiar with libraries in the area and encourage their use.
20. Engage in continuing planning with the media specialist.
21. Subscribe to and actively support the media specialist's request for more supportive personnel so that there is more time for reading guidance for individual students.
22. Discontinue formal book reports in favor of informal book sharing (See Suggested Ways to Share Books— Appendix XIV.)
23. Emphasize the students' strengths.
24. Discontinue the practice of using required reading lists.
25. Let the students participate in setting their individual goals, implementing them, and evaluating progress.
26. Make use of student and volunteer tutors to provide

253

more individualized instruction.

*Preventive measures by the media specialist:*
1. Give much individual help to students.
2. Coordinate and plan activities with teachers.
3. Develop an understanding of the teaching of reading by taking courses, by observing the reading specialist in action, and by reading professional journals and books.
4. Use a positive approach in working with students, and emphasize successes.
5. Serve as a member of teaching teams and be involved in planning and implementing the reading program.
6. Hold picture book and storytelling sessions with students on a continuing basis.
7. Develop objectives for the media program that mesh with the objectives of the total instructional reading program.
8. Coordinate student and volunteer adult tutoring program.
9. Gear instruction of media center skills to the ability and reading levels of students.
10. Develop with teachers learning centers and learning packages on reading skills with clearly defined objectives.
11. Encourage small groups to come to the media center with a common need or a common interest.
12. Sponsor the research-oriented facet of the reading program: Students define a reading topic, select and use pertinent materials, and produce a report in written or non-print format.
13. Make using the media center an enjoyable and satisfying experience.
14. Advise the use of various lists of *suggested* books on a number of interests instead of one required reading list.

15. Help students select books on their independent and/or instructional reading level.
16. Encourage the circulation of filmstrip viewers and tape recorders for home use.
17. Discourage the use of formal book reports and suggest creative book sharing.

## Undue Pressure To Learn Mechanical Skills

*Preventive Measures You Can Take:*
1. Teach only the technical skills that are necessary.
2. Stress reading for enjoyment and allow extra time for browsing and reading in the classroom and the media center.
3. Provide easy reading materials for practice of skills.
4. Have a recreational reading center in the classroom with a variety of books and magazines selected from the media center collection.
5. Let students talk about the books they have enjoyed.
6. Give students more time to practice skills independently by *reading*.
7. Sponsor with the media specialist a large collection of carefully selected paperback books.
8. Let students record on tape the stories they have enjoyed.
9. Make use of the adapted versions of the classics.
10. Use a variety of techniques in teaching skills.

*Preventive measures by the media specialist:*
1. Encourage more visits to the media center for reading, book selection, and/or reference work.
2. Let students help in the evaluation and selection of new books.
3. Introduce appropriate magazines to students and stimulate their use.
4. Suggest a variety of ways for students to share the books

they have read. (See Appendix XIV.)

5. Help students become skillful in locating and using media center resources.
6. Teach students the skills of designing and producing non-print materials and indicate ways these skills can be used.
7. Develop projects and activities that result in increased student reading.
8. Develop projects that will lead students to enjoy books of recognized worth and to improve the quality of their reading.
9. Send teachers notices of professional books and magazine articles on ways to increase student interest in reading.
10. Suggest that teachers vary their skills teaching by reading more often to students, and offer to assist with this.
11. Review for a class a special selection of books on the students' interests and reading levels.
12. Encourage teachers to record stories for students and make these tapes available for use in the listening centers.
13. Hold workshops for teachers on the books children enjoy reading.

## INAPPROPRIATE READING MATERIALS

*Preventive measures you can take:*
1. Carefully review instructional and supplementary texts for undesirable features such as concepts too difficult for students' comprehension, vocabularies too difficult, selections too long.
2. Check readability of materials by using the Fry readability graph.
3. Have available a great variety of books, magazines, and skill exercises.

4. Foster student self-selection of materials as much as possible. Permit a student to read a book he selects which is too difficult for him. His strong interest in the book may motivate him to read it.
5. Use many mechanical aids to give practice.
6. Utilize every opportunity to support and assist the building of an excellent media center.
7. Participate in the selection of new media in cooperation with the media specialist.
8. Be receptive to the practice of students bringing materials from home.
9. Be familiar with recognized book selection aids.
10. Be well informed about the books in the media center of high interest and low vocabulary and other instructional materials for the disabled readers.

*Preventive measures by the media specialist:*
1. Have available a collection of the most dependable book selection aids and introduce them to teachers.
2. Orient new teachers to media resources for teaching reading.
3. Alert all teachers to new materials as they are received.
4. Involve teachers and students in the selection of new materials.
5. Organize all materials in the media center to be easily accessible.
6. Rotate specially selected collections to the classrooms after consultation with teachers.
7. Purchase books and other media as requested by the reading specialist for clinical use.
8. With the assistance of the teachers and/or reading specialist, evaluate the collection of materials periodically and build a collection which is outstanding in quantity and quality and which is appropriate to the needs, reading levels, ability levels, interests, and goals of the students.

9. Make teachers aware of other resources in the school district for the teaching of reading, and help obtain them.
10. Become familiar with materials for teaching reading and develop a chart indicating which materials are suitable for teaching the varous skills.
11. Provide a rich background of films, filmstrips, video and audio tapes and transparencies, and develop a community resource file.
12. Promote the student use of the public library.
13. Make available an abundance of paperback books and circulate collections to the classrooms.

## INADEQUATE EVALUATION TECHNIQUES

*Preventive measures you can take:*
1. Identify a student's successful activities which enable him to gain status with his peers.
2. Assess students' progress in comparison with their past records.
3. Keep a cumulative account of students' progress.
4. Let students check progress in oral reading by using the tape recorder.
5. Report students' progress in a descriptive form rather than in letter or percentage grades.
6. Use evaluation techniques which improve the student's self-image.
7. Make value judgments without determining causal factors.
8. Initiate student self-evaluation of progress.
9. Employ a variety of evaluation procedures: observation, parent conferences, anecdotal records, questionnaires, etc.
10. Make a careful appraisal of the student's independent, instructional, and frustration reading levels, using informal measures.

*Preventive measures by the media specialist*:
1. Observe whether or not the student enjoys reading.
2. Note how often the student comes to the media center.
3. Ascertain whether the student actually reads the books he selects.
4. Observe how effectively the student locates and uses reference materials.
5. Assess the students' mastery of media skills.
6. Note the kinds of books the students select.
7. Gear materials and activities to reading levels of students so that they will experience success.
8. When calling attention to students' errors, always find something worthy of positive comment.
9. Exhibit high expectations of students.
10. Contribute to discussions of teachers and counselors when evaluating a student's behavior or progress.

The activities described above reflect the eight principles underlying treatment of disabled reading listed by Bond and Tinker. These principles specify that instruction must

1. Be based on understanding of the child's instructional needs.
2. Be highly individualized.
3. Be organized instruction.
4. Be meaningful to the learner.
5. Consider the child's personal worth.
6. Be encouraging to the child.
7. Utilize materials and exercises suitable to reading ability and instructional needs.
8. Employ sound teaching procedures. (2)

Several times in the above lists of activities references have been made to media specialist/teacher-designed special projects and programs to foster student reading. These activities are limited only by the creativity of the planners, and the duration depends upon the type of project. The significant feature of these and a determinant of their success is the extent of cooperation between teacher and media specialist. The teacher is knowledgeable about reading level and ability and can specify relevant objectives; the media specialist knows available materials and can indicate those which will implement objectives. Together they can devise activities which will motivate students. The following are listed as samples of these projects which have been successful. The first three are described in a leaflet, *Reading Motivation and the Media Specialist*, issued by the Supervisors Section of the American Association of School Librarians.(1)

"One elementary school initiated a 'Books Across the Worlds' project. . . . The project began with an international book exhibit which included materials written by the students themselves, books published in other countries, rare books, and books borrowed from community sources, faculty members and parents. Each class selected a particular people or country to study in depth and identified the book which had been most useful and interesting in its study. A bulletin board featured these favorites. A new copy of each of these books was sent with a letter from the children to a school in the chosen area or country. The replies, including some from several ambassadors and one governor, were later exhibited with artifacts and realia. A video tape was prepared and presented to interested adults, including school board members, at a PTA meeting.

"The highlight of this project was a newspaper published by some forty students in the Media Center Club. They visited newspaper offices, book publishers, museums, the TV station, the mayor, and the city council. Small groups went to all kinds of places to get their stories. . . . 'We feel that the program is improving individual reading abilities . . . and offering a diversity of curricular involvement to a could-be apathetic student body.'

"A cooperative effort called *Power of Words* or POW involved an entire school district and Central Missouri State University. Radio and television featured the students as well as performances by rock, jazz, country and folk musicians from the university. Community people came in for a special career day. All activities in the project were designed to lead children to books through other media and to increase their interest in the use and *Power of Words.*"

A special report published by the International Reading Association notes this interesting project: "Senior citizens in a High Rise Community for the Elderly look forward to afternoon visits from students at the nearby Jefferson Elementary School. The students visit the elderly community members for a sharing time, during which the 'listening grandparents' hear the children read, and often return the favor by reading aloud to the youngsters. Deep bonds have developed between the adults and children."

The teachers in this school system used scripts of TV shows as reading textbooks. Students read the scripts before and after viewing the show. The motivation was high, and students gained one and a half years in reading.(5)

These teachers used the subject matter of science and the "hands on" experiences with science materials as stimulation for "experience stories" that were used as material for reading and language arts programs. "Verbal response is a natural outgrowth of personal involvement of the child. The initial interest expressed through experience stories ties together listening, spelling, reading, and writing skills."(9)

The following two projects are described in *Profiles of ESEA Title III Projects*, issued by the South Carolina Department of Education:(20)

The first project focused on the motivation to read rather than on reading skills. The title of the project, *Reading, Response, and Responsibility*, reflects the methodology used. Activities are centered in three areas:

261

1. Letting students read—students are allowed to read the books, papers, and magazines that interest them.
2. Initiating response from the teachers to their reading.
3. Placing the responsibility for reading and learning on the student through contracts.

The project is implemented through multimedia, multi-level learning centers, social studies classes in the seventh and eighth grades, and English classes in the ninth grade.

The second project, *Visual Arts in Reading Development* is one in which art techniques and visual arts are used to increase the students' interests, perception, and comprehension by bringing the students in contact with the objects associated with the words they read. Sensory awareness, art field trips, and vocabulary expansion through exposures to new colors, geometric forms, and textures are used to stimulate student participation in the learning process. Students are encouraged to use their imaginations by making up stories to illustrate works of art and real-life pictures.

Many reading programs have been criticized because they are not related to the world of the students, but Rupley describes a program that corrects this fault. The materials used are newspapers. Students apply reading in an actual reading situation with which they are familiar. The aims are "to help students become informed about the world, learn to read newspapers intelligently, develop lasting interest in newspapers, increase and strengthen skills and vocabulary, develop dictionary skills, skills of drawing inferences, and critical analysis." This program may be used with both elementary and secondary slow and advanced students.(22)

McClosky reports a program to improve reading which was developed for a mixed high-school class from four grades with a variety of problems. Two strategies were employed. First, the teacher projected the belief that the students were able to succeed, and second, a weekly period of writing was required. Students were asked to write for forty-five minutes on their own choice of subjects. Selected pieces were published in a magazine to give recognition to their efforts. This class was held in a reading laboratory with much equipment and a collection of books from the media center.(17) (For other more simple suggestions see Appendix XV, *Suggested Library Activities for Reading, Viewing and Listening,* and *Personal Guidance.*)

Psychological and socioeconomic factors that affect reading motivation and reading development are far more complex and far more difficult for teachers and media specialists to grapple with than are the educational factors, over which school people can have a good deal of control. Psychological problems are often the result of social and economic pressures in the family and in the community. Many psychological counselors, in fact, see most reading problems as being, at least in part, psychological. Children often demonstrate resistance by failure, especially failure in reading, which is more apt than any other to gain the attention of both parents and teachers.

At a workshop on shared responsibility for reading development by the teacher-media specialist team in the Stamford, Connecticut, public schools Dr. Hendricks, a psychological counselor working with children in the middle schools, outlined pressures to which children often respond by resistance to reading. Cultural, ethnic, and linguistic differences, resulting in problems of self-identity and self-worth, headed the list. "There is nothing a child does that there is no reason for," Dr. Hendricks reminded teachers and school library media specialists. "Perhaps he is not lazy, but has given up; maybe he is not so much tough as he is scared." He urged workshop participants to remember that where problem readers are concerned they must work through layers of fear and the results of the lack of constructive adult attention, adult models of learning behavior, and psychological deprivation often coupled with other types of deprivation as well. He recommended the use of games to help children learn to think, to make responsible decisions and choices. He suggested the periodic use of rewards as extrinsic motivational tools for use until intrinsic motivation could be established. Children disabled from reading development especially need a sense of structure to what they are doing, and a way to measure their performance.

A provider of input in the same professional development workshop was the director of the Child Care Center and the citywide preschool program, Mrs. Jeanne Ellis. Mrs. Ellis made a plea for teachers and media specialists to find out about, and utilize as a base for the beginning of reading instruction and interest, some of the experiences with which a young child enters school, the growth or stunting of language skills, and the preschool child's struggle to express himself. She talked about some of the experiences, directly related to later reading abilities, that should be a part of preschool and early elementary programs: storytelling, poetry, singing, reading aloud, playing with animals, and dramatic play. Teachers in her center jot down some of the expressions children use, record a child's speech patterns periodically during an hour of play, in order to find a place to "plug in" for learning growth.

Mrs. Ellis stressed the importance of parent participation in learning and developing a base for reading, and affirmed that even the most apathetic, crisis-oriented, or alienated parents usually respond to persistent efforts to involve them. Parents can be helped, through the joint efforts of teachers and media specialists, to raise their expectations of their children's success in learning, especially learning to read. They begin to take their part in achieving it by talking to their children, being willing for them to bring books home, watching and discussing TV programs with them.

Parents of youngsters of all grades, K–12, should be helped to understand the need for their support in developing their children's reading ability. Too often parent conferences take place only when a child is doing poorly; they reconfirm failure and thrust the child deeper into a defensive, failing role. There should be individual conferences and group discussions scheduled about reading, its value in today's communications-oriented world, and what kinds of support parents can provide, depending on the age of the child. Most parents, especially those from educationally deprived backgrounds who may lack good reading skills themselves, know well the economic and social advantages of good reading abilities, and want them for their youngsters.

Parents should be encouraged to become active in school affairs, such as volunteer programs, grade-mother activities, parent-teacher study groups, school-community entertainments, children's paperback book sales, speakers' presentations, exhibits, field trips, literature discussion group led by the media specialist, etc. As parents become involved in school activities, they will arrive at a better understanding of educational goals and how they apply to their children. For working parents, who are unable to attend school functions, an attractive, simply written school bulletin might be issued each month with accounts of current learning activities and available school resources. Much of this information can be passed along also during the individual parent-teacher conferences, where the unique progress in reading skills and other learning experiences of a particular student can be communicated.

Books going from the school into the homes is another channel of information concerning the value of reading. Students should be able to check out books from the media center for home use from the first day of school. Kindergarten and first-grade teachers might delay this practice for a few days until children have been given lessons on the care of books. A plan should also be developed to allow parents to check out books from the media center. Special books purchased for parent interests could be publicized and a shelf set aside for these. The media specialist should have available a list of books on various grade levels and interests which are suitable for gifts to children, and could offer to compile a bibliography for a parent's special interest.

A workshop could be offered for parents on how to stimulate their children's interest in reading, stressing the adverse effects of pressure to read and the value of motivation. Also, for parents with children in the early grades a workshop on the technique of reading picture books aloud to children would point out the value of this activity.

Parents should be advised of the value of giving their children many new experiences, e.g., trips to different environments, visits to the circus, beach, post office, mountain craft fairs, and the importance of linking these experiences to follow-up reading. Also, parents should be encouraged to watch TV with their children and use programs, characters, events, and places as springboards to follow-up reading.

Opportunities should be seized to remind parents that their children's attitude toward books and reading can be influenced by having books, magazines, newspapers in the home and by seeing them used.

The cooperative efforts of parents, teachers, and media specialists can underpin the sound teaching of reading skills with a strong foundation of motivation to read, reading habits, and a lifelong interest in reading. As Kumble states: "Thus I have grown up feeling strongly that reading for pleasure ought to be just that—free, spontaneous, joyous. To organize it; to hedge it about with rules and lists and schedules; to reward it with anything but itself is to defeat its purpose. The most useful reading, in the long run, is apt to be that which the child does because he wants to, not because he has to."(14)

Finally, it is essential that the *concept* of the reading development team approach be discussed, understood, and *subscribed* to by administrators, school psychologists and guidance counselors, and reading specialists, as well as by classroom teachers and media specialists. Reading skills laboratories should be physically located in or close to the media center so that learning reading skills is not separated, as it too often is, physically and psychologically, from the reason for reading, the practice of reading, and the enjoyment of reading. It is highly recommended that the reading development team of teacher and media specialist play a major role in the formal training of all categories of aides, paraprofessionals, tutors, and volunteers who are or will be at any time or in any manner concerned with reading instruction, practice, or motivation.

Development of lifetime reading habits for students is so important that if the media specialist and the media staff were to devote full time to assisting teachers with it, this could be justified. It is well to remember that, according to recent studies and surveys, a greater number of adults than ever before who learned in school the technical skills of reading cannot be qualified as fully literate. The have allowed the skills once learned to atrophy through disuse, because they never became *readers*. Media specialist and media resources involvement, with the teacher, in the development of reading skills can help to reverse this trend by instilling the lifetime reading habit.

TEACHER'S RESERVATION: There is a definite need . . . for a cooperative effort between parents, teachers, and media specialists in working with children who show disinterest in reading. Motivating such a student is extremely important but difficult to achieve. The suggestions offered in the chapter are helpful.

The lists of preventive measures made by the authors are excellent and thorough. Teachers ideally do not want to give a letter grade for progress, but in many schools this is the required form of evaluation.

It would be difficult for the media specialist to determine whether or not each child has read every book he selects.

Likewise, it would be an impossible task to send home a book from the media center with each child on the first day of school.

WRITERS' RESPONSE: The authors assume that the requirement for a letter grade as evaluation pertains only to reading in basal readers. We would hope that no grade would be given for general recreational or exploratory reading. Enjoyment of reading is the paramount concern in this case. A grade could be counterproductive.

In this chapter we suggested that kindergarten and first-grade teachers "might delay [the practice of sending library books home] for a few days until children have been given lessons on the care of books." The purpose for suggesting that books be carried home the first day was to emphasize the importance of having media center services available from the very first day of school. No rigid policy was intended.

Regarding the suggestions that the media specialist try to determine whether each child has read every book he selects, it has been our experience that a media specialist can often determine this by low-key discussion—never interrogation. Certainly the media specialist wants to encourage the reading of books selected, but again no rigid policy was intended.

### BIBLIOGRAPHY

1. American Association of School Librarians, Supervisors Section. *Reading Motivation and the Media Specialist*. Chicago, The Association, 1973.
2. Bond, Guy L. and Miles A. Tinker. *Reading Difficulties, Their Diagnosis and Correction*. New York, Appleton-Century-Crofts, 1957.
3. Carter, Homer J. and Dorothy J. McGinnis. *Diagnosis and Treatment of the Disabled Reader*. New York, Macmillan, 1970.

4. Cleary, Florence. *Blueprints for Better Reading: School Programs for Promoting Skill and Interest in Reading.* New York, H. W. Wilson, 1972.

5. Criscuolo, Nicholas P. "The Reading Program: Media to the Rescue." *School Media Quarterly*, 1:316–17, Summer, 1973.

6. Dalzell, Bonnie. "Exit Dick and Jane?" *American Education*, 12:9–13, July, 1976.

7. DiGiambattista, J. "School Media Services and the Reading Program." *Ohio Media Spectrum 80*, 4:3–6, 1978.

8. Ekwall, Eldon E. *Diagnosis and Remediation of the Disabled Reader.* Boston, Allyn and Bacon, 1976.

9. Esler, William K. and King Merritt, Jr. "Teaching Reading Through Science Experience Stories." *School Science and Mathematics*, 76:203–06, March, 1976.

10. Fenwick, Sara Innis. "Getting Along With Reading Teachers." *Wilson Library Bulletin*, 45:273–277, November, 1970

11. Gallup, George H. "Sixth Annual Gallup Poll of Public Attitudes Toward Education." *Phi Delta Kappan*, 56:27– 32, September, 1974.

12. Kennedy, Eddie C. *Classroom Approaches to Remedial Reading.* Itasca, Illinois, F. E. Peacock Publishers, 1971.

13. Koenig, D. "Developing Reading Encouragement Areas." *Hoosier School Libraries*, 17:49–50, April, 1978.

14. Kumble, Vrinda. "Root-Room for Delight." *The Horn Book*, 41:247–51, June, 1965.

15. LaBudde, Constance and Richard J. Smith. "Librarians Look at Remedial Reading." *Reading Teacher*, 27:263–69, December, 1973.

16. Leviton, Harvey S. and Annette King Thompson. "Person or Machine in Remedial Reading?" *Academic Therapy*, 11:455–59, Mid-Fall, 1975.

17. McClosky, Mildred G. *Teaching Strategies and Class-*

*room Realities*. Englewood Cliffs, New Jersey, Prentice-Hall, 1971.

18. Inovshow, Rae S. "Reluctant Reader." *Elementary English*, 52:364–65, March, 1975.

19. Paulin, Mary Ann. *A Study of the Materials Used in the Teaching of Reading by Teachers with and without a Library Media Center with a Full-time Media Specialist*. Kalamazoo, Western Michigan University. 1971.

20. *Profiles of ESEA Title III Projects*, prepared by the Office of Federal Programs. Columbia, South Carolina Department of Education, 1976.

21. *Reading Ladders in Human Relations*, edited by Virginia M. Reid and the Committee on Reading Ladders for Human Relations of the National Council of Teachers of English. Washington, D. C., American Council on Education, 1972.

22. Rupley, William H. "Using Newspapers to Teach Reading." *Reading Teacher*, 30:346–47, December, 1976.

23. Savage, John F. "Technology in Reading Instruction." *Educational Technology*, 12:18–20, June, 1972.

24. Smith, James A. *Creative Teaching of Reading and Literature in the Elementary School*. Boston, Allyn and Bacon, 1967.

25. Spache, George D. *Good Reading for Poor Readers*, revised, 9th ed. Champaign, Illinois, Garrard Publishing Company, 1974.

26. Stauffer, Russell G. "A Reading Teacher's Dream Come True." *Wilson Library Bulletin*, 45:285–92, November, 1970.

27. Sterenson, Bertha. "The Role of the Librarian in the School Reading Program." *Education*, 93:271–72, February, 1973.

28. Suderman, Hazel Kirbie. "Accept the Negative, Accen-

tuate the Positive." *Reading Teacher* 24:251-56, December, 1970.

29. Zintz, Miles V. *Corrective Reading*, 3rd ed. Dubuque, Iowa, William C. Brown Company, 1977.

# PART IV

## PROFESSIONAL GROWTH

# 11

## "I Would Benefit From Encouragement To Grow Professionally And From More Information About In-Service Education Opportunities."

There has never been a time when more opportunities for professional growth and continued training were available to teachers than at present. Nor has there ever been a greater need for systematic continuing education and professional development. The knowledge explosion has caused rapid changes. More and more is being discovered about how children learn, resulting in many changes in the educational process. Teachers can no longer rely on what they learned in their preservice education to carry them through the situations they must deal with on the job. Whether through a return to a formal classroom situation and academic work, through occasional workshops or training sessions, or through personal reading and studying, it takes some effort for teachers to stay in touch with current information and trends in their respective fields. Equally important, they must continually update their knowledge of teaching methods that enhance the learning process for today's students.

In most states teacher certification boards have required for some years that teachers receive some type of continuing education as a prerequisite for recertification. For example, a state may require six credit hours of college training every five years for renewal of certification. Many colleges and universities gear their summer programs to meet recertification requirements. Professional organizations offer a large number of conferences and publications designed to acquaint teachers with issues in their field and to keep them abreast of new developments, and some have developed a structured program of workshops and seminars. More school districts are offering in-service programs, collections of materials (professional libraries), teacher centers, and so forth. Some districts have a system of certification renewal via in-service points rather than college credits. In these districts a system for awarding in-service credits is worked out, and a full-staff development program is made available to teachers. (For example, one hour of approved participation earns one credit. Sixty credits is equivalent to one three-hour college course. A hundred and twenty credits earns certification renewal.) In any case, opportunities available to teachers are numerous. Keeping track of the many different possibilities is the first task most teachers face.

The media specialist in the school is a natural choice to serve as a "clearinghouse"of information regarding professional opportunities and in-service offerings. Some media specialists take more initiative than others in informing teachers of such opportunities, but all are prepared to provide this information when asked. Most media specialists can provide quite a range of services designed to promote professional growth. An aware teacher, by becoming familiar with the possibilities, may be able to help inaugurate new or expanded services.

In the general field of education, as well as in the various disciplines, there are numerous professional organizations with their respective publications. Some, such as the National Education Association, are composed of a broad membership encompassing all subject areas. Others are very specific in nature, such as the National Council of Teachers of English, the Council for Exceptional Children, or the Association for Supervision and Curriculum Development. Media specialists are generally informed about these various groups and their activities and can pass the word along through personal notes, announcements in a faculty newsletter, or bulletin board notices. Numerous bulletins, newsletters, journals, and yearbooks are among the publications provided by these organizations to their members. Obviously one cannot join every organization of value, but the media center probably subscribes to many of the publications available from these organizations.(3) These publications feature articles about recent issues in education, new laws that affect teachers, book reviews, teaching ideas, even resource materials. Copies of current issues may be circulated among interested teachers, while past issues are kept for reference or research. Articles of interest to teachers from other publications such as *Newsweek*, *Reader's Digest*, *National Geographic*, or *Saturday Review* may be circulated, or perhaps will be clipped for inclusion in the vertical file. Making known an interest in such materials to the media specialist can insure a constant flow of current information.

Most professional organizations schedule conferences on an annual basis, if not more frequently. At these meetings leading educators conduct work sessions, dialogues, previews of materials, debates on current issues, and so on. There are usually elaborate exhibits of materials and continuous film showings to give participants an opportunity to see the newest materials on the market. Attendance at one of these conferences is usually a stimulating, productive experience. Media specialists in some schools keep a "calendar of events" of such meetings so that teachers can make early plans to attend. Many school systems provide released time

277

for at least a few of these.

Professional journals are beneficial to teachers, and so are many other materials that foster professional growth. Curriculum guides, courses of study or study units, books on pertinent issues, "how-to" publications, catalogs of various media (print and non-print), lists of free and inexpensive materials, bibliographies on specific topics are all important to the professional growth and awareness of teachers. Media centers usually have a collection of professional materials. The media specialist can circulate a catalog of such materials as are available in your school. Most media centers have a self-charging system to facilitate use. For books or other publications not available in the school the media specialist can provide interlibrary loan services. Highly specialized materials are usually acquired in this manner.

Occasionally there may be a topic on which information is needed but for which there is no specific reference. For example, you may want to learn more about setting up learning centers or developing learning packages. You may need information on teaching methods appropriate to youngsters with learning disabilities. The media specialist is trained to locate materials for such specific needs, and can put teachers in touch with various groups or organizations that may assist. It is the media specialist's job to provide this kind of information. Teachers should learn to expect and not hesitate to seek assistance.

Unfortunately, little attention is given to training teachers in media skills during preservice education. (See Chapter 12 for a detailed list of media skills teachers need to develop.) Media specialists can contribute to the professional growth of teachers by providing workshops and training sessions that help to fill in the gaps left by preservice training in this area. One service provided by media specialists is an orientation session for new teachers, designed to acquaint them with the physical layout of the media center, overall characteristics of the collection, specialized materials, types of equipment available, and services provided. During the course of the year the media specialist may organize workshops around specific skills, such as making and using transparencies, using U-film (blank filmstrip) to make a filmstrip, or operating the video tape recorder (VTR) equipment. Teachers who want assistance in learning a specific skill or technique should let the media specialist know. Even if a learning session to fit your needs isn't offered, information can be provided concerning a suitable workshop planned elsewhere. The media specialist may also schedule work sessions periodically to introduce teachers to new acquisitions, to consult teachers on materials ordered, or to discuss scheduling problems. Working through the media specialist in previewing new, commercially produced materials, is a very productive endeavor. The media specialist can help screen possible materials for viewing and can facilitate ordering, receiving, and returning procedures. You are then better able to advise the media specialist when it is time to order new materials for your specific subject area or grade level.

Media specialists in individual schools are prepared to work closely with district and school personnel in organizing in-service programs for their respective faculties. The extent to which such planning is done often depends on teacher interest. If there are specific needs, teachers should by all means talk to the media specialist or encourage the grade/department chairman to do so. Sessions that acquaint teachers with district resources and services are very valuable. Many districts have a central collection of films for districtwide use; some have centralized examination centers for new materials. Teachers need opportunities to preview films before they use them, opportunity and stimulus to use a district-level professional library, supplementary book center, resource center, or whatever. Opportunities need to be provided for teachers to learn what is in a collection, how it can help them, and how to go about ordering titles for specific use. The media specialist is the key to more productive teacher use of all of these collections. The same is true for any centrally located production facilities that house laminating machines, dry-mount presses, photocopiers, collators, and so forth.

Work sessions or presentations that inform teachers on issues and trends in their respective fields are tremendously worthwhile. Such topics as mainstreaming, modular scheduling, diagnosing pupil problems, adapting teaching to varied learning styles, involving parents in individualized instruction are examples of matters of great concern to teachers. Discussion of these issues in an open, give-and-take atmosphere is vital. More specific areas of controversy, like "the new math," the relationship of social studies to the "basics," or the appropriate age for beginning the study of foreign languages, also need to be debated by teachers. Teachers profit intellectually by exposure to debate on issues, but teachers are also a vital source of creative *solutions* to issues actually plaguing school districts, and they should be involved in decision-making about them.

Many types of information about issues, controversies, materials, and methods can be disseminated by media specialists without organizing formal meetings or work sessions. A regular staff bulletin or newsletter is an excellent way to circulate information. A centrally located bulletin board is also useful. Personal notices to individuals may sometimes suffice. Information about field trip possibilities for students, summer institutes for teachers, local cultural events, ETV presentations, special programming on closed circuit TV, new materials in the school district may be supplied via written notice. Bulletin boards may "advertise" college courses being offered, speakers whom teachers ought to hear, meetings they should attend. Announcements about the professional accomplishments of faculty members can also be posted. Circulation of "how-to" publications, teaching models, or resource suggestions is always appreciated. Other services to teachers may include making photocopies of articles, providing work space in the media center for producing materials, assisting in the development and production of materials, holding specific materials in reserve for teachers or students. A particularly helpful service is the posting of a chart (weekly, bimonthly, or monthly) that indicates by teacher the topics being studied, equipment that has been reserved, visits scheduled to the media center, and perhaps even specific materials in use. This type of chart helps prevent conflicts in use of equipment, space, materials, and is important in helping teachers gain an overall perspective of what students are learning.

Figure 10 is a summary list of media center services that encourage and facilitate the professional growth of teachers. Any opportunities afforded to teachers that increase their knowledge, skills, expertise, or effectiveness are important. Media centers offer more such opportunities than most teachers ever realize or take advantage of. Now that you know what some of these are, your use of them will undoubtedly give impetus to the development of many more valuable professional opportunities.

FIGURE 10

MEDIA CENTER SERVICES THAT
PROMOTE PROFESSIONAL GROWTH

I. Providing Information
    —Notices about professional organizations, publications, meeting dates
    —Notices about college courses, summer institutes, seminars, workshops, special conferences, speakers, cultural events
    —Announcements of new materials, free and inex-

pensive materials, field trip options
—Announcements of district-level resources or
services

II. Providing Materials
—Housing a collection of professional materials
including Newly published books and nonprint
materials
professional journals, yearbooks, bulletins
"how-to" publications
teaching models
curriculum guides, study units, etc.
—Housing a collection of catalogs from publishers,
producers, etc.
—Maintaining an up-to-date file of articles,
pamphlets, brochures, circulars of professional
interest
—Development of original multimedia materials

III. Providing In-service Opportunities
—Organizing orientation sessions for new teachers
—Organizing periodic work sessions to introduce new
acquisitions, plan future acquisitions, etc.
—Organizing in-service workshops according to needs
of teachers to update media skills
—Organizing in-service sessions on pertinent topics or
issues such as
parent-teacher relationships
media skills
teaching centers
mainstreaming
individualized instruction
independent study
classroom management
—Informing teachers of district-level or other in-service
opportunities available

IV. Providing Personal Services
   —Interlibrary loan services
   —Material production facilities and assistance
   —Photocopying articles, etc.
   —Holding materials on reserve
   —Setting up chart of topics, equipment, materials, etc. in use by teachers
   —Recognition of teacher accomplishments
   —Assisting in research, planning, production of materials, etc.
   —Securing ERIC materials as requested


TEACHER'S RESERVATION: This chapter is instructive and informative. I agree that staying informed about the many opportunities available is a problem for teachers. But the *real* problem is that teachers do not have time to do even all they know how to do.

I think there is not enough emphasis on the role teachers themselves play in demonstrating successful teaching techniques, discovering solutions to educational problems, and affecting the direction in which development of the profession takes place.


WRITERS' RESPONSE: Teachers must be selective about the in-service opportunities they pursue and the professional activities they are involved in. But selection will be most satisfactory if made from a broad knowledge of possibilities for a wide range of opportunities.

We support teacher involvement in in-service programs not only as learning participants but also as instructors. Implied in our recommendation that media specialists participate in planning in-service programs is the assumption that they know the capabilities of their faculties and can draw on these as appropriate.

# Bibliography

1. Adams, Elizabeth. *In-Service Education and Teachers' Centres*. New York, Pergamon Press, 1975.
2. Clay, Katherine, and J. Jeffrey Dietz. "Building a Human Resources File: A Model." *Clearing House*, 50:337–40, April, 1977.
3. Davies, Ruth Ann. *The School Library Media Center: A Force for Educational Excellence*. New York, R. R. Bowker, 1974.
4. Duane, James E. "An Individualized Approach to Teaching Media Utilization." *Educational Technology*, 12:31–32, July, 1974.
5. Gaver, Mary Virginia. *Services of Secondary School Media Centers*. Chicago, American Library Association, 1971.
6. Goodlad, John J. *Facing The Future: Issues in Education and Schooling*. New York, McGraw-Hill, 1976.
7. Gorman, Don. "Classroom Teachers Use Media to Learn Media." *Audiovisual Instruction*, 22:15–17, January, 1977.
8. Joyce, Bruce R. "Learning Strategies for Learning Centers." *Educational Leadership*, 32:388–91, March, 1975.
9. Mann, Dale. "The Politics of Inservice." *Education Digest*, 44:19–22, January, 1979.
10. *Media Programs: An Evaluation Guide*. Columbia, South Carolina, State Department of Education, 1978.
11. Prostano, Emanuel T. and Joyce S. Prostano. *The School Library Media Center*. Littleton, Colorado, Libraries Unlimited, 1971.
12. Schiller, Jeanette. "Inservice Teacher Training in Media Skills." *Audiovisual Instruction*, 22:58, April, 1977.
13. Waltzer, Margaret Allen. *Library In-Service Program for Teachers*. New Orleans, St. Mary's Dominican High School, 1978.

# 12

## "My Media Skills Need Updating So That I Can Function Effectively in a Multimedia Learning Environment."

The students whom teachers face in their classes each day represent an enormous variety in learning styles. They may also represent great diversity in ability. Some will be visual learners, others, aural learners; some will learn quickly, others, slowly. Some students may be able to learn from reading assignments. Others will need to organize and write information before they can learn it. Some require a great many of "hands on" experiences, others an active, physical involvement in activities; and most students will need a great deal of reinforcement. And all students need motivation. In order to meet all of these different learning needs one must rely on a wide range of materials, techniques, and activities. Fortunately, diverse materials are abundant, and strategies limited only by the imagination. Figure 11 provides a partial list of resources, materials, and equipment you may utilize.

285

## Figure 11
### Media and Activity Suggestions for Diversified Teaching

| | | |
|---|---|---|
| Albums | Filmstrips | Poetry |
| Album covers | Flannelboard | Pastels |
| Artifacts | Games | Puppets |
| Artworks | Gameboards | Puzzles |
| Bibliographies | Globes | Radio |
| Biographies | Graphs | Realia |
| Book covers | Inquiry | Records |
| Bulletin Boards | Interviews | Reports |
| Cameras | Learning Centers | Research |
| Caricatures | Learning Packages | Role-playing |
| Cartoons | Magazines | Scrapbooks |
| Charts | Maps | Simulations |
| Collages | Mobiles | Slides |
| Costumes | Models | Stamps |
| Creative Writing | Murals | Stories |
| Diagrams | Music | Study Prints |
| Diaries | Newspapers | Tape Cassettes |
| Dioramas | Observation | Tape Recorders |
| Dictionaries | Outlines | Television |
| Drawings | Pen Pals | Time Lines |
| Exhibits | Photographs | Transparencies |
| Field Trips | "Pictionaries" | Travel Folders |
| Films | Pictures | Worksheets |

Selection from among these options requires a rather sophisticated knowledge of media. Unfortunately, many teachers are "media illiterates," for two basic reasons: First, little emphasis is placed on learning media skills in most preservice teacher education programs; although instructors presumably expect these skills to be learned, a systematic program of training in media skills may not be provided. Secondly, technology is advancing so rapidly that teachers cannot devote the necessary time to keeping up with all the new developments. The learning of media skills has become by its very nature an ongoing process. As pointed out in Chapter 11, providing continuing opportunities for teachers to develop these skills is one very important aspect of the school media center program. In this chapter the authors will detail the areas of skill and knowledge that teachers will need in order to make the best use of the materials and resources available to them in the school media center.

The obvious starting point is to know the physical layout of the media center. Most media specialists provide orientation to the media center for all new faculty members. But occasional browsing to refresh the memory is useful. It may seem insignificant on the surface, but it is important to know where reference books are shelved, where non-print materials are housed, and how they are arranged, where fiction is located, or which stacks contain biography. In order to be able to put your hands on materials quickly and easily, you should know the classification system used. Knowing how to use the card catalog is essential. The cross-referencing built into the card catalog by the use of three cards per selection (author, title, subject), plus inclusion of "see" and "see also" cards, enables you to make full use of the card catalog in compiling bibliographies, readings lists, research assignments, and so forth. The more adept the teacher, the better the example provided for students and the easier it will be to help students develop these skills.

Some drawers in the card catalog may be reserved for listing specialized materials, such as the filmstrip collection, a paperback book collection, or the list of periodicals available (current and past issues). It is useful for the teacher to learn where the various indexes to materials are kept, e.g., the *Readers' Guide to Periodical Literature*, as well as knowing where the collections themselves are shelved. Such things as the location of the vertical file, the housing of multimedia kits, and the location of games and simulations are important to know. It is also important to be familiar with what is in a specific collection. What recordings does the media center have? To which magazines and newspapers does the center subscribe? No teacher can know every title in every collection, but everyone should have a general familiarity with the materials. Teachers need to know what reference materials are available and which ones are suitable for which groups of students; to be familiar with the transparency, filmstrip, record, and tape collections, the multimedia kits, the print collection and the extent of the equipment available. Such information makes it possible not only to offer suggestions for acquisitions to each collection, but, more important, to make appropriate use of the materials. Knowing the materials enables the teacher to plan meaningful research for students.

Selection of materials for specific teaching/learning is a skill that teachers often learn by making mistakes! Mistakes can often be avoided by following a few simple rules: (1) be familiar with all materials put in the hands of students; (2) consult the media specialist about specific titles or selections; (3) use only materials that fit the overall purpose. There is a variety of selection aids for teachers, as well as countless lists of specific criteria to apply in making selections (see Chapter 6). Things to consider include the credibility of the author, reading level, vocabulary, appropriateness of subject matter to the chronological and developmental age of the students(s), accuracy and validity of content, relevance to specific learning objectives, and appeal of the format to students.

Reference works are utilized by students probably more than any other materials in the media center. Students need to be taught to use them properly. Many are highly specialized. Familiarity with specialized sources in one's subject area (see Appendix XVII) is necessary in order to help students learn to use them. Other skills you will need to help students develop include listening and viewing skills, critical reading, paraphrasing, comparing and contrasting information from multiple sources, note-taking and outlining, compiling bibliographies, problem-solving, analyzing, drawing conclusions, summarizing, and evaluating. Careful consideraton should be given to matching skill assignments or exercises to appropriate materials or resources. The

288

media specialist can assist in making such selections, but it is important for *you* to know the materials yourself. The more familiar you are with the media collection, the more you can tailor your teaching to student needs. The more you use a variety of media, the more you are enabling your students to become skilled in using media as tools of learning.

In making formal research assignments teachers will need to acquaint students with the correct form for note-taking, for footnote references, for bibliographic citations, etc. There are several different style sheets students can consult. There should be a standard form adopted by the school district. If there is not, establishment of a school standard should probably be considered, as this eliminates confusion for students.

Proficiency in the use of equipment as well as materials is helpful. Film and filmstrip projectors, slide projectors, overhead and opaque projectors, tape player/recorders, record players and video tape recorders are examples of some of the equipment you should be using in class. Teachers often rely on students to operate such equipment, but for good supervision, should know the operation themselves, too. Other types of equipment make it possible to produce a variety of teaching materials tailored to specific objectives. These include a copier for making ditto masters and transparencies, a ditto machine, a mimeograph machine, a dry-mount press, a laminating machine, photographic equipment, and a tape recorder. None of these is difficult to operate. If any one of them is available in school the media specialist can demonstrate how to do it. Some districts have equipment to copy slides and other more elaborate equipment.

There are also production techniques to be learned— some sophisticated, some very simple. The media specialist can organize workshops for teachers to acquaint them with these techniques and procedures and/or to work with individual teachers. Transparencies or slides can be made using transparent contact paper, filmstrips can be made using the commercial U-film. Old filmstrips can be bleached in order to make new ones. The media specialist has information about these techniques if they are new to you.

Effective use of media includes more than simply learning how to operate equipment and how to select or produce materials. Careful planning is needed when any materials (print or non-print) are presented to students as learning tools. In using a film, for example, it must be previewed, study questions prepared, explanation given to the students about why they are viewing the film and what they should be looking for, and reactions to the film thoroughly discussed once they have viewed it. (3) The same careful planning should precede the use of any visuals—filmstrips, transparencies, pictures, charts, posters, photographs, and others (see Figure 12). Activities involving these materials should be thoughtfully organized. Sometimes stopping the action on a film is desirable; sometimes that is frustrating to students. Some pictures can be used in sequencing activities. Some can be used to illustrate definitions. (11) Teaching aids should be used only when they help accomplish the desired objectives.

FIGURE 12

SKILLS FOR TEACHER USE OF NON-PRINT MATERIALS

I. Reasons for Using
   —encourage discovery learning
   —develop concepts
   —arouse interest
   —provide vicarious experience
   —reinforce earlier learning
   —enrich reading
   —develop viewing and listening skills
   —provide background for role-playing
   —stimulate discussion

II. Teacher must prepare in advance
    —teacher previews materials
    —material must fit lesson(s)
        objectives selected
    —material must be appropriate
        for students
    —material must be illustrative of
        content, concepts being taught
    —material should reinforce previous
        learning
    —room set up, equipment ready for use, etc.

III. Class should be prepared in advance
    —given objectives of lesson
    —given reasons for activity
    —told what to look for
        all students look for same information
        small groups look for different things
    —write major points on board or hand out
    —write vocabulary on board

IV. Presentation
    —teacher observes students' reaction
    —teacher may use stop-action techniques

V. Follow-up
    —students have opportunity to react
    —teacher leads discussion based on
        questions or directions given to
        students prior to showing
    —reports
    —creative projects
        poems
        collages

Very few schools today are without television and radio equipment. In most schools television sets are available for receiving educational and commercial programs. Media specialists usually facilitate scheduling of programs for teachers. They can assist also in assembling supportive materials and designing follow-up activities for programs that are viewed. If a school has closed circuit viewing capabilities, programming flexibility is greatly enhanced. A few schools have their own VTR equipment, and the possibilities for using it as a teaching/learning tool are nearly endless. However, such equipment is sensitive and complex, and the media specialist should be involved in the planning of all activities involving the VTR equipment.

Figure 13 is a summary list of the areas of skill teachers must develop in order to enjoy maximum benefits of the media center resources. The media specialist is always willing to give assistance. As familiarity with the media center resources develops, more and more possibilities for creative and effective use of media in the classroom will be apparent.

FIGURE 13
MEDIA CENTER SKILLS FOR TEACHERS

I. *Knowledge of physical layout*
    Arrangement of book collection
    —location of reference materials
    —location of circulating nonfiction
    —location of fiction
    —location of indexes

    Location of nonbook collections
    —films, filmstrips
    —multimedia kits
    —periodicals, newspapers
    —print collection
    —simulations, games
    —tapes, records
    —transparencies, slides
    —vertical file

II. *Knowledge of classification and cataloguing system*
    Use of Card Catalog
    Use of indexes to various collections

III. *Media Selection*
    Knowledge of selection aids
    Knowledge of criteria to apply in selecting

IV. *Use of reference materials*
    General works
    Specialized materials (See Appendix XVII)

Information retrieval
—bibliographic form
—footnote form
—note-taking
—outlining

V. *Knowledge of use of equipment*
Computers
Ditto, mimeograph
Dry-mount press
Laminating machine
Photo copier
Photographic equipment
Previewer
Projectors (film, filmstrip, slide, overhead, opaque)
Tachistoscope
Tape player/recorder
Television, radio
Video tape recorder

VI. *Knowledge of production techniques*
Activity folders
Filmstrips
Gameboards
Simulations, Games
Slides
Sound/filmstrip production
Sound/slide production
Sound/visuals production
Tapes
Transparencies
Visuals and graphics

TEACHER'S RESERVATION: Several excellent reference sources
and materials that should be given consideration are barely
mentioned in this chapter. The ERIC system of information
retrieval is available to school media centers through college
and university libraries or through state department of
education connections. Teachers and students alike need to
be familiar with the ERIC system. Public radio is an increasingly useful teaching tool and should be called to the
attention of teachers at all levels. For elementary teachers

there are reference books which give detailed information about the Newbery and Caldecott award winners. These are excellent resources. The chapter mentions the importance of previewing films before using them, but it needs to be reiterated.

WRITERS' RESPONSE: The ERIC system is an excellent reference resource. Radio and television equipment are discussed in one paragraph of the chapter, with the emphasis on television. Radio programs for instructional use are increasing. The media center should have program guides and teaching suggestions for these programs as well as the equipment itself. No attempt was made to include *all* of the excellent reference books available.

## BIBLIOGRAPHY

1. Alcorn, Marvin D., James S. Kinder, and Jim R. Schunert. *Better Teaching in Secondary Schools.* New York, Holt, Rinehart, Winston, 1970.
2. Biggs, Mary. "A Proposal for Course-Related Library Instruction." *School Library Journal*, 26:34-37, January, 1980.
3. Bryan, Sam. "Effective Use of Films in Social Studies Classrooms." *How To Do It Series*, No. 2. Washington, D.C., National Council for the Social Studies, 1977.
4. Davies, Ruth Ann. *The School Library Media Center: A Force for Educational Excellence.* New York, R. R. Bowker, 1974.
5. Gorman, Don. "Classroom Teachers Use Media to Learn Media." *Audiovisual Instruction*, 22:15–17, January, 1977.
6. Harding, Nelson. "Utilizing Closed Circuit Television." *American Libraries*, 1:165–66, February, 1970.
7. Hedges, Sally. "Nuts and Bolts." *Learning Today*, 7:77– 78, Fall, 1974.

8. Henne, Frances. "Learning to Learn." *School Libraries*, 15:15–23, May, 1966.

9. Hopkinson, S. L. *Instructional Materials for Teaching the Use of the Library*. San Jose, California, Claremont House, 1975.

10. Jay, Hilda. "Increasing the Use of Secondary School Libraries." *School Libraries*, 20:23–26, Summer, 1971.

11. Kenworthy, Leonard S. "Reach for a Picture." *How To Do It Series*, No. 3. Washington, D. C., National Council for the Social Studies, 1977.

12. "Living: Pushbutton Power." *Time*, 111:46–49, February 20, 1978.

13. Lubans, John, ed. *Educating the Library User*. New York, R. R. Bowker, 1974.

14. Merryman, Donald. "Mobile Educational Technology." *School Libraries*, 20:24–28, Spring, 1971.

15. Schiller, Jeanette F. "Inservice Teacher Training in Media Skills." *Audiovisual Instruction*, 22:58, April, 1977.

16. Waltzer, Margaret Allen. *Library In-Service Program for Teachers*. New Orleans, St. Mary's Dominican High School, 1978.

# 13

## "I Am Interested In The Design, Creation, And Production Of Non-Print Materials Related To Instruction."

Children grow up in a world in which they are immersed in a flood of electronically produced sight and sound. In view of this fact teachers feel the need to develop instructional strategies that help students become intelligent, appreciative, discriminating consumers of these forms of media and also give them the skills of communicating with others through visual and aural means as well as verbal. Students should be given the tools and helped to acquire the expertise that makes it as easy, and often more enjoyable, to produce a slide-sound presentation as to write an essay or deliver a speech. If these alternate and reinforcement forms of communication are neglected, it is possible that schools will graduate visual and aural illiterates who have not learned to realize the potential of their multisensory world.

At this point it is necessary to repeat the definition of "media." Many people who should know better continue to use the word "media" to mean only *non-print* materials. As defined in the 1975 publication of the American Association of School Librarians and the Association for Educational Communication and Technology, *Media Programs, District*

296

*and School*, "media" includes "*all* forms and channels used in the transmittal process and their accompanying technologies." (24) Thus "media" refers to both print and non-print materials and the various types of technical apparatus needed to record and transmit them, such as the book, camera, and recording and receiving mechanizations.

For years teachers have concentrated on media in print format and have expended much effort in teaching students to decode and comprehend it properly. No one denies that children should still be taught to read and write, but they should also become effective senders and receivers of other forms of communication. Teachers find that the student production of non-print materials often promotes the skills of reading and writing. Miller, an experienced teacher, states: "I can say with some authority that there can be few better ways to teach reading, writing, and oral expression on the secondary level than working with students in producing sound filmstrips and slide productions."(26) The same can be said for elementary school children. (See Appendix XVI for suggested bibliography.)

Although teachers in recent years have used audio-visual materials as instructional aids, they have not moved into the production area to any great extent. There are two possibilities: teacher production and student production.

An investigation of teacher production starts with the fact that teachers need to learn various technical processes, and this instruction requires "hands on" experiences. Many universities offer this type of course, and many media specialists sponsor workshops which help teachers acquire these skills. Also, the media specialist is conveniently available to give individual instruction as needed.

After teachers have learned the "how," they must also consider the "why" before they begin to turn out sets of transparencies, sound-slide sequences, super 8mm films, etc. They should consider whether these materials are useful in meeting instructional objectives or student needs, whether they provide some information not available in other materials, and whether they are too costly, too time-consuming, or too difficult to justify. They should balance any disadvantages with the advantages. Materials teachers design and produce are geared to a particular situation and the identified needs of certain students; they are apt to be more current, important in a time when information is changing and expanding so rapidly.

After the advantages and disadvantages of teacher-made materials have been reviewed, teachers might like to appraise the various uses of these materials. In mathematics problems on transparencies allow students as a group to see solutions and proofs. Tape recordings provide make-up work for class absentees or remedial help for the slower students. In social studies teachers can share summer travel experiences with students via slides or film. Transparencies can bring significant maps, graphs, tables, or other illustrative material to the class. Teacher-taped interviews with resource people such as bankers, policemen, members of the city council, or those who have traveled or who live in foreign countries provide enrichment for a study. The teacher who video-tapes a class discussion helps students critique their performance. In the teaching of a foreign or second language, a slide series may serve as a backdrop for role-playing. A teacher may make cassette tapes for individuals or small groups to pace and explicate reading and may design an 8mm film to stimulate the development of speaking and writing skills. To introduce unfamiliar reading materials or more complex conversational patterns, hand-drawn filmstrips, slides, transparencies with accompanying recordings, will enhance retention of meaning and context and vary the monotony of drill. In vocational education teacher-produced, individualized multimedia presentations combining printed and pictorial material free the teacher from whole-class teaching. Filmstrips in combination with cassette tapes can be set up in individual carrels so that students can learn at their own pace and can manipulate an apparatus while they listen and learn. The teacher can video-tape a student practice of a skill, and the playback can be studied for evaluation. The whole class can discuss a process when the teacher makes transparencies using diagrams and illustrations.

The media specialist can assist with the planning and designing of the materials described above. In schools where the number of the personnel on the media staff is adequate, the media specialist can probably schedule enough time to produce the materials. One media specialist in Arlington, Virginia, during the summer made multimedia kits related to historical or current events in the community. One kit included a correlated slide-tape set, an overhead transparency map, a taped interview with a local historian, a brief study guide with objectives and questions, and artifacts from the historical site. The kits were circulated among classes in the schools.(9)

Students also could have adopted as a project the making of these kits. But when student production of materials is ventured, it becomes a "whole new ball game." Teachers have established behavioral routines that provide class stability and control. They hesitate to introduce activities which turn a passive group of students into active, inquiring, investigating, experimenting individuals. Teachers must be willing to abandon some of the authority role and to participate in mutual exploration and learning. The rewards are likely to outweigh the risks.

What are some of the rewards? The following have been observed by teachers and media specialists:

A joy in accomplishment which leads to the desire for mastery and learning in other areas.
An increased interest in research and inquiry.
Increased opportunities for expression. Students are given the chance to say who they are, how they think, and

how they see the world.

A motivation to succeed and an increased interest in learning. Successful production of materials brings a marked improvement in the students' self-images, and there is a carry-over to more desirable behavior and better social relationships.

These rewards will be realized only if certain sequential steps are taken. The purpose must be clearly established and a careful plan made by the student for every sound-slide sequence, set of transparencies, 8mm film, video tape, filmstrip, proposed. The teacher and student confer about the plan, about background information the student must acquire, and the technical skills the student must learn. The media specialist must be available to advise the student about materials and to teach the skills. Sometimes general orientation lessons on certain production skills may be given to a whole class, but most often the media specialist will work with small groups and individuals.

Teachers must be alert to those students who are not visually oriented and who need the constant direction of the teacher. Some students with very poor self-images may feel threatened by the excellence of some other student productions and fear that their own efforts will suffer by comparison. Although production experiences should not be provided routinely for all students, teachers have found that students both slow and advanced in all grades, K-12, can be successful. The National Society for the Study of Education's publication states: "Teachers who have worked extensively with non-print media in their classrooms report that previous scholastic ability has little or nothing to do with whether a student can handle media equipment efficiently or express himself or herself through film or videotape."(27)

As students begin to express their thoughts, interpretations, and feelings by creating non-print materials, they usually, in their first attempts, imitate the work of others or

300

copy pictures and maps. Later they might try to modify or adapt some materials. Finally, as they become more skillful, they become truly creative and express ideas in an original way. Teachers should encourage students to become inventive and original in their productions.

Student productions fall into three categories. Some are in the sight area, others are limited to sound, and still others combine sight and sound.

Those in the sight category include filmstrips and slides without sound, transparencies, opaque projections, and still pictures, charts, etc. Some students like to make slides and filmstrips and accompany them with an oral commentary. These can be made from commercially available write-on film or from bleached-out filmstrips. The use of water-based, felt-tipped pens makes these films reusable. Visual presentations are simple and easy on transparencies, and students are often ingenious in the ideas and designs they create in this way. Teachers for years have had students summarize their research, describe events, or illustrate books read by making posters, charts, or using other graphic means. Presenting a collection of still pictures cut from magazines or photographs is another relatively easy way for students to use a visual means of communication. Even young children can make photograms. Objects such as leaves, cutouts, scissors, rulers, etc., are placed on a piece of photograph paper, exposed to light for about three seconds, and developed in the regular manner. Many students already know how to operate simple Instamatic cameras, and many teachers, even in kindergarten classes, help children to become expert in this form of expression. Students can also exhibit much creativity in the way they select and arrange opaque projections to illustrate their ideas.

The sound category of student productions includes radio programs and tape recordings. Students might give a weekly radio program on the school intercom or review a new book. The teacher might plan with the local radio station for students to give a short program. In the area of tape recordings there are many opportunities for student creativity. Students might produce a parody of old-time radio shows or produce an original play with sound effects on tape. An activity that stimulates the imagination is the production of an audio tape to update an old filmstrip. A common use of the tape recorder is the student-made tape of short descriptions of books they have read for other students to review.

As students work in the sight-sound area of productions, they have a wide range of means, including 8mm films and video tapes. The advent of small portable video-tape equipment and video cassettes offers many possibilities. In the 8mm films students may lip-sync in sound and put the sound effects on the recorder part of the projector, or a processing laboratory may put the sound on a magnetic sound track. Also a sound-stripping machine may be purchased. However, it is easier, simpler, and less expensive for students to make an audio tape to accompany the film. The film-making or the making of a slide-sound program or video tape can be quite elaborate, with the teacher assigning script writers, appointing a cameraman, sound man, prop man, and also supervising the shooting of the film and advising the editors. On the other hand, a small group may choose this as a project and work out their own procedures. Also, the film-making can be a one-person affair when one student wants the film to be exclusively an expression of unique creativity.

There are many different ways that students can use sight-sound productions:

Dramatization of historical events.

Descriptions of community problems, e.g., pollution, crime, etc.

Investigations of community services, e.g., fire department, social welfare services, government, health services, etc.

Description of school educational program to show to
   parents.
Surveys of community occupations for vocational guid-
   ance.
Documentaries of field trips to show to other classes.
Weekly newscasts on video tape with news, editorial, ad-
   vertisements, and simulated live coverage.
A video-taped game show.
Creative designs or colors on filmstrip with appropriate
   music.
Slides or film to illustrate favorite popular lyrics.
The filming of a segment of a book being studied.

These, of course, are only a few of the ways students can
expand their learning and deepen their perceptions through
the creation of non-print materials. The possibilities are
limited only by the versatility and ingenuity of teachers and
students.

As they work with different non-print media they will
learn certain skills. These are listed in Figure 14.

FIGURE 14
PRODUCTION SKILLS

Still photography (35mm or Instamatic cameras)—for
   still pictures, slides, and filmstrips:
   Preventive camera maintenance, such as dusting lens,
      oiling, care of batteries, etc.
   Preplanning
   Holding camera correctly
   Lighting
   Focusing
   Composition of picture
   Types of lenses
   Shutter speed
   Use of camera stand (Ektographic Visual Maker)
   Editing

Motion photography—for motion pictures, video tapes:
Preventive equipment maintenance, such as cleaning
heads, lens and shutter, oiling, etc.
Planning procedures
Script writing
Operation of equipment
Selecting locale
Composing shots
Lighting
Sound
Captions and art work
Editing

Transparency production:
Preventive equipment maintenance, such as cleaning
and oiling regularly
Composition of layout
Methods of using color
Lettering and art work
Overlays
Color lifts
Use of thermocopier
Use of diazo
Dry photo copying
Use of developer-printer
Mounting

"U-Film" production (writing or drawing on blank
35mm sprocketed film):
Planning procedures
Composition
Appropriate lettering
Art work—use of fine-tipped, water-soluble colored
markers

Since acquiring these skills requires direct use of the

equipment, they must be learned either through experience or through workshops structured for a specific skill and including practice time. Much informal instruction is given by the media specialist or by experienced practitioners to individuals or to small groups.

In the process of producing these materials it may be necessary to copy both visual and aural items. Teachers and media specialist should be knowledgeable about the revised copyright law which took effect in January, 1978, and especially the meaning of the term "fair use." An ad hoc committee of the American Association of School Librarians working with the Washington office of the American Library Association has prepared a media-oriented guide to permissible copying for the schools. "The Committee believes the guidelines are a reasonable interpretation of the minimum standards of fair use. The teacher will know that copying within the guidelines is fair use." A copy of this document, entitled *Copyright, Media, and the Librarian*, may be obtained from AASL, 50 E. Huron Street, Chicago, Illinois, 60611. The Committee urges users to consider this publication an interim guide, since changes will undoubtedly occur as time goes by.

Another publication useful to teachers and media specialists was issued by the Copyright Office, Library of Congress, Washington, D.C. 20559. This is Circular R 21, with the title *Reproduction of Copyrighted Works for Educators and Librarians*, and contains "some of the most important legislative provisions and other documents dealing with reproductions by librarians and educators."

If it seems that certain copying is not "fair use," teachers and/or media specialists must write to the producer of the material seeking permission to duplicate their copyrighted property. An informative pamphlet about writing for permission is available free of charge from the Association of American Publishers, 1920 L Street, N.W., Suite 750, Washington, D.C. 20036. The title is *Copyrighted Permis-*

*sions: A Guide for Non-Commercial Use.* The pamphlet includes a simple, tested one-page form which may be duplicated for school use.

With an understanding of the copyright laws you may feel more secure about bringing vibrant, meaningful, exciting learning experiences to your students via student production of non-print materials. As this strategy is initiated here are a few suggestions to consider:

The students' interests, instructional and personal needs and welfare must be kept at the center of the activities.

Your own caring and enthusiasm will promote success.

Preplanning of the projects is vital.

Careful organization of the class will ensure a smooth operation.

Behavior guidelines should be planned with the class and limits set.

The purposes and objectives of proposed productions should be clear to students.

The media specialist can help to provide the needed instruction in skills. Remember that students who have learned techniques can teach others.

Production activities should be fully integrated with the total instructional program.

A large outlay of funds is not necessary. Where school-owned equipment is minimal, some may be borrowed from students or the school staff or may be available in the community.

Adult consultants in the community can provide much help.

Descriptions of successful production programs and explicit technical directions are found in current professional literature. These will be helpful. (See Appendix XVI.)

A file of student-made materials in the school media center will stimulate others.

Students "learn by doing." Don't overemphasize technical instruction and extensive film study. Kohl says, "Trust the natural talent of children."(19)

Remember that the end product is not as important as the benefit students derive from the process of producing these materials.

Students' everyday lives are filled with multisensory experiences, and they may experience difficulty when confronted with a school curriculum which is overwhelmingly print-oriented. Students may be "turned off" and cry "Irrelevant!" or "Boring!" Teachers would be wise to add new sensory experiences to their teaching and to help students become literate in *all forms* of communication. This strengthens the hand of the teacher and educators generally by demonstrating that even knowing well, and being familiar with, the values of non-print media, they still insist that confident use of reading and writing skills are *essential* to those who would lead in the world's tomorrows.

TEACHER'S RESERVATION: I agree with the thrust of the chapter, which, as I see it, advocates using non-print material to motivate and develop critical thinking in students. However, there are some assumptions in the chapter I question.

The thrust of the chapter is basically an advocation that all children will benefit equally from non-print activities. Yet Jerome Kagan has done a series of studies on the styles of conceptualization manifested by different children, and his research needs to be taken into account. It indicates that some types of learners may not be able to deal effectively with inquiry-oriented, non-print activities. Secondly, the time-consuming aspects are also in need of close study. B. F. Skinner points out that often such activities are inefficient in public education. Often these activities are not more effective because the necessary "verbal associations" have not been taught previously.

I seriously question the extent to which most "media

specialists" have the skills and knowledge necessary to implement the varied program described here. Faced with a general "belt-tightening" in education, I suspect that teachers will still hesitate to venture into non-print production endeavors.

WRITERS' RESPONSE: It is our view that many different techniques and strategies should be used by teachers precisely because children do learn differently. No single teaching strategy or single type of media should be used exclusively. Non-print materials are used in connection with other strategies of instruction, which should include "verbal associations."

Teachers who work with children as they produce non-print materials are aware that the youngsters must acquire a great deal of information prior to beginning the production activity. Some children gain knowledge more readily this way; others may need different activities.

The writers know many media specialists who *do* have skills and competencies for teaching production skills. Where there are weaknesses, all staff members need to work together to strengthen instructional programs. Belt-tightening is indeed a problem. However, there are many inexpensive ways to achieve instructional goals. Numerous articles have been written about the implementation of student-production of materials in an economical way. Using PTA funds, borrowing equipment from community resources, using people from the community are some ways to circumvent shortage of funds.

BIBLIOGRAPHY

1. Belland, John C. "Educational Media; Why Bother?" *School Media Quarterly*, 3:219–22, Spring, 1975.

2. Brinton, Martha. Student Produced Media and Children. Hoosier School Libraries 17:9–13, February, 1978.
3. Brown, James Wilson, Richard B. Lewis, and Fred F. Harcleroad. *AV Instruction Technology and Methods.* New York, McGraw-Hill, 1973.
4. Brudner, Harvey J. "Gedanken Experiments in Educational Cost-Effectiveness." *The Journal: Technological Horizons in Education*, 5:32–37, March/April, 1978.
5. Busse, Norman. "Revealed: How Classroom Teachers Use Media." *Audiovisual Instruction.* 21:45, October, 1976.
6. Charp, Sylvia and Robert N. Sebastian. "Cost Effectiveness Considerations in the Use of a Combined CAJ/CMJ System." *The Journal; Technological Horizons in Education*, 5:42–46, March/April, 1978.
7. Davies, Ruth Ann. *The School LIbrary Media Center, a Force for Educational Excellence.* New York, R.R. Bowker, 1974.
8. Dodge, Martin, Robert Bogden, Nancy Bragden, and Richard Lewis. "How Teachers Perceive Media." *Educational Technology*, 14: 21–24, January, 1974.
9. Doerken, William E., Jr. "Putting Podunk in the Projector." *Learning Resources*, 2:3–5, February, 1975.
10. Duane, James E. "An Individualized Approach to Teaching Media Utilization." *Educational Technology*, 12:31–32, July, 1974.
11. Duane, James E. "Media as Applied to Individualized Instruction." *Audiovisual Instruction*, 19:33–36, May, 1974.
12. Erickson, Carlton W. and Carid H. Curl. *Fundamentals of Teaching with Audiovisual Technology.* New York, Macmillan, 1972.
13. Ferguson, Roy and Jon Shorr. "Seeing is Believing: Visual Communication and the Social Studies." *Social*

*Education*, 40:274; 280–81, May, 1976.

14. Gorman, Don A. "Classroom Teachers Use Media to Learn Media." *Audiovisual Instruction*, 22:15–17, January, 1977.

15. Hall, Karen and Larry L. Palmatier. "Radio in the Classroom: Fibber McGee and Who?" *Educational Technology*, 16: 57–58, January, 1976.

16. Haney, John B. and Eldon J. Ullmer. *Educational Media and the Teacher*. Dubuque, Iowa, William C. Brown Company, 1970.

17. Harding, Nelson. "Utilizing Closed Circuit Television." *American Libraries*, 1:165–66. February, 1970.

18. Harrod, Norma M. "Media Read, Media Write, Media Teach." *Audiovisual Instruction*, 21:54–55, March, 1976.

19. Kemp, Jerold E. "Developing Your Own Instructional Materials." *High School Journal*, 59:332–37, May, 1976.

20. Kohl, Ed. "Creative Filming in School." *Educational Media International*, 2:20–24, June, 1975.

21. Laybourne, Kit, ed. *Doing the Media; a Portfolio of Activities and Resources*. New York, The Center for Understanding Media, 1972.

22. Lum, Lillian A. "Instructional Material Development at the School Level." *High School Journal*, 59:321–26, May 1976.

23. Maryland State Department of Education. *Media and Instruction*. Baltimore, The Department, 1976.

24. *Media Programs, District and School*. Prepared by the American Association of School Librarians, ALA and The Association for Educational Communications and Technology. Chicago, American Library Association, and Washington, Association for Educational Communications and Technology, 1975.

25. Merryman, Donald. "Mobile Educational Technology." *School Libraries*, 20:24–28, Spring, 1971.

26. Miller, Doris P. "The Case for Filmstrips: Producing Filmstrips in the Classroom. *English Journal.* 66:70–72, October, 1977.
27. National Society for the Study of Education. *The Teaching of English:* edited by James R. Squire Seventy-Sixth Yearbook, Part 1. Chicago, The Society, 1977.
28. Opdahl, Viola Woodruff. "Student-made Audiovisual Productions." *Social Education,* 40:275–79, May, 1976.
29. Reeder, Alan F. and Jacqueline M. Bolen. "Match materials to the learner." *Audiovisual Instruction,* 21:24–25, December, 1976.
30. Ross, Samuel B. "Steps Toward 'Visual Literary.'" *School Media Quarterly* 1:205–08, Summer, 1973.
31. Schillinger, Julius F. "Media Are Tools for Children." *Audiovisual Instruction,* 21: 67–69, March, 1976.
32. Taylor, Kenneth J. "Media in the Context of Instruction." *School Media Quarterly,* 4:224–28, 237–41, Spring, 1976.
33. Turner, Pater. "Present and Future Trends for Audio-Visual Resources." *School Librarian,* 26:309–14, December, 1978.
34. Vento, Carla J. "A Peanut Butter Disaster." *Audiovisual Instruction,* 21:64–65, March, 1976.

# 14

## "My Greatest Weakness is the Promotion of Good School/Community Relationships."

There has probably never been a time in the history of public education when educators and the instructional process were more suspect in the public eye than at the present time. Faith in and support of public education are at an all-time low. The Ninth Annual Gallup Poll of the Public's Attitudes Toward The Public Schools (1977) showed a continued decline in the percentage of people who gave the schools a rating of average, above average, or excellent, and an increase in those giving a rating of poor to public school programs.(12) Among the specific groups identified in the poll giving the lowest ratings to schools were young adults, aged eighteen to twenty-nine, the most recent products of the education programs. Public clamor for tax cuts, denial of millage increases to support new school programs, and growing enrollment in private schools are all indications of the alarming disenchantment of the citizenry and its disengagement from active and positive support of public education.

In such a climate it is understandable that many teachers are concerned about ways to enhance their image with the public and, more important, to foster better relations be-

312

tween the school and the community it serves. The purpose of this chapter is to suggest ways teachers and media specialists can work together to improve school-community relations.

At the heart of good school-community relations is the one-on-one relationship the teacher has (or should have) with the families of the students. While the responsibility for initiating this relationship between teacher and parent should be shared, all too often parents fail to initiate any contact until a serious problem with their child develops, if then. You are often handicapped in making contacts with parents because of the large number of students in a class, the small amount of free time available, and the inaccessibility of working parents. So the one-on-one aspect of public relations must be augmented by broader-based efforts to involve the community in school affairs and to convince the citizenry of the value and the integrity of the school program. The media specialist is in a particularly advantageous position to assist teachers in these broader-based efforts.

Certainly a beginning point for improving school-community relations is to learn as much as possible about the community served by the school. This can be the immediate neighborhood of a school, or it can be the broader political community where decisions for financial support of a total district are made. There are valid reasons for being well informed about both. A systematic approach to gathering information about the community and disseminating it to teachers is probably best organized by the media specialist. Starting with a large map of the district or the area served by the school, the media specialist can locate areas of concentrated residence, using color codes to indicate average age of residents, predominant socioeconomic level, sections where there are many (or few) school-age children, major industries or businesses in which residents are employed, and so forth. The resulting community profile can guide efforts of school personnel in publicity campaigns, in organizing community services, and in seeking citizen involvement in school programs.(27) Schools where such a study has actually been done and the resulting information used in planning for better public relations have shown marked success in gaining public support and participation in school concerns.

Most schools have to prepare a written "portrait" of the community served when applying to a regional association for accreditation. The full report submitted to the evaluating committee and the committee's response should be available in the school's media center. The introductory information describing the school community should be useful to school staff members seeking ways to bridge the gap that often exists between the school and the citizenry.

Many media specialists attempt to provide an ongoing community awareness through updated, widely circulated newspaper files highlighting articles of community interest. Others organize forum discussions led by guest speakers from the community. Bulletin boards calling attention to community events and concerns also add to the overall knowledge.

There are many reasons why active support of citizens is desirable, not the least of which is the fact that children learn best when there is a sound partnership between school and home, one in which the efforts of the school reinforce those of the home and vice versa.(2, 19) Cooperation is the key to effective partnerships. Problems in schools are usually lessened in direct proportion to the degree of parental involvement; those problems remaining are more easily resolved by the better ideas and resources made possible by active citizen participation. Where teachers and parents act as partners, children will learn better. Where school personnel and concerned citizens act as a team, education will achieve impressive results.

How can the media program foster this partnership of parents and teachers? It has been accomplished in diverse ways. One media specialist developed a volunteer program

314

that eventually spread throughout the entire district. She began by inviting a few parents to assist her in staffing a story-hour program. She soon found herself swamped with offers of a wide variety of skills. Within a short time there were volunteers tending the circulation desk, shelving books, assisting students in finding books, writing overdue notices, binding periodicals, creating bulletin boards. Some volunteers learned to operate closed circuit television equipment and VTR machines. It didn't take long for the volunteer program to spread beyond the media center. The media specialist developed a catalog classifying volunteers according to their skills, and circulated the catalog among teachers. Now there are volunteers dry-mounting and laminating materials for teachers, grading papers, tutoring slow learners, assisting in reading programs, or acting as advisers to student clubs. The teachers see repeatedly a dramatic improvement in student performance and behavior when parents get actively involved in the school program, and they hear less criticism of education. Parents or other citizens actively involved in schools are not blinded to problems or shortcomings, but as they become better informed about school programs, they also become more aware of the reasons for some of the problems and the complexity of demands made on schools. Understanding the situations school personnel must deal with makes parents and citizens less critical of the school's efforts.

Other means of achieving parent-teacher contact and community involvement in the schools include visitation programs, open houses, and specific community services. Whether through the media center or by some other personnel, parents and citizens should be actively and continually invited into the school. Not many will respond to a general invitation, at least not often, so specific occasions for visits need to be created when appropriate occasions do not exist. Obviously, American Education Week, National Library Week, and similar observances afford ready-made oppor-

315

tunities to invite the public in. But book fairs, craft displays, musical programs, open houses, etc., can provide equally good occasions for visits. The more often people from the community come into the schools to see firsthand what is going on, the more involved and supportive they will become. Book fairs and craft shows can have the added advantage of being fund-raising activities to benefit school clubs or organizations, and they are also ways to encourage student reading and student creativity.

One secondary media program achieved very favorable public notice through its forum series. Periodically the media specialist circulated notices that a guest speaker would appear in the forum for lecture and discussion on a given topic (these varied each week). Students who were not behind on their work and who had shown interest in the week's topic were given permission by teachers to attend the discussion. Topics varied from such current issues as minority rights to the phenomenon of eclipses of the sun to reviews of best seller titles. The discussions were well attended. Guest speakers left the school impressed by the students' interest and ideas. The students got to know adults from the community they would not have known otherwise. And parents were pleased that the discussions stimulated serious thinking and debate on the part of the students. The effort of organizing the program paid off in positive repercussions in the community. Teachers and the media specialist can work effectively together to organize this type of program. It is probably preferable to allow students to select topics (in consultation with teachers), invite speakers, and generally organize the forum sessions. These sessions should be scheduled as often as is compatible with maximum interest and involvement. Since media centers are usually centrally located within the school building, the media specialist is in an ideal position to publicize the sessions, and to locate books and articles related to the current topic for students to read either in advance of or as a follow-up to the discussion session.

Much more widespread in school districts is maintenance of the community resource file, a classified list of people in the community who will speak to students in regular classes on subjects in which they have expertise. The file also lists places in the community which have educative value and are recommended for students to visit. Bankers will talk on interest rates to economics classes. Authors discuss writing styles with English classes. An industrial chemist will demonstrate safety techniques in a chemistry lab. A good media specialist keeps an updated list and makes recommendations to teachers about the approach or the effectiveness of a specific speaker for a particular group of students. The by-product of the successful use of community human resources is similar to that of the forum series described above. The gap between school and community is bridged, if not eliminated.

The media center can provide a variety of services on behalf of the school to the community that will enhance the relations of the two and encourage a sense of "ownership" in the public—the feeling that this is *their* school and that their interests are at stake in multiple ways. The use of school facilities for community meetings, for recreational activities, or for adult education is common to many districts around the country. The problems that arise in providing these services, however, can sometimes prove to be insurmountable. Media center services provided on a more modest scale prove to be more manageable, yet yield very satisfying benefits.

One of the most effective community services offered by a school media center is a story hour for preschool age children. This is *not* a baby-sitting service, but it does free mothers for a while, perhaps to do volunteer work in other parts of the school while the young children are attending the story hour. Starting preschool children in an enjoyment of a reading program pays big dividends when they start to school and accustoms them to the media center, its organization, its resources.

Another service that can be provided to the community is an extended-hours program when the media center is open and accessible to students and their families. Professionals are often unable to man the media center after regular school hours, so this service can be provided by community volunteers who are under the supervision of the media specialist. This service is particularly important in secondary schools where teachers are likely to assign research or independent study projects and which require evening hours, and the accessibility of the media center to busy students becomes a problem. If such a service is not normally provided, teachers and the media specialist might work together to provide it on a temporary basis when such projects have been assigned.

Teachers and the media specialist should also collaborate in planning training sessions for school volunteers. Many schools request the assistance of volunteers without providing much training or direction. Proper use of A-V equipment, an explanation of the school schedule and organization, methods of record-keeping, and many other skills or areas of information need to be provided to volunteers if their assistance is to be really meaningful and effective in the media center or classroom.

A number of media specialists have received recognition from the public for information services provided. Newsletters to parents are particularly appreciated. A newsletter can contain book reviews, movie reviews, recommended reading suggestions for specific age groups, annotated bibliographies on pertinent topics, a calendar of events, announcements of new acquisitions, even recommendations for games or records that have educational value. Alerted by teachers concerning subject or content areas about which students should be reading at a given time, the media specialist can select appropriate recommendations for inclusion in the newsletter. Any of the features of a newsletter listed above can be published individually for parents by teachers and media specialists alike. Informal afternoon or evening sessions with parents telling them about what their children are learning, about skills they need to develop, or about books they should be reading are very valuable. Home-teaching packages designed to help parents coach children in specific content or skill areas could be available for check-out use.(18) Any information given to parents by school personnel which enables them to help their children is always a plus in public relations.

Recently in New York State a symposium was held for administrators, teachers, librarians, and community members on the "School Library Media Center: A Powerful Force for Learning."(28) It could serve as a model for similar programs in community schools. The participants—educators, parents, community leaders—were the planners and organizers. Seminars planned by educators, parents, professionals, and community leaders on such topics as parenting skills, parent-teacher partnerships, the effects of TV on children, the value of a sensible diet, and many other issues could be enormously productive in many important ways. Teachers provide the impetus for organizing such seminars, perhaps in cooperation with the media specialist, perhaps through the PTA organization, or through other channels. Public involvement in solving such problems as vandalism, absenteeism, and declining test scores is badly needed.(17) Teachers and media specialists willing to take the lead in organizing opportunities for input from the public will enjoy the cooperative spirit that such teamwork engenders.

If there is resistance by the public to coming into the schools to see what is going on, then perhaps the school needs to go to the public. More than one teacher has met with success in taking a presentation of a school program to civic

319

groups around the community. Even more effective is a student-made A-V presentation which highlights the diverse programs of a school, the accomplishments of students, and the hopes of students for the future. Such a presentation is usually welcomed by civic organizations of all types. Teachers, media specialist, and students can work together, and enlist the advice and interest of the principal, to develop a presentation that informs the public of the strengths of the school program and highlights ways in which community involvement can improve and enhance it.

Proposition 13 in California and its counterparts in other states have caused citizens and politicians to look at places where tax support can be cut. One prime target, of course, is the schools. The inefficiency of the nine-month calendar and the overlapping of services of school and public libraries are among frequently cited problems which directly affect school media services. A broader concept of the role of public schools in a community education program is developing, and this may mean that major changes in education are coming. Meanwhile, teachers and media specialists can meet some public criticism by fostering cooperation between school and public libraries and may at the same time be able to help the public see how these two programs are inherently different and complementary. Some areas where cooperation needs to be encouraged include provisions for interlibrary loan services, planning for materials acquisitions, development of summer reading programs for students, joint use of film and filmstrip collections, and combined in-service programs designed to help school and public library personnel work together more effectively.(11)

A final word needs to be said regarding action-learning projects in the community. At a time when poor public relations are matched by apathy among students who see education as irrelevant, action-learning projects offer at least one way of addressing both problems simultaneously. Action-learning projects are those programs which take students

out of the classroom and put them to work in the community providing needed services or helping to find solutions to
community problems.(3) Educators and community
members alike need to study the feasibility of such projects
and move positively toward the tapping of student talents in
meeting community needs.

Good school-community relations will come about only
when all involved—educators, students, parents, and non-
parent citizens—are satisfied with the value and the product of the educational system. The teacher can do many
small things to reach out into the community and establish
positive contacts, and in concert with the media specialist
and with other teachers can extend the reach into the community. If all parties together were to work toward productive educative programs, we would not only bridge the gap,
but perhaps be able to eliminate it altogether.

TEACHER'S RESERVATIONS: This chapter is filled with sound
goals for any media specialist. It is to be hoped that one outcome of such an endeavor could be improved school/com-
munity relationships.

WRITERS' RESPONSE: We intended to point out that the goal of
improved school/community relations should be every
teacher's goal as well as the goal of the media specialist. The
teacher may be the catalyst for inaugurating some media
center services to the community. Even where a strong program of media center services is not provided there are ways
the teacher can work to improve school/community relationships.

## BIBLIOGRAPHY

1. Abramowitz, Elizabeth A. "When Parent Cares About
   School, So Does Child." *Christian Science Monitor*,
   March 6, 1978.

2. Anselmo, Sandra. "Parent Involvement in the Schools." *Clearing House*, 50:297–99, March, 1977.

3. Aronstein, L. W. and E. G. Olsen. *Action Learning: Student Community Service Projects*. Washington, D.C., Association for Supervision and Curriculum Development, 1974.

4. Ascough, Larry. "Reconnecting the School and the Community: Mission Possible," *National Association of Secondary School Principals Bulletin*, 63:58–64, January, 1979.

5. Balzek, Ron. *Influencing Students Toward Media Center Use*. Chicago, American Library Association, 1975.

6. Barron, Daniel. "Role of the School Media Program and Specialist in Community Education." *School Media Quarterly*, 7:12–17, Fall, 1978.

7. "Blueprint Suggested to Revise School Concepts." *Christian Science Monitor*, May 18, 1978.

8. Byrne, Robert, and Edward Powell. *Strengthening School-Community Relations*. Reston, Virginia, National Association of Secondary School Principals, 1976.

9. Chang, Robert L. "A Systematic Approach to Your P.R. Program." *Audiovisual Instruction*, 22:20–21, February, 1977.

10. "The Changing Picture of School-Community Relations." *Education Digest*, 45:6–9, November, 1979.

11. Fleming, Lois. "Public and School Libraries: Partners in The Big Picture." *School Media Quarterly*, 7:25–30, Fall, 1978.

12. Gallup, George H. "Ninth Annual Gallup Poll of the Public's Attitudes toward the Public Schools," *Phi Delta Kappan*, September, 1977.

13. Gelms, Kenneth J. "The Overlooked Communications Tool: Building-level Publications." *NASSP Bulletin*, 63:39-45, January, 1979.

14. Giondomenica, William T. "What Makes A Good

Media Center?" *The Instructor*, 85:64, November, 1975.

15. Goodlad, John J. *Facing the Future: Issues in Education and Schooling.* New York, McGraw-Hill, 1976.

16. Henne, Frances. "Learning to Learn." *School Libraries*, 15:15-23, May, 1966.

17. Hitchens, Howard B. "Technology, Libraries and Public Relations." *Audiovisual Instruction*, 22:9-16, February, 1977.

18. "Home Teaching Packages for Parents." *Audiovisual Instruction*, 21:45, December, 1976.

19. Hover, Margot. "School as a Resource for Families." *Clearing House*, 50:415-16, May, 1977.

20. Hug, William E. *Instructional Design and Media Program.* Chicago, American Library Association, 1975.

21. McCauley, Elfrieda. "Volunteers? Yes!" *School Library Journal*, 22:29-33, May, 1976.

22. Neal, Marnie. "Education: Today and Tommorrow." *School and Community*, 61:8.39, May, 1975.

23. Ossefort, Joan. "Teamwork Tells at Woodrow Wilson Junior High Library." *Illinois Libraries*, 58:363-65, September, 1976.

24. Schmid, William T. "P.R. Techniques for Media Center Managers." *Audiovisual Instruction*, 22:54-61, February, 1977.

25. Stroud, Janet. "The Shape of Public Relations: Performance Plus Communication." *Audiovisual Instruction*, 22:16-17, February, 1977.

26. Sullivan, Tim. 'What Makes a Good Media Center?" *The Instructor*, 85:65-66, November, 1975.

27. Tait, Susan F. "In the YA Corner." *School Library Journal*, 24:42, February, 1978.

28. Thomas, Lucille T. "Insights: School Library Media Program Support." *School Library Journal*, 23:19-25, September, 1976.

# Summary of Guidelines For Use of Media Center

The following list is a summary of the principles included in this handbook for teachers. With these principles as guidelines, you should find that use of the services and resources of the media center constitutes an invaluable element of the instructional program.

1. Communicate periodically with the media specialist on an ongoing basis.
2. Become knowledgeable about materials and related equipment in the media center relevant to your subject area.
3. Become informed about the variety of media services now available, and request those that should be available.
4. Involve the media specialist in designing programs of study for individuals and small groups.
5. Seek assistance from the media specialist in creating individual programs of study for students with special needs.
6. Plan with the media specialist in developing new units or study programs.
7. Consult and cooperate with the media specialist in teaching media skills.
8. Seek assistance from the media specialist in updating

your own media skills.

9. Plan cooperatively with the media specialist in designing special projects.
10. Include the media specialist in all departmental planning sessions.
11. Encourage media center programs that promote establishing the habit of reading for pleasure and enjoyment.
12. Extend students' ability to communicate in a multimedia world by providing many experiences in using and producing non-print materials.
13. Provide many opportunities for purposeful student use of media resources to assure complete integration within the instructional program.
14. Solicit input from the media specialist on the evaluation of progress in the instructional program.
15. Participate in efforts of the media specialist to evaluate and improve the media program.
16. Use the services of the media specialist to keep informed about opportunities for professional growth.
17. Participate with the media specialist in activities to improve school community relations.

# APPENDIXES

# I

## Selected References On Learning Packages

Blackburn, Jack E. and W. Conrad Powell, *One at a Time All at Once. Teachers' Guide to Individualized Instruction without Anarchy.* Pacific Palisades, California, Goodyear Publishing Company, 1976.

Duke, C. R. "Learning Activity Package: Discovering Dialects." *English Journal,* 62:432–40, March, 1973.

Dunn, Rita Stafford and Kenneth Dunn. *Practical Approaches to Individualized Instruction: Contracts and Other Effective Teaching Strategies.* West Nyack, New York, Parker Publishing Company, 1972.

Dunn, R. and K. Dunn. "Seeing, Hearing, Moving, Touching Learning Packages." *Teacher,* 94:48–51, May, 1977.

Gibbons, Maurice and Gary Phillips. "Case for Negotiated Learning Contracts." *National Association of Secondary School Principals Bulletin* 63:66 ff. December, 1979

Hoffer, Beth. "Planning A Contract-based Reading Program." *School Library Journal* 26:40–41, 1979.

Jackson, Pat. *The Writer's LAP.* Fort Lauderdale, Florida, Educational Associates, 1971.

Johnson, Stuart R. and Rita B. Johnson. *Developing Individualized Instructional Material: A Self-Instructional Material in Itself.* Palo Alto, California, Westinghouse

Learning Press, 1970.

Kapfer, Philip G. and Glen F. Ovard. *Preparing and Using Individualized Learning Packages for Upgraded, Continuous Progress Education.* Englewood Cliffs, New Jersey, Educational Technology Publications, 1971.

Miller, J. R. and P. A. Gonyar. "Learning Activity Packages." *Social Studies*, 65:120–25, March, 1974.

Raymond, A. R. "Contract as an Alternative." *Social Studies*, 66:54–55, March, 1975.

Smith, James E. *The Activity Package.* Fort Lauderdale, Florida, Educational Associates, 1971.

Talbert, E. Gene and Larry E. Frase. *Individualized Instruction: A Book of Readings.* Columbus, Ohio, Charles E. Merrill Publishing Company, 1972.

# II

## SELECTED REFERENCES ON LEARNING CENTERS

Bierly, K. "Taking a New Look at Learning Centers." *The Instructor*, 87:80+ January, 1978.

Candler, Ann C. and Virginia Sowell. "Gameplan for Learning Centers: Steps to Achievement. *Reading Improvement* 16:215–18 Fall, 1979.

Creating Learning Centers: Ideas for Language Arts, Math, Science, and Social Studies. (Card File) Set 1; Intermediate Level, 1973; Set 2. Primary Level, 1974. Monterey Park, California, Creative Teaching Press, nd.

Don, Sue and others. *Individualizing Reading Instruction with Learning Stations and Centers.* Riverside Learning Association, 1973.

Forte, Imogene and Joy Mackenzie. *Nooks, Crannies, and Corners.* Nashville, Incentive Publications, 1972.

Forte, Imogene, Mary Ann Pangle and Robbie Tupa. *Pumpkins, Pinwheels, and Peppermint Packages: Learning Centers to Make Every Day a Special Day.* Nashville, Incentive Publications, 1974.

Greff, Kasper N. and Eunice N. Askov. *Learning Centers: An Idea Book for Reading and Language Arts.* Dubuque, Iowa, Kendall/Hunt, 1974

Guenther, John and Patricia Hansen. "Social Studies Activity Centers." *Social Studies*, 68:65–69 March, 1977.

Hirschman, Dorothy. "Center Center; Learning Centers." *Learning* 8:40 April, 1980.

Horton, Lowell and Phyllis Horton. *The Learning Center: Heart of the School.* Minneapolis, Denison, 1973.

Jernigan, M. L. "Centers Approach to Reading Instruction." *Elementary English* 51:859–60, September, 1974

McCarthy, M. M. "How and Why of Learning Centers." *Elementary School Journal,* 77:292–99, March, 1977.

Manning, Patricia. "Creating Science Inquiry Centers." *Science and Children* 17:37 April, 1980.

Ukens, L.L. "Learning Stations and Science Teaching." *Science and Children,* 14:13–14, November, 1976.

Vacca, J.A.L. "Learning Stations: How to in the Middle Grades." *Journal of Reading,* 19:563–67, April, 1976.

Voight, Ralph Claude. *Invitation to Learning 1. Invitation to Learning 2.* Washington, D. C., Acropolis Books, 1974.

# III-A

## Independent Study Guidelines for Students

As independent study students you have been given special privileges, but along with these privileges come certain responsibilities. You are expected to use your time wisely and to organize your work efficiently. You should also avoid interfering with the work of other independent study students or students who are working in the media center. This doesn't mean that if two of you are working on the same topic, you cannot confer with each other quietly for short periods of time. It is a good idea, as we discussed earlier, to utilize the carrels for your work. By doing this, other students will not disturb you and you can work more effectively.

If you have difficulty in locating resources or material, you should contact any member of the media staff and/or your adviser for assistance. You should become aware of all resources in the media center that can help you in your independent study project. This means check the card catalog carefully, review the pamphlet file thoroughly, and use the *Readers' Guide* to see if there are magazine articles applicable to your work.

Another point that should be emphasized is the use of community resources and field trips. Several of you have done outstanding work in this area. As you schedule field trips or interviews, remember to speak slowly and clearly. One appropriate way to begin your telephone conversation is:

"Hello, this is Robert Ector. I am an eighth grader at GJHS, and I am working on an independent study project. The topic of my project is 'Sports and Recreation in South Carolina.' If possible, I am interested in arranging an interview with you. Would you suggest some appropriate dates and times? Thank you for your help." (Always add this remark at the end of your conversation.)

After returning from an interview or a field trip, you are reminded that two things must be done. First, a letter thanking the individual, group, or organization with whom you met should be written. This helps to promote a good image of our school and to insure that if other students would like to utilize this same resource, it may be arranged. The secretary of the media staff will be glad to help you in locating addresses and organizing your letter. Next, two written evaluations of the field trip should be completed. One copy should be filed with me, and the second one should be included in your written report. This should be done regardless of the type of community resource you use. Please include your opinion of the value of this resource. Also, three outside activities per student should be sufficient.

Finally, I want to compliment you on your work up to this point. There are some areas in which we can improve, but you have accomplished some very good things thus far. Let's continue to work hard.

INDEPENDENT STUDY COORDINATOR

# III-B

## COMMITMENT OF TEACHER-CONSULTANT

I have seen and approved _____'s plan of Independent Study. I understand that if accepted, the student will be released from his class obligation to undertake this study on a full-time basis. I agree to serve as his teacher-consultant for this project and understand that he/she will check with me at least two times weekly to keep me informed on his progress and so that I may offer advice and suggestions for continuance of his project. I will serve as part of the committee which evaluates this student during the week of _____ . Please return this commitment to the Coordinator of Independent Study.

_____          _____

Teacher-Consultant's Signature                              Date

# III-C

## Teacher Recommendation Form

Student's Name _____

Independent Study Topic _____

    The student above is applying for Independent Study, a program of self-directed learning.

    Will you please help us evaluate the student by completing this recommendation form and returning it to Miss Lochridge no later than _____ .

The information you provide will remain confidential

    Thank you.

Course for which you have this student: _____

Grade student is now making in your class: _____

1. Does he require much assistance in organizing ideas? Materials? or does he take initiative and make decisions regarding his work?

2. Does he regularly attend your class?

3. Is the student a leader in class discussion?

4. Is he able to maintain interest in long-term projects?

5. Does he possess imagination and originality?

6. Do you feel this student is reliable and responsible when left on his own?

7. Do you consider him an acceptable candidate for the Independent Study program?

# III-D

## INDEPENDENT STUDY APPLICATION

Name: _____

Date: _____ Address: _____

Parent Approval: _____ Committee Approval:_____

Topic for Study:_____

Teacher Consultant: _____

As well as written evidence of the work you do in independent study, you must also present oral, visual, or aural evidence of your work. Which of these forms do you anticipate your final presentation will take? _____

Please fill in your schedule for the current semester:

| PERIOD | COURSE | TEACHER |
|--------|--------|---------|
|        |        |         |
|        |        |         |
|        |        |         |
|        |        |         |
|        |        |         |

Give a brief outline or explanation of your plan for this study. (Use back of this page for additional comments.)

Signatures of approval of application:
I approve this applicant's participation in Independent Study.

_____          _____
Teacher-Consultant                              Parent or Guardian

# III-E

## SELECTED REFERENCES ON INDEPENDENT STUDY

Devitt, Tjomàs O. "Personality and Motivational Factors in Student Choice of Independent Study." *Educational Technology* 19:52–56 April, 1979.
Copeland, Amanda. *Community-based Projects in Business Education; Independent Study Projects.* National Business Education Yearbook 17:180–86, 1979.

# IV-A

## Tutorial Program Letter To Parents

Dear Parent or Guardian:

This year your child may have the opportunity to participate in a supervised tutorial program. Your son or daughter has been recommended by his teachers as a possible student tutor. Through this program we think that the student tutors will learn for themselves the values of planning, organizing, evaluation, and working with others.

These students will be working at a nearby elementary school or here at our school during their related arts period. No academic class would be missed. The student tutors will be asked to work in the tutorial program for an eighteen-week period instead of being involved in the subjects they had selected for related arts courses. They will be tutoring Monday through Friday for one period each day. They will receive a pass-fail grade for participating in the program.

Teachers at both our school and the elementary school have agreed to help each tutor in setting and attaining goals, utilizing materials, and evaluating their work. We hope that this program will help the student tutors to become more self-directed and responsible.

Please discuss the tutoring program with your child and let us know about his/her involvement. Please sign and return the bottom portion of this sheet.

If you have any questions or comments concerning the program, please call the coordinator's office at the school.

_ _ _ _ _ _ _ _ _ _ _ _ _ _ _ _ _ _ _ _ _ _ _ _ _

I do _____ do not _____ want my child to participate in the tutorial program.

SIGNED _____

# IV-B

To:      Teachers
From:    Coordinator
Re:      Student Tutorial Program

We wish to organize our tutorial program for the year as soon as possible. In order to do this efficiently, we need your help.

This year, we want to pull our student tutors mainly from *enrichment* classes so as not to place a burden on academic teachers. Many names have already been submitted as possible student tutors. Please check over the names listed. This list will be given to you on Friday morning. If you have objections to any of these students, please comment by their name. Also, if you know of a student who would be a good tutor, but his/her name does not appear on the list, please add his/her name. We use seventh and eighth grade students.

The success of this program has many contributing factors, but one factor is good scheduling from the beginning. On the attached sheet, please write your name, the number of students you need by periods, the subject or subjects they will be tutoring in, grade preference, days needed, if you would like to use tutors.

After the tutorial students have been identified, separate meetings will be held for the students and teachers involved in the program. Details will be discussed at those times.

This program can really be effective if everyone—students and teachers—are enthusiastic and can plan ahead.

Please return forms to Room 304 or Mrs. Goble's teacher box by Thursday afternoon, September 27th.

# IV-C

## Selected References on Student Tutors

Bessal, Frederick and Con Cozack. "Gains of Fifth and Sixth Grade Readers from In-school Tutoring." *Reading Teacher* 33:567–70 February, 1980.

Clarkson, D. M. "Children as Teachers: Some Fundamental Operations." *Arithmetic Teacher*, 22:495–97, October, 1975.

Elliot, A. H. "Turning it around in Education with Student Tutoring." *Clearing House*, 50:285–90, March, 1977.

Hymovitz, L. "Children 'Helping Children.'" *National Elementary Principal*, 54:41–43, May 1975.

Larsen, S. C. and S. Ehly. "Peer Tutoring: An Aid to Individual Instruction." *Clearing House*, 49:273–77, February, 1976.

"When Big Kids Work With Little Kids, Everyone Learns: Symposium." *The Instructor*, 85:98–104, November, 1975.

Melaragno, R. T. "Pupil Tutoring: Directions for the Future." *Elementary School Journal*, 77:384–87, May, 1977.

National Commission on Resources for Youth Incorporated, Supervisor's Manual: Youth Tutoring Youth. New York, The Commission, 1968.

Smith, C. C. "Partner Learning: Peer Tutoring Can Help

343

Individualization." *Educational Leadership*, 34:361–63, February, 1977.

Steinberg, Zina D. and C. B. Cazden. "Children as Teachers: of Peers and Ourselves." *Theory into Practice* 18:258–66 October, 1979.

Thelen, Herbert A. *Learning by Teaching—The Helping Relationship in the Classroom.* Chicago, University of Chicago Press, 1968.

*Youth Tutoring Youth: A Manual for Trainers.* National Commission on Resources for Youth, Inc., 36 West 44th St., New York, New York, 10036.

# V

## Selected References on Simulations

Boocock, Sarene S. and E. O. Schild. *Simulating Games in Learning.* Beverly Hills, California, Sage Publications, 1968.

Burgess, Philip M., Lawrence E. Peterson, and Carl D. Franz. "Organizing Simulated Environments." *Social Education,* 33:185–92 + , February, 1969.

Ellman, Neil. "Before Simulation Fails." *Social Studies,* 58:251–53. November/December, 1977.

Glenn, A. D. "Simulations in the Instructional Sequence." *Social Studies,* 68:23–26, January, 1977.

Guetzkow, Harold, ed. *Simulation in Social Science: Readings.* Englewood Cliffs, New Jersey, Prentice-Hall, 1972.

Hulsey, J. A. "New Insights into Simulation as an Effective Method of Teaching Social Studies." *High School Journal,* 60:243–46, March, 1977.

Inbar, Michael and Clarence S. Stall. *Simulation and Games in Social Science.* New York, Free Press, 1972.

Nesbitt, William A. *Simulation Games for the Social Studies Classroom.* Foreign Policy Association, 1971.

Olmo, Barbara G. "Simulations: Do It Yourself." *Social Studies,* 57:10–14, January/February, 1976.

"Simulations: Symposium" *Social Education* 44:22–31, January, 1980.

Wright, Emmett L. "Energy Program Simulation." *School Science and Mathematics* 79:275–78, April, 1979.

Zuckerman, David W. and Robert E. Horn. *The Guide to Simulation Games for Education and Training.* Lexington, Massachusetts, Information Resources, 1973.

# VI

## Selected References on Inquiry and Discovery

Allen, Rodney F. *Inquiry in the Social Studies: Theory and Examples for Classroom Teachers.* Washington, National Council for Social Studies, 1968.

Armstrong, T. and M. Heikkinen. "Initiating Inquiry through Open-end Problems." *Science and Children*, 14:30–31, March, 1977.

Azbell, Wayne. "Supervising the Inquiry Method." *Social Studies*, 68:189–92, September/October, 1977.

Beyer, Barry K. *Inquiry in the Social Studies Classroom: A Strategy for Teaching.* Columbus, Ohio, Charles E. Merrill Publishing Company, 1971.

Collinge, J. "Teacher's Role in Discovery Learning." *Reading Improvement*, 13:92–95, Summer, 1976.

Herrick, M. J. "Guide for Developing a Discovery Curriculum." *Clearing House*, 51:274–77, February, 1978.

Hurst, Joe B. and Daniel L. Merritt. "Pre-structured and Semi-structured Role-Playing." *Social Studies*, 67:14–18, January/February, 1976.

Morine, Harold and Greta Morine. *Discovery: A Challenge to Teachers.* Englewood, New Jersey, Prentice-Hall, 1973.

Rice, A. H. "Relationship of Teacher Opinion to Student Inquiry." *High School Journal*, 59:163–68, January, 1976.

346

# VII

## Guidelines For Group Leadership

*Primary Purpose of the Leader*
   To guide discussion along its course from analysis to decision.
   To help the group realize its fullest potentialities in the thinking process.

*Suggestions for Effective Leadership*
   1. Inform yourself about the subject to be discussed.
   2. Know your group, their needs, abilities, and expectations.
   3. Know what is expected of you as a leader. Stimulator? Coordinator? Mediator? Degree of formality?
   4. Plan the discussion. Sample outline:
      I. Analysis of question or problem: extent, importance, causes, etc.
      II. Desirable goals in this area.
      III. Possible solutions or decisions and selection of preferred solution.
      IV. Methods of achieving preferred solution.
      V. Conclusion.
   5. Distribute any available resource material to group members. Arrange for resource people to be present at discussion.
   6. Provide for physical comfort of group.

347

Arrange for comfortable light, ventilation, and temperature.

Seat members in circle or semi-circle if possible.

Eliminate distractions.

7. Open the discussion with brief introduction.

Focus group's attention on subject, pointing out importance, timeliness, pertinence, etc.

Define terms.

Clarify purpose of discussion.

8. Promote progressive development of group thinking.

Refrain from imposing your ideas upon the group.

Try to have all of the important facts brought out.

Call attention to points of agreement.

Draw attention away from irrelevant issues by means of questions or summaries.

Limit discussion of issues on which it is plain no agreement can be reached.

Summarize and interpret discussion at various times.

Instead of answering questions directed to you, refer them to the group.

Use stimulating questions to move discussion along.

Have significant points recorded on chalkboard.

9. Promote evenness of participation.

Keep all contributions short. Break in with minor summaries and comments.

Accept each contribution as worthy of thought.

Encourage the noncontributor with a nod or word, a request for his opinion, or a question which can be answered yes or no.

10. Prevent confusion, unnecessary disagreement, and antagonism.

Clarify or ask for clarification of vague terms.

Intervene in cases of misinterpretation or misunderstanding.

348

11. Close the discussion, or appoint a participant to do this.

    Summarize discussion points.

    Reveal extent of agreement or disagreement.

    State any solutions, decisions, or plans of action decided upon.

    Give participants opportunity to confirm this summary.

# VIII

## Selected References on Small Group Work

Amidon, Edmund J. *Self-directed Group Work*. (Tape Cassette) Minneapolis, Paul S. Amidon and Associates, n.d.

Andersen, Charles and David Butts. "Comparison of Individualized and Group Instruction in a Sixth-grade Electricity Unit." *Research in Science Teaching* 17:139-45 March 1980.

Berchard, Joseph E. *The Process of Small Groups* (Pamphlet) Fort Lauderdale Florida, The Edutronics Corporation, 1971.

Hart, Gordon. "Preparing Students for Small Group Work in the Classroom." *Education*, 95:351-53, Summer, 1975.

Hunsakey, J. S. and W. Roy. "Group Centered Classroom: Alternative to Individualized Instruction?" *Educational Leadership*, 34:366-69, February, 1977.

Lyon, T. "On Small Group Teaching." *American Education*, 12:35, August, 1976.

McNeil, J. H. *Some Guidelines for Small Group Discussion*. (Pamphlet) Fort Lauderdale, Florida, The Edutronics Corporation, 1971.

Schuncke, George M. "Using Groups in Social Studies Classes." *Social Studies* 70:38-41 January/February, 1979.

Schuncke, George M. and T. R. Bloom. "Cooperative Groups: From Theory to Practice." *Social Studies*, 68:208–10, September/October, 1977.

Smola, J. K. and A. Mandell, "Using Group Dynamics in the Classroom." *Science Teacher*, 41:28–31, April, 1974.

Valentine, C. A. "Using Small Group Methods in Education." *Clearing House*, 50:115–17, November, 1976.

# IX

## Selected References on Oral History

Cutler, William W. III. *Oral History as a Teaching Device, The Fourth National Colloquium on Oral History, 1969,* edited by Gould P. Colman. New York Oral History Association, 1970, pp. 160–66.

Hirsch, R. and M. Lewinger. "Oral History: The Family is the Curriculum." *Teacher*, 93:60–62, November, 1975.

Lehane, S. and R. Goldman. "Oral History: Research and Teaching Tool for Educators." *Elementary School Journal*, 77:173–81, January, 1977.

Mazuzan, G. T. and G. Tuomey. "Oral History in the Classroom." *Social Studies*, 68:14–19, January, 1977.

Mehaffy, George, and T. Sitton. "Oral History: A Strategy that Works." *Social Education*, 41:378–81, May, 1977.

Nelson, M. and H. W. Singleton. "Using Oral History in the Social Studies Classroom." *Education Digest*, 42:58–61, September, 1976.

# X

## SCHOOL LIBRARY BILL OF RIGHTS FOR SCHOOL LIBRARY MEDIA PROGRAMS

The American Association of School Librarians reaffirms its belief in the Library Bill of Rights of the American Library Association. Media personnel are concerned with generating understanding of American freedoms through the development of informed and responsible citizens. To this end the American Association of School Librarians asserts that the responsibility of the school library media center is:

To provide a comprehensive collection of instructional materials selected in compliance with basic, written selection principles, and to provide maximum accessibility to these materials.

To provide materials that will support the curriculum, taking into consideration the individual's needs, and the varied interests, abilities, socio-economic backgrounds, and maturity levels of the students served.

To provide materials for teachers and students that will encourage growth in knowledge, and that will develop literary, cultural, and aesthetic appreciation, and ethical standards.

To provide materials which reflect the ideas and beliefs of religious, social, political, historical, and ethnic groups and their contribution to the American and world heritage and culture, thereby enabling students to develop an intellectual integrity in forming judgments.

To provide a written statement, approved by the local Boards of Education, of the procedures for meeting the challenge of censorship of materials in school library media centers.

To provide qualified professional personnel to serve teachers and students.

# XI-A

## Book Selection Aids

(Revised editions are issued periodically for some of the following titles, and prices are subject to change)

American Association for the Advancement of Science. *The AAAS Science Book List*, 3d ed., compiled by Hilary J. Deason. Miscellaneous Publication 70-8. Washington, D. C., The Association, 1970. $10.

American Association for the Advancement of Science. *The AAAS Science Book List for Children*, 3d. ed., compiled by Hilary J. Deason. Washington, D. C., The Association, 1972. $8.95.

American Association of School Librarians. *Paperback Books for Children*. New York, Citation, 1972. $.95. Paperback.

American Library Association. *Books for Elementary School Libraries: An Initial Collection*, compiled by Elizabeth Hodges. Chicago, The Association, 1969. $7.50. Paperback.

American Library Association. *Let's Read Together: Books for Family Enjoyment*, 3d ed. Chicago, The Association, 1969. $1.50. Paperback.

American Library Association. *Reference and Subscription Books Reviews, 1970–1972*. $3.50. Paperback.

American Library Association. *Reference and Subscription Books Reviews, 1972–1974*. $4. Paperback.

Association for Childhood Education International. *Bibliography: Books for Children*. Washington, D. C., The Association, 1974. $2.75.

*Children's Catalog*, 12th ed., 1971. $25. Includes four annual supplements, 1972–1975.

Dodds, Barbara. *Negro Literature for High School Students*. Champaign, Illinois, National Council of Teachers of English, 1968. $2.20.

*The Elementary School Library Collection*, 11th ed., edited by Phyllis Van Orden and Lois Winkle. (Contains multimedia items) Newark, New Jersey, The Brodart Foundation, 1977.

Hirschfelder, Arlene. *American Indian and Eskimo Authors*. New York, Association on Indian Affairs, 1973. $4.

Information Center on Children's Cultures. *Africa: An Annotated List of Printed Materials Suitable for Children*. New York, The Center, 1968. $1.

Information Center on Children's Cultures. *Latin America: An Annotated List of Materials for Children*, edited by Elena Mederos de Gonzalez and Anne Pelowski. New York, The Center, 1969. $1.

Information Center on Children's Cultures. *Near East and North Africa*. New York, The Center, 1970. $1. (20% discount on 20 or more copies).

Irwin, Leonard B. *Black Studies: A Bibliography*. Brooklawn, New Jersey, McKinley Publishing Company, 1973. $6.50.

Jackson, Miles, ed. *A Bibliography of Negro History and Culture for Young Readers*. (Books and audio-visual materials.) Pittsburgh, University of Pittsburgh, 1969. $2.50.

*Junior High School Library Catalog*. 2d ed. 1970. $30. Includes four annual supplements. 1971–1974.

National Association of Independent Schools. Library Committee. *Books for Secondary School Libraries*, 4th ed. New York, R. R. Bowker, 1971. $9.95.

National Council for the Social Studies. *American History Booklist for High Schools: A Selection for Supplementary Reading*, edited by Ralph and Marion Brown. Bulletin 42. Washington, D. C., The Council, 1969. $3.

National Council for the Social Studies. *World Civilization Booklist: Supplementary Reading for Secondary Schools*, edited by Morris Gall and Arthur E. Soderlind. Bulletin 41. Washington, D. C., The Council. 1968. $4.20.

National Council of Teachers of English. *Adventuring With Books: 2,400 titles for pre-K-grade 8*, edited by Patricia J. Cianciolo. New York, Citation Press, 1977. $1.95. Paperback.

National Council of Teachers of English. *Books for You: A Reading List for Senior High School Students*, rev. ed. by Kenneth L. Donelson. New York, Washington Square, 1976. $ 2.95.

National Council of Teachers of English. *High Interest-Easy Reading for Junior and Senior High School Students*, edited by Marian E. White. New York, Citation Press, 1972. $ .95. Paperback.

National Council of Teachers of English. *Picture Books for Children*. The American Library Association, 1973. $5.95 Paperback.

National Council of Teachers of Mathematics. *The Elementary and Junior High School Mathematics Library*, 3d. ed., compiled by Clarence Ethel Hardgrove and Herbert F. Miller. Washington, D. C., The Council, 1973. $1.50.

National Council of Teachers of Mathematics. *The High School Mathematics Library*, 5th ed., compiled by William L. Schaaf. Washington, D. C., The Council, 1976. $1.50.

Posner, Arlene, and Arne J. deKeyzer, eds. *China: A Resource and Curriculum Guide*. Chicago, University of Chicago Press. 1973. Cloth $6.50. Paperback $2.95.

*Reference and Subscription Book Reviews, 1974-75.* Reprinted from *Booklist*. Chicago, American Library

Association, 1976. (Earlier issues available)

Reid, Virginia M. *Reading Ladders for Human Relations*, 5th ed. Washington, American Council on Education, 1972. $3.95. Paperback.

Reinhart, Bruce, ed. *Vocational-Technical Learning Materials; Books and Manuals for Schools and Community Colleges*, 2d. ed. Williamsport, Pennsylvania: Bro-Dart, 1974. $35.

Rollins, Charlemae, ed. *We Build Together: A Reader's Guide to Negro Life and Literature for Elementary and High School Use*, 3d ed. Champaign, Illinois, National Council of Teachers of English, 1967. $1.65.

*The School Library Journal Book Review, 1968–69; 1969–70.* New York, R. R. Bowker. $10.95 each volume.

*Senior High School Library Catalog*, 10th ed., 1972. $30 in U. S. and Canada; $35 elsewhere. Includes five annual supplements, 1973–1977.

Spache, George D. *Good Reading for Poor Readers*, 9th ed. Champaign, Illinois, Garrard Publishing Company, 1974. $5.75.

Spache, George D. *Good Reading for the Disadvantaged Reader.* (Multiethnic resources.) Garrard Publishing Company, 1970. $4.75. Paperback.

Sutherland, Zena K., ed. *The Best in Children's Books: The University of Chicago Guide to Children's Literature 1966–1972.* 1973. $9.95.

Wynar, Christine L. *Guide to Reference Books for School Media Centers.* Littleton, Colorado, Libraries Unlimited, 1973. $17.50.

# XI-B

## CURRENT SELECTION AIDS

American Library Association. *Choice*. Published monthly, 11 times a year, with combined July–August issue. The Association. $25 a year for initial subscription; available back issues, $2 a copy.

American Library Association. *Booklist*. Published semi-monthly, September through July; one issue in August. The Association. $20 a year, $1 a copy

*Appraisal: Science Books for Children*. Children's Science Book Review Committee. Published 3 times a year $4 a year; $1.50 a copy; foreign, $3.75 a year.

*Bulletin of the Center for Children's Books*. Published monthly except August. University of Chicago Press. Critical reviews of a selected number of children's books. $8 per year.

*Educational Technology*. Educational Technology Publication, Inc., 140 Sylvan Avenue, Englewood Cliffs, New Jersey 07632. $21 per year.

*Film News*. 250 West 57th Street, New York, New York 10019. Reviews both non-print materials and books in this field. 6 issues. $6 per year.

*The Horn Book Magazine*. The Horn Book, Inc. Published bimonthly. Discriminating reviews of books for children and young people and articles on children's literature. $8.50 per year.

*Kirkus Reviews*. Published semimonthly. The N.Y. Review, Inc. $36 a year to school libraries.

*Media and Methods*. North American Publishing Company, 134 North 13th Street, Philadelphia, Pennsylvania 19107. Contains articles and reviews of non-print materials and books in the audiovisual field. Monthly September–May. $7 per year.

*Media Review*. University of Chicago Laboratory Schools, 1362 East 59th Street, Chicago, Illinois 60637. A monthly review of many types of media examined in the Center for Educational Media for Children and Young People. $6 per year.

*Previews*, Monthly September through May. New York, R.R. Bowker. Non-print software and hardware news and reviews. $5 per year.

*School Library Journal*. Monthly September through May. New York, R. R. Bowker. Critical reviews of print and non-print materials. $10.80 per year.

# XI-C

## Free and Inexpensive Materials Selection Aids

*Elementary Teachers Guide to Free Curriculum Materials*, edited by Patricia H. Suttles, 29th ed., Educators Progress Service, 1972. $9.75.

*Educators Guide to Free Social Studies Materials*, compiled and edited by Patricia H. Suttles, 14th ed., Educators Progress Service, 1974. $10.50.

*Educators Guide to Free Science Materials*, compiled and edited by Mary H. Saterstrom, 13th ed., Educators Progress Service, 1972. $9.25.

*Educators Guide to Free Health, Physical Education and Recreation Materials*, compiled and edited by Foley A. Horkheimer, 7th ed., Educators Progress Service, 1974.

*Free and Inexpensive Learning Materials*, 17th ed. Division of Surveys and Field Services, Nashville, George Peabody College of Teachers, 1974. $3.50.

Kenworthy, Leonard. *Free and Inexpensive Materials on World Affairs*. New York, Teachers College, Columbia University, 1969. $1.95.

# XII

## Selection Aids for Non-print Materials

Anderson, Robert, Robert Hemenway, and Janet W. Anderson. *Instructional Resources for Teachers of the Culturally Disadvantaged and Exceptional.* Springfield, Illinois. Charles C. Thomas, 1971. $11.

*Audiovisual Instruction.* Association for Educational Communications and Technology, 1201 Sixteenth Street, N.W., Washington, D. C. 20036. Monthly September–June. Contains articles, information about newer hardware, and cites reviews of new audiovisual materials. $12 per year.

*Core Media Collection for Secondary Schools.* Lists and annotates 2,000 of the most highly recommended audiovisual items between 1965 and 1974. New York, R. R. Bowker. $16.95.

Downes, Patricia, comp. *Negroes in American Life: An Annotated Bibliography of Nonprint Media.* Rockville, Maryland: Evaluation and Selection Division, Department of Educational Media and Technology, Montgomery County Public Schools, 1971. $2.00.

Educational Film Library Association. *Film Evaluation Guide.* New York, The Association. Supplement, 1965–1967, (c) 1968. $12. *Supplement* 1967–1971. $12.

*Educators Guide to Free Filmstrips*, 24th ed., Educators

Progress Service 1972, compiled and edited by Mary Foley Horkheimer and John C. Diffor. $8.50.

*Educators Guide to Free Tapes, Scripts, Transcriptions*, compiled and edited by Walter A. Wittich. 19th ed., Educators Progress Service 1972. $7.75.

*The Elementary School Library Collection*, edited by Phyllis Van Orden, 9th ed., 1975. The Bro-Dart Foundation, 744 Broad Street, Newark, New Jersey 07102. (Contains multimedia items.)

Greene, Ellin, and Madalynne Schoenfeld. *A Multimedia Approach to Children's Literature: A Selective List of Films, Filmstrips and Recordings Based on Children's Books*. Chicago: American Library Association, 1972. $3.75. Paperback.

Jackson, Miles, ed. *A Bibliography of Negro History and Culture for Young Readers*. Pittsburgh: University of Pittsburgh, 1969. $2.50.

Johnson, Harry. *Multimedia Materials for Afro-American Studies*. New York, R. R. Bowker, 1971. $15.95.

Lekan, Helen A., ed. *Index to Computer-Assisted Instruction*. 3d ed. New York, Harcourt Brace Jovanovich, 1971. $20.50.

*Listening Post*. Bro-Dart, Inc., 15255 East Don Julian Road, City of Industry, California 91749. Critical reviews of current recordings. Published ten times a year. $9 per year.

McDaniel, Roderick, ed. *Resources for Learning: A Core Media Collection for Elementary Schools*. New York, R.R. Bowker, 1971. U. S. and Canada, $16. Elsewhere, $17.60.

Markham, Lois, ed. *New Educational Materials, a Classified Guide*. New York, Citation Press, 1970. $3.75.

*National Center for Audio Tapes Catalog, 1969–71*. Boulder, Colorado, National Center for Audio Tapes, 1969–71. $4.50.

National Information Center for Educational Media. *Index*

*to Black History and Studies—Multimedia*, 2d ed. Los Angeles, University of Southern California, 1973. $19.50.

National Information Center for Educational Media. *Index to 8mm Motion Cartridges*. New York, R.R. Bowker, 1969. $19.50.

National Information Center for Educational Media. *Index to 16mm Educational Films*. New York, R.R. Bowker, 1969. $39.50.

National Information Center for Educational Media. *Index to Overhead Transparencies*. New York, R.R. Bowker, 1969. $22.50.

National Information Center for Educational Media. *Index to 35mm Educational Filmstrips*. 2d ed. New York, R.R. Bowker, 1970. $34.

New York Library Association. Children's and Young Adult Services. *Records and Cassettes for Young Adults*. The Association, 1973. $2.50.

New York Library Association. Children's and Young Adult Services. *Recordings for Children. A Selected List of Records and Cassettes*, 3d ed. $2.50.

New York Library Association. *Films for Children*. New York, The Association, 1970. $1.

New York Library Association. *Films for Young Adults. A Selected List and Guide to Programming*, rev. ed. New York, Educational Film Library Association, 1970. $2.

Posner, Arlene, and Arne J. de Keyzer, ed. *China: A Resource and Curriculum Guide*. Chicago, University of Chicago Press. 1973. Cloth $6.50; Paperback, $2.95.

*Previews*, monthly, September–May. New York, R.R. Bowker. Critical Reviews of print and nonprint materials. $10.80 per year.

Raab, Joseph A. *Audiovisual Materials in Mathematics*. Washington, D. C., National Council of Teachers of Mathematics, 1971. $1.80.

Roach, Helen. *Spoken Records*, 3d ed. Metuchen, New Jersey, Scarecrow Press, 1970. $7.50.

Rufsvold, Margaret I., and Carolyn Guss. *Guides to Newer Educational Media: Films, Filmstrips, Kinescopes, Phonodiscs, Phonotapes, Programmed Instruction Materials, Slides, Transparencies and Videotapes*, 3d. ed. Chicago, American Library Association, 1971. $2.50.

San Francisco Unified School District. *The North American Indian and the Eskimo*. San Francisco, The District, 1972. $3.29.

*U. S. Government Films: A Catalog of Motion Pictures and Filmstrips for Sale by the National Audiovisual Center.* Washington, D. C. National Archives and Records Services, General Services Administration, 1969. Free.

*U. S. Government Films: 1971 Supplement; A Catalog of Motion Pictures and Filmstrips for Rent and Sale* by the National Audiovisual Center. Washington, D. C. National Archives and Records Service, General Services Administration, 1971. Free.

# XIII

## Sources Of Information And Materials For The Handicapped

*General References*
1. Bureau of Education for the Handicapped, Regional Office Building—GSA, 7th and D Streets, S.W., Washington, D.C. 20202
2. Closer Look, P. O. Box 1492, Washington, D.C. 20013
3. Council for Exceptional Children, 1920 Association Drive, Reston, Virginia 22091
4. Instructional Materials Center Network for Handicapped Children and Youth, 3116 S. Mill Avenue, Tempe, Arizona 85282
5. Media for the Exceptional, 6345 Clyburn Avenue, North Hollywood, California 91606
6. National Media Center for the Handicapped, Chemical Abstracts Building, Ohio State University, Columbus, Ohio 43215

*Hearing Impairment*
1. Alexander Graham Bell Association for the Deaf, 1537 35th Street, N.W., Washington, D.C. 20007
2. American Speech and Hearing Association, 9030 Old Georgetown Road, Bethesda, Maryland 20014
3. Captioned Film for the Deaf Project, Bureau of Educa-

366

tion for the Handicapped, Regional Office Building—GSA, 7th and D Streets, S.W., Washington, D.C. 20202

4. Council of Organizations Serving the Deaf, 4201 Connecticut Avenue, N.W., Suite 210, Washington, D.C. 20008
5. National Advisory Committee on Education of the Deaf, 330 Independence Avenue, S.W., Washington, D.C. 20201
6. National Association of the Deaf, Suite 321, 2025 Eye Street, Washington, D.C. 20006
7. Specialized Office for the Deaf and Hard of Hearing, University of Nebraska, 175 Nebraska Hall, Lincoln, Nebraska 68508

*Visual Impairment*

1. American Association of Instructors of the Blind, 711 14th Street, N.W., Washington, D.C. 20005
2. American Foundation for the Blind, 15 W. 16th Street, New York, New York 10011
3. American Printing House for the Blind, P. O. Box 6085, 1839 Frankfort Avenue, Louisville, Kentucky 40206
4. Bureau of Education for the Handicapped, Regional Office Building—GSA, 7th and D Streets, S.W., Washington, D.C. 20202
5. Clovernook Printing House for the Blind, 7000 Hamilton Avenue, Cincinnati, Ohio 45231
6. Division for the Blind and Physically Handicapped, Library of Congress, Washington, D.C. 20542
7. Howe Press, Perkins School for the Blind, Watertown, Massachusetts 02172
8. National Braille Book Bank, 85 Goodwin Avenue, Midland Park, New Jersey 07432
9. National Braille Press, Inc., 88 St. Stephen Street, Boston, Massachusetts 02115
10. Recording for the Blind, Inc., 215 East 58th Street New York, New York 10022

*Neurological or Orthopedic Impairment*
1. American Orthopsychiatric Association, 1790 Broadway, New York, New York 10019
2. Division for the Blind and Physically Handicapped, Library of Congress, Washington, D.C. 20542
3. Muscular Dystrophy Association of America, 1790 Broadway, New York, New York 10019
4. National Institute of Neurological Diseases and Blindness 9000 Rockville Pike, Bethesda, Maryland 20014
5. National Easter Seal Society for Crippled Children and Adults, 2023 West Ogden Avenue, Chicago, Illinois 60612
6. United Cerebral Palsy Association, 66 E. 34th Street, New York, New York 10016

*Learning Disabled*
1. Association for Children with Learning Disabilities, 2200 Brownesville Road, Pittsburgh, Pennsylvania 15210

*Mentally Retarded*
1. American Association on Mental Deficiency, 5201 Connecticut Avenue, N.W., Washington, D.C. 20015
2. National Association for Mental Health, 10 Columbus Circle, New York, New York 10019
3. National Association for Retarded Citizens, 2709 Avenue E East, Arlington, Texas 76011
4. President's Committee on Mental Retardation, South Building, Room 5064, Washington, D.C. 20201

*Emotionally Handicapped*
1. American Psychological Association, 1200 17th Street, N.W., Washington, D.C. 20036
2. National Institute of Child Health and Human Development, 9000 Rockville Pike, Bethesda, Maryland 20014

3. National Institute of Mental Health, 5454 Wisconsin Avenue, Chevy Chase, Maryland 20015

# XIV

## Suggested Ways to Share Books

CONVERSATION that might take place between the characters in two different books.

TRANSPARENCIES made by student to illustrate his books.

HEADLINED NEWSPAPER REPORT of some event in the book.

FILMSTRIP OR MOUNTED PICTURES to illustrate a talk.

OVERHEAD PROJECTOR used to show illustrations from a book while student talks about it.

SKIT, WITH COSTUMES, illustrating some dramatic part of the book.

POSTERS illustrating characters, map of county, or locale, or some scene in book. These should be accompanied by analytical talk.

IMAGINARY NEWS CORRESPONDENT TELEVISION REPORT.

ILLUSTRATED BOOK REVIEW—a brief synopsis illustrated with pictures.

A TELEVISION QUIZ PROGRAM—pupil giving report interviewed by other students.

MOCK RADIO SHOW—several scenes rewritten as short radio plays.

A TABLEAU representing scenes from a book.

A SALES-TALK TECHNIQUE—Student given a designated
length of time in which to make his classmates want to
read the book he has just read.

IMAGINARY TELEPHONE CONVERSATION during
which the plot of the book is described.

IMAGINARY CONVERSATION between two historical
characters during which part of the content of the book
read is revealed.

A TALK based on one or more of the following questions:
If such an experience happened to me, what would I have
done? Do I know anyone like the people in the story?
Would I like to be like the book character? Have I ever
seen anything like this happen?

DIORAMA representing various book events.

PANEL DISCUSSIONS—several books of the same kind
(biography, historical novel, etc.) or on the same subject
(sports, American Revolution, etc.), discussed by a
group, followed by questions from the class.

GENERAL CLASS DISCUSSIONS of various books concerned with the same interest; i.e., books about sports
which might include fiction, biography, and informational biography, play, poetry, essays, etc.

DEBATE on a topic such as "Resolved, That the reading of
travel books is more broadening to the mind than the
reading of biography," with students giving examples
from books they have read.

PUPPETRY—Hand puppets made by the student dramatize
the action of the story.

READING OF BEST-LIKED CHAPTERS and pages by
students who also give a brief summary of the preceding
part of the book.

FIVE-MINUTE TALKS given by each student about a
book he has read, in effort to get the class members to
vote for his book for Book-of-the-Month selection.

A LETTER written to the author, stating why the book was

enjoyed and suggesting improvements, to a character in the book or from the character to a person in today's world.

A DISCUSSION OF THE BOOK followed by a description of what could happen after the story ends.

A WRITTEN ADVERTISEMENT stressing the good features of the book.

"LIFE" STORY—Imagine *Life Magazine* doing a feature story on the book, and describe the photographs they would take and write captions for each.

LETTER—Write a letter to a foreign student, discussing why the book is or is not representative of American Life.

ANALYSIS BY A MAN OF THE FUTURE—In a time capsule or in the ruins on the planet Earth, some man of the future finds the book and writes a paper on what it reveals of life of an earlier time.

A LETTER WRITTEN ON THE ROLE OF A BOOK CHARACTER—Example: The hero of *Lost Horizon* writes a letter about his final return to Shangri-la, explaining his purposes and his hopes for the future.

THE SCHOLARLY CRITICAL PAPER—Honors classes may combine research on "what the critics and authorities think of the author" with critical opinion on "what I think about those of his books which I have read."

ROUND-TABLE DISCUSSION UNDER A STUDENT CHAIRMAN—Four or five students read the same book. Part of a period is given before the day of report for each group to confer on questions for discussions.

GROUP PERFORMANCE IN THE STYLE OF "THIS IS YOUR LIFE." This procedure lends itself to reports on biographies.

REPORTER AT THE SCENE—While it's happening, a crucial scene from the book is described on the spot by a TV or radio reporter.

THE TRIAL OF A MAJOR CHARACTER—Defendant,

prosecuting attorney, defense attorney, and witnesses
may participate in the case. The charge should preferably
be one of acting unethically, unfairly, or even unwisely,
rather than one of breaking a law.

THE AUTHOR MEETS THE CRITICS. Three, four, or
five students may form a group. A student posing as
Charles Dickens may defend his *Tale of Two Cities*
against critics as they ask questions.

QUIZ PROGRAM—Use this when the class has read only
one book, or when several groups have each read a single
book. A quizmaster asks questions of two teams, each
composed of half the class or group.

USE OF TAPE RECORDER—Students tape a description
of their books, and these are used for individual or group
listening.

MONOLOGUE—"I am John Ridd, and I appear in a book
that Blackmore wrote about Lorna Doone and me. I'm
the kind of person who. . . ."

COUNSELING BY EXPERTS—A character explains his
crucial problem to three social workers who specialize in
guidance, family counseling, and psychological
rehabilitation. They ask questions and offer advice. Note
that the "social workers" need not have read the book.

OUTLINE OF A TV OR MOTION-PICTURE VER-
SION—This may be oral or written, including major
scenes, sets, casting, and other aspects. Students enjoy
telling "how I would dramatize this book if I were a TV
or motion-picture producer."

MOVIE TRAILER OR PREVIEW OF COMING AT-
TRACTIONS—Each student clips magazine or
newspaper pictures—or sketches his own—showing
scenes similar to those of significant moments in his book.
He displays the pictures in organized sequence and supplies a commentary on the action and characterization.

TWENTY QUESTIONS—Most successful when subject is
familiar to class. The reviewer chooses a fact from his

book and the class must guess it in twenty questions to which the reviewer may answer only "yes" or "no."

SIMULATED INTERVIEW WITH AUTHOR—One pupil poses as author, another as interviewer.

OPAQUE PROJECTOR—Use book or original illustrations.

ORIGINAL POEM—It might be about the main character.

MAPS—Useful for tracing a route, indicating episodes or landmarks.

PANTOMINE—Present characters in action. Audience participation might include guessing what they're doing. One student might tell a story while others act out the action.

FLANNEL BOARD—For elementary pupils a synopsis might be woven around a few figures placed on a simple background.

CHALKBOARD SKETCH—For the artistically talented. He or she might sketch while talking about the book.

A VIDEOTAPE of scenes from a book.

MOBILE of characters, setting, events of a book.

MURAL depicting events in a book.

PHOTOGRAPHIC DISPLAY related to a book.

ESSAY telling why a book should be included in a capsule to be buried today for retrieval in a hundred years.

DIARY OF A CHARACTER in the book.

ALTERNATE ENDING of a book, rewriting the last chapter.

COMIC STRIP drawn of the action in a book.

POEM written to express reactions to a book.

"DEAR ABBEY" LETTER written by one of the characters in the book.

COLLAGE based on the scene, mood, or character of the book.

GAME invented based on a book—a puzzle, scrambled words, bingo, etc.

374

FAVORITE CHARACTER IN A BOOK—Come to class
dressed to represent the character chosen.
BOOKMARK designed to depict characters or events in a
book.

# XV

## SUGGESTED LIBRARY ACTIVITIES FOR READING, VIEWING, LISTENING, AND PERSONAL GUIDANCE

ROLE PLAYING

Use a familiar story. Read several times.

Let children volunteer for different parts. If no volunteers, ask for suggestions as to how a character would act or look.

Let children originate interpretations. Don't tell them what to do. Show appreciation of the efforts of each one.

Show that you're enthusiastic and having fun.

Sometimes use a story that lends itself to group participation so that the shy child will join in.

Let children suggest props.

STORY HOURS OR PICTURE BOOK HOURS

Remember the short attention span of the younger children. Select story carefully.

Gather children close around you. Be enthusiastic. Show children that you're having a good time.

Relate story to children's experiences before you read or tell it.

Allow time for children to react to the story and to talk

about it after you have finished.

Encourage upper grade children to read or tell stories to primary grade children. Be sure the story has been reviewed first and that it is told or read clearly and well.

Take time to show the book's illustrations as you read. Talk about them. Compare the different styles, colors, designs, media, and the degree to which the pictures help tell the story. Let children tell what they like about them.

Consider the use of a continued story for older children.

Use recordings and filmstrips related to stories.

Use fairy tales, folk tales, myths.


ACTIVITIES WITH RECORDINGS

Review recording before using it.

Discuss good listening skills. Let children make suggestions.

Limit other distractions.

Decide what to listen for:
    Directions
    Sequence of thought
    Details
    Main ideas
    Rhythms
    Descriptive phrases or story
    Instruments used
    Repetition and themes

Play part of recording. "What did you hear?"

Be considerate of your neighbors.

Relate recording to children's experiences.

Always talk about related books.

Use recording as background for a story or poetry.

Let children sing along with music, or say poetry with the narrator.

Let children react to music:

"How does this music make you feel?"
"What is this music saying?"
"What rhythms express the music?"
Show picture book as record is being played.
Encourage children to evaluate the recording on the following criteria:
  Clear sound
  Proper length
  Pleasing narration
  Good technical qualities
  Adequate content

## SHARING READING EXPERIENCES

Let children talk informally about their reading:
  "The best book I've read."
  "The last book I've read."
  "What I like about it."
  "The book character I like best."
Encourage reactions other than just the plot of the story:
  Have you ever known anyone like that?
  What would you have done?
  Would you like to have a friend like that?
  What part did you like the best?
  Did he (or she) do the right thing?
Tell children about a book you have read and enjoyed.
Encourage creative reactions to books:
  Draw a picture
  Act out a scene
  Write a poem
  Write a skit for puppets
Stress care in handling books.
Encourage children to speak clearly and interestingly.
Let children find some information in the library about the authors of the books they've read.
Stress the courtesy and skill of listening to each other as they share reading experiences.

See "Sharing Book Experiences" Appendix XIV, for other suggestions.

POETRY ACTIVITIES

Select poems on the children's level.

Repeat favorites.

Let children participate, all saying a poem together or different groups saying different lines.

Let children read favorites.

Use poetry in connection with a filmstrip.

Tell something about the poet.

Use poetry which suggests a book. For example, for the book *Whistle for Willie* by Ezra Jack Keats, use the following poem:

"I want to learn to whistle
I've always wanted to
I fix my mouth to do it
The whistle won't come through."

Relate poem to children's experiences.

Use related recordings.

Teach listening skills.

Encourage creative interpretation of poetry:

Art work

Dramatics

Rhythms

Read poetry carefully and enthusiastically.

ACTIVITIES WITH FILMSTRIPS

Always preview.

Show filmstrip slowly

Show part of filmstrip. Ask "How do you think it should end?" Use only a part of a filmstrip to illustrate or to emphasize a point.

Let children have time to react. Let them talk or plan art work or dramatics.

Show filmstrip. Talk about related books.

Let the class develop good viewing standards according to their maturity level. Have them practice these as filmstrips are shown. Let children make suggestions for standards.

Identify a purpose for viewing.

Provide an environment which is comfortable and free from distractions.

Concentrate on understanding what is being seen.

Have an alert, interested attitude.

Locate central idea and subordinate ideas of what is being seen.

Summarize mentally.

Distinguish between the true and make-believe.

Plan to verify what has been seen by consulting various sources of information.

Show a frame - turn off - "What did you see?"

Remind children to be considerate of neighbors.

Encourage children to evaluate the filmstrip on the following criteria:

Clear and pleasing pictures
Satisfactory captions
Good technical qualities
Proper length
Adequate content

Read story before showing filmstrip. Let children tell the story.

# XVI

## SELECTED REFERENCES ON PRODUCTION OF NON-PRINT MATERIALS

Bullough, Robert U. *Creating Instructional Materials.* Columbus, Ohio, Charles E. Merrill Publishing Company, 1974.

Brune, B. and J.E. Splaine. "Student Production: Getting Started." *Audiovisual Instruction,* 21: 35-37, October, 1976.

Cromer, N. "Making a Videotape: a Group Experience." *English Journal,* 65: 94-95, May, 1976.

Langford, Michael. *Visual Aids and Photography in Education.* New York, Hastings House, 1973.

Lanier, V. "Simple Multi-media: Slide Making." *Arts and Activities,* 79:25, April, 1976.

Lundy, L.L. "How to Make Your Own Transparencies." *Industrial Education,* 64:65, September, 1975.

"Media of, by, and for Students: Symposium." *Audio visual Instruction,* 21: 59-65, March, 1976.

Miller, D.P. "Case for Filmstrips: Producing Filmstrips in the Classroom." *English Journal,* 66: 70-72, October, 1977.

Minor, Edward. Techniques for Producing Visual/Instructional Media. New York, McGraw-Hill, 1970.

Nikirk, F.M. "Filmmaking: a Seventh Grade Experience."

*School Arts*, 75: 16-17, December, 1975.

Oles, H.J. "Super 8 Comes of Age." *Audiovisual Instruction* 22: 16-17, May, 1977.

Ryan, M. "Preparing a Slide-Tape Program: A Step-by-Step Approach." *Audiovisual Instruction*, 20: 36-38, September, 1975; 36-39, November, 1975.

Wileman, R.E. "Local Production of Instructional Materials." *High School Journal*, 59: 320-61, May, 1976.

Yeamans, George T. Projectionists' Programmed Primer. Muncie, Indiana, Ball State University, 1975.

# XVII

## SOME BASIC REFERENCE MATERIALS FOR TEACHERS TO KNOW

I. *General References*
Atlases, Gazeteers, Guidebooks:
    Goode's World Atlas. Rand-McNally.
    International Atlas. Rand-McNally.
    National Geographic Atlas of the World. National Geographic Society.
    New York Times Atlas of the World. Quadrangle.

Biographical Dictionaries:
    Current Biography. H.W. Wilson.
    Dictionary of American Biography. Scribners.
    Dictionary of National Biography. Oxford University.
    Webster's Biographical Dictionary. Merriam.
    Who Was Who in America. A.N. Marquis.
    Who's Who in America. A.N. Marquis.
    Who's Who of American Women. A.N. Marquis.

Dictionaries:
    New Roget's Thesaurus of the English Language in Dictionary Form. Putnam.
    Thorndike-Barnhart Beginning Dictionary. Doubleday.

Webster's Seventh New Collegiate Dictionary. Merri-am.

Webster's Third New International Dictionary of the English Language, Unabridged. Merriam.

World Book Dictionary. Field Enterprises Educational Corporation.

Encyclopedias:

Childcraft. Field Enterprises Educational Corp.

Collier's Encyclopedia. Crowell-Collier.

Compton's Encyclopedia and Fact Index. Encyclopedia Britannica.

Encyclopedia Americana. Grolier.

Encyclopedia of Careers and Vocational Guidance. Doubleday.

Lincoln Library of Essential Information. Frontier Press.

New Book of Knowledge. Grolier.

New Encyclopedia Britannica. Encyclopedia Britannica.

World Book. Field Enterprises Educational Corp.

Handbooks and Manuals:

Anniversaries and Holidays: A Calendar of Days and How to Observe Them. American Library Association.

Bartlett's Familiar Quotations. Little.

Contemporary Quotations. Crowell.

Emily Post Book of Etiquette for Young People. Funk and Wagnalls.

Homebook of Quotations. Dodd, Mead.

Hoyt's New Cyclopedia of Practical Quotations. Funk and Wagnalls.

Robert's Rules of Order. Scott, Foresman.

Indexes to Periodicals:

National Geographic Cumulative Index. National
    Geographic Society.
Readers' Guide to Periodical Literature. H.W. Wilson.
Subject Index to Children's Magazines. Madison, Wis-
    consin.

Yearbooks and Annuals:
    Facts on File. Facts on File, Inc.
    Famous First Facts. H.W. Wilson.
    Guinness Book of World Records. Sterling.
    Information Please Almanac, Atlas, and Yearbook.
        Simon & Schuster.
    Statesman's Yearbook. St. Martin's.
    World Almanac and Book of Facts. Doubleday.


II. *Specialized References*
    Art:
        Art Through the Ages. Harcourt Brace Jovanovich.
        Dictionary of Art and Artists. Praeger.
        Encyclopedia of World Art. McGraw-Hill.
        Famous Artists of the Past. Platt & Munk.
        McGraw-Hill Dictionary of Art. McGraw-Hill.
        Praeger Encyclopedia of Art. Praeger.
        Who's Who in American Art. Bowker.

    Drama:
        Bibliography of Costume. H.W. Wilson.
        Concise Encyclopedia of Modern Drama. Horizon
            Press.
        Costume Book. Lippincott.
        Guide to Play Selection. Bowker.
        Index to Plays in Collections. Scarecrow Press.
        McGraw-Hill Encyclopedia of World Drama. Mc-
            Graw-Hill.
        Play Index. H.W. Wilson.

Education:
  Barron's Profiles of American Colleges. Barron's Educational Services.
  Dictionary of Education. McGraw-Hill.
  Education Directory. U.S. Office of Education.
  Educator's Guides (to free films, free filmstrips, etc.). Educators Progress Service.
  Encyclopedia of Education. Macmillan.
  Lovejoy's College Guide. Simon & Schuster.

Foreign Languages:
  New Cassell's German Dictionary: German-English, English-German. Funk and Wagnalls.
  Cassell's Spanish Dictionary: Spanish-English, English-Spanish. Funk and Wagnalls.
  Larousse's Modern French-English, English-French Dictionary. Macmillan.
  New Cassell's French Dictionary. Funk and Wagnalls.

Language Arts:
  Dictionary of Contemporary American Usage. Random House.
  Dictionary of Slang and Unconventional English. Macmillan.
  A Manual for Writers of Term Papers, Theses, and Dissertations. University of Chicago Press.
  MLA Style Sheet. Modern Language Association Materials Center.
  Roget's International Thesaurus. Crowell.
  Synonyms, Antonyms, and Prepositions. Funk and Wagnalls.
  Webster's New Dictionary of Synonyms. Merriam.
  Wood's Unabridged Rhyming Dictionary. World.

Literature:
  American Authors, 1600-1900. H.W. Wilson.

Anthology of Children's Literature. Houghton Mifflin.
British Authors before 1800. H.W. Wilson.
Bulfinch's Mythology. Crowell.
Dictionary of Fictional Characters. The Writer.
Favorite Poems Old and New. Doubleday.
Golden Treasury of Poetry. Golden Press.
Granger's Index to Poetry. Columbia University Press.
Guide to Historical Literature. Macmillan
Guide to Modern World Literature. Funk and Wagnalls.
Index to Fairy Tales, Myths and Legends. F.W. Faxon.
Junior Book of Authors. H.W. Wilson.
Library of Literary Criticism. Frederick Ungar.
More Junior Authors. H.W. Wilson.
Oxford Companion to American Literature. Oxford University.
Oxford Companion to English Literature. Oxford University.
Penguin Companion to English Literature. McGraw-Hill.
The Readers Encyclopedia. Crowell.
The Readers Encyclopedia of Shakespeare. Crowell.
Readers Handbook of Famous Names in Fiction, Allusions, References, Proverbs, Stories, and Poems. Lippincott.
Science Fiction Story Index. American Library Association.
Short Story Index. H.W. Wilson.
Stevenson's Home Book of Verse. Holt, Rinehart, & Winston.
Subject and Title Index to Short Stories for Children. American Library Association.
Subject Index to Poetry for Children and Young People. American Library Association.

Mathematics:
  James and James Mathematics Dictionary. Van Nostrand.
  Mathematics Dictionary. Reinhold.
  Universal Encyclopedia of Mathematics. Simon & Schuster.
  World Weights and Measures. United Nations Statistical Office.

Music:
  Encyclopedia of the Opera. Hill and Wang.
  Everyman's Dictionary of Music. Dutton.
  Great Composers, 1300-1900. H.W. Wilson.
  Grove's Dictionary of Music and Musicians. St. Martin's.
  Milton Cross' Encyclopedia of the Great Composers and Their Music. Doubleday.
  Music Dictionary. Doubleday.
  New Edition of the Encyclopedia of Jazz. Horizon.
  Stories of Favorite Operas. Crowell.

Physical Sciences:
  American Men of Science. Bowker.
  Applied Science and Technology Index. H.W. Wilson.
  Aviation and Space Dictionary. Aero.
  The Book of Popular Science. Grolier.
  Compton's Dictionary of Natural Sciences. F.E. Compton.
  Dictionary of Scientific Biography. Scribner.
  Encyclopedia of Biological Sciences. Van Nostrand.
  Encyclopedia of Chemistry. Van Nostrand.
  Encyclopedia of Physics. Van Nostrand.
  Field Guide to Rocks and Minerals. Houghton Mifflin.
  McGraw-Hill Dictionary of Life Sciences. McGraw-Hill.

McGraw-Hill Encyclopedia of Science and Technology. McGraw-Hill.
McGraw-Hill Encyclopedia of Space. McGraw-Hill.
Modern Men of Science. McGraw-Hill.
Penguin Dictionary of Science. Penguin.
The Peterson Field Guide Series. Houghton Mifflin.
Pictorial Encyclopedia of Plants and Flowers. Crown.
Sourcebook of Biological Names and Terms. Thomas.
Van Nostrand's Scientific Encyclopedia. Van Nostrand.
Young People's Science Encyclopedia. Children's Press.

Social Sciences:
American Book of Days. H.W. Wilson.
American Heritage Pictorial Atlas of U.S. History. American Heritage.
American Negro Reference Book. Prentice-Hall.
American Political Parties: A Selective Guide to Parties and Movements of the 20th Century. Libraries Unlimited.
Anniversaries and Holidays. American Library Association.
Biographical Directory of the American Congress. U.S. Government Printing Office.
Book of Festivals. Gale Research Company.
Book of Superstitions. Taplinger.
The Concise Encyclopedia of Archaeology. Hawthorn.
A Dictionary of Comparative Religion. Scribners.
Documents of American History. Appleton-Century-Crofts.
Encyclopedia of American Facts and Dates. Crowell.
Encyclopedia of American History. Harper & Row.
Encyclopedia of Human Behavior. Doubleday.
Encyclopedia of Philosophy. Macmillan.

Encyclopedia of Psychology. Herder & Herder.

Encyclopedia of the Social Sciences. Macmillan.

Encyclopedia of World History. Houghton Mifflin.

Everyman's United Nations. United Nations, Dept. of Public Information.

Flags of the World. Narne.

Historical Statistics of the United States, Colonial Times to 1957. U.S. Government Printing Office.

The Negro Handbook. Johnson.

Occupational Outlook Handbook. U.S. Bureau of Labor Statistics.

Recent Historical Atlas. Macmillan.

State Names, Flags, Seals, Songs, Birds, Flowers, and Other Symbols. H.W. Wilson.

Statistical Abstract of the United States. U.S. Government Printing Office.

Stories of the States: A Reference Guide to the 50 States and the U.S. Territories. Crowell.

Webster's Geographical Dictionary. Merriam.

# Index

Action-learning projects, 320-21

Activities to promote reading, 259-66
parental involvement, 264-66

Book Selection Aids, 355-60
Evaluation criteria for books, 139-41

Classroom management, 177-78, 214-15
Community profile, 313-14
Community relations. *See* School/Community relations
Community Resource File, 317
Community Resources, 119-20, 192-93
Community services of media center, 317-19
Computer technology, 121-22
Contracts
for slow learners, 201
Creative teaching strategies, 99-127
evaluation, 125
Formula for Creativity, 126
Criteria for evaluating books, 139-41
Criteria for selection of equipment, 150-51
Curriculum development, 73-81
role of Media Specialist, 73, 81-95
six elements of, 73-74

Educational games, 113
Educational Goals
translated to objectives, 75-76
Emotionally handicapped students, 231-35
behavior modification, 235
bibliotherapy, 234
characteristics of, 232
Evaluation of unit studies, 80-81

Field trips and community resources
use with gifted students, 192-93

Gifted students, 178-96
*Bloom's Taxonomy*, 186
characteristics, 181
creative writing, 188-89
planning for, 182
reading guidance, 186-87
role of media specialist, 184-88, 195-96

Handicapped students, 212-39
sources of information and materials, 366-69
Hearing-impaired students, 222-26

Independent study, 108-09, 193
evaluation, 194
for gifted students, 193-4
for slow learners, 201-202
guidelines, 333-39
Inquiry methods, 116-17
bibliography, 346
In-service education for teachers, 275-93
role of media specialist, 279-83
Instruction
creative learning experiences, 99-127, 286
individualized, 38-39, 72, 198
inequality in teaching, 92
Instructional goals, 77-78
See also Instructional Objectives
Instructional Objectives
evaluation, 79-81
formulating of, 75-78
implementation of, 52-66

Language Arts
suggestions for role-playing, 111
See also Media Center, use in Language Arts instruction
Learning centers, 106-108
bibliography, 322-32
Learning disabled, 235-38
characteristics, 236
Learning packages, 104-06
bibliography, 329-30

Mainstreaming, 212-13
Media, 16, 286
production, 21
selection, See also Selection

of media. 134-52
selection policy, 135-36
use of equipment, 289-90
Media Center
description, 15-24
effective use, 45-65
student use, 46-47
teacher's role, 49, 64-65, 324-25
use in Language Arts instruction, 61-64
use in Science instruction, 57-61
use in Social Studies instruction, 52-57
use of, 17-19, 45-66
Media Skills, 285-93
teacher training, 278-79
summary list, 292-93
Media Specialist, 27-42
curriculum planning, 73, 81-95
job description, 27
role in reading instruction, 249-59
work with handicapped students, 212-39
work with slow learners, 199-207
work with students, 29-40
work with teachers, 29-40
Mentally retarded students, 227-31
Moral development
Kohlberg's stages of, 161-62
Morals education. See Values education.

Non-print materials
bibliography, 381-82
production, 296-308
reproduction of copyrighted works, 305-06

use of, 290-91

Oral history, 120-21
  bibliography, 352
Orthopedically and neurologically impaired students,
  226-27

Parent-teacher contacts, 314-
  16
Professional growth, 275-83
  media services for teachers,
  281-82
Public Law 94-142, 212-14

Reading, 246-67
  educational factors, 248-59
  methods of sharing books,
  370-75
  role of media specialist,
  248-59
  role of parents, 264-66
  role of teacher, 248-59
Reference materials, 287-89
  list of basic reference materials, 383-90
Reinforcement of learning
  through curriculum planning, 78-79
  for slow learners, 204-05
Role-playing, 110-13

School/community relations,
  35-36, 312-21
  role of media specialist,
  316-19
School Library Bill of Rights,
  353-54
Science
  suggestions for role-playing,
  112
  See also Media Center, use
  in Science instruction.

Selection of media
  evaluation of free and inexpensive materials, selection aids, 151-52;361
  evaluative criteria for
  books, 139-41; See also
  Book selection aids.
  evaluative criteria for curriculum packages, 149
  evaluative criteria for
  equipment, 150-51
  evaluation criteria for non-
  print materials, selection
  aids, 142-48; 362-65
  policy, 31-32
  role of media specialist, 137-
  38
  role of teacher, 137-38
Simulation games, 113-16
  bibliography, 345
Slow learners, 196-206
  contracts, 201
  description, 196-97
  independent study, 201-202
  principles of instruction,
  198
  selection of suitable
  materials, 200
  summary of teaching
  techniques, 207
Small group work, 18
  for gifted students, 189-92
  guidelines for group leadership, 347-49
  bibliography, 350-51
Social studies
  suggestions for role-playing,
  111
  See also Media center, use in
  social studies instruction.
Student tutoring, 109-10, 340-
  42
  bibliography, 343-44

Student-produced materials, 301-304
Students
consultations with media specialist, 22
developing desirable attitudes, 159-73
emotionally-handicapped, 231-35
hearing impaired, 222-26
learning disabled, 235-38
mentally retarded, 227-31
orthopedically and neurologically impaired, 226-27
visually-impaired, 218-22

Teacher-made materials
for handicapped students, 216-17
various uses for, 298-99
Teachers
consultations with media specialist, 22, 81-95
media skills, 278-79, 285-93
professional growth, 275-93
work with gifted students, 178-96
work with slow learners, 196-206
Teaching techniques
educational games, 113
independent study, 108-09
inquiry and discovery methods, 114-18
learning centers, 106-08
learning packages, 104-06
oral history, 120-21
peer teaching, 109-10
role-playing, 110-12
simulations, 113-15
small group work, 118-19
student production of nonprint materials, 120-21

use of community resources, 119-20
Television and radio equipment, 291-92

Values education, 159-73
Kohlberg's moral reasoning, 161-64
objectives, 165-66
role of media specialist, 168, 170-72
suggested activities, 166-71
value clarification, 160-61
Visually-impaired students, 218-22
Volunteer programs, 314-15

Writing instructional objectives, 75-77